Swift™
in the Cloud

Swift™
in the Cloud

Leigh Williamson

John Ponzo

Patrick Bohrer

Ricardo Olivieri

Karl Weinmeister

Samuel Kallner

WILEY

Swift™ in the Cloud

Published by
John Wiley & Sons, Inc.
10475 Crosspoint Boulevard
Indianapolis, IN 46256
www.wiley.com

Published by John Wiley & Sons, Inc., Indianapolis, Indiana

Published simultaneously in Canada

ISBN: 978-1-119-31937-5
ISBN: 978-1-119-36853-3 (ebk)
ISBN: 978-1-119-36847-2 (ebk)

Manufactured in the United States of America
10 9 8 7 6 5 4 3 2 1

For general information on our other products and services please contact our Customer Care Department within the United States at (877) 762-2974, outside the United States at (317) 572-3993 or fax (317) 572-4002.

Wiley publishes in a variety of print and electronic formats and by print-on-demand. Some material included with standard print versions of this book may not be included in e-books or in print-on-demand. If this book refers to media such as a CD or DVD that is not included in the version you purchased, you may download this material at http://booksupport.wiley.com. For more information about Wiley products, visit www.wiley.com.

Library of Congress Control Number: 2017946220

Karl would like to dedicate this book to his supportive wife, Samantha, and their crazy kiddos, who still gave him enough time to write.

Leigh dedicates this book to his wife, Cheryl, always his compass through life, and his daughter, Claire, the light of his life.

About the Authors

Leigh Williamson is an IBM Distinguished Engineer who has been working in the company's Austin, Texas lab since 1989, contributing to major software projects for IBM, including OS/2, DB2, AIX, Java, WebSphere, Rational, and MobileFirst products. He is currently leading a cross-disciplinary team of IBM Cloud Consultants who assist clients with cloud computing strategy and execution. Leigh is an active mentor and leader in the IBM technical community, working with international mentees; working in the Advanced Technical Eminence program; leading multiple patent brainstorming teams; publishing technical blogs and articles; conducting external broadcast webinars; and speaking at IBM and non-IBM conferences.

This is the fourth IBM Press book on which Leigh has collaborated over the past 15 years, with works covering Java standards, WebSphere Application Server, and enterprise-class mobile application development. He holds a B.S. in Computer Science from Nova University and an M.S. in Computer Engineering from The University of Texas at Austin.

You can follow Leigh on Twitter at @leighawillia. His LinkedIn address is `https://www.linkedin.com/in/leigh-williamson-9048654`.

John Ponzo is an IBM Fellow and Chief Technology Officer for Mobile who has shaped the future of IBM business in mobile computing and delivered innovative products and services to web browser and server-based standards. He is a pioneer in technology that promotes end-user interaction through mobility, web programming, web application middleware, and software tools. John led the development of key software technologies including HTML/JavaScript runtime libraries, XML middleware, web services runtime libraries, Eclipse Web Integration, and Web 2.0 enterprise collaboration services. He also authored the "Enterprise Mobile" and the "Mobile First" theses that are the cornerstone of mobile strategy and execution at IBM. John also serves as the IBM technology ambassador to Kenya.

John is the primary technical collaborator between Apple and IBM in the effort to define and enhance the Swift programming language for both mobile client development and cloud services development.

Patrick Bohrer is a Distinguished Engineer in the IBM Cloud division. His responsibilities include serving as the technical lead for the company's global efforts around Swift@IBM (`developer.ibm.com/swift`). He formerly served as the technical lead of the Mobile Innovation Lab in Austin, Texas. Patrick also helped lead IBM Research's Mobile Research agenda after co-leading the 2012 Global Technology Outlook topic entitled "Mobile First," which helped set the technical direction for current mobile and cloud efforts at IBM. Patrick received a B.A in Computer Science from The University of Texas at Austin.

Karl Weinmeister is the Program Director for Swift@IBM Engineering, based in Austin, Texas. He is passionate about improving people's lives and experiences with technology. In his role, he has helped to enable Swift to extend from its mobile roots to become a full-stack language ecosystem.

Previously, Karl led engineering for the IBM Mobile Innovation Lab. He is a diehard Duke basketball fan and enjoys spending time with his family.

Ricardo Olivieri is a Senior Software Engineer at Swift@IBM Engineering. His areas of expertise include gathering and analyzing business requirements, architecting, designing, and developing software applications. Ricardo has extensive experience in the complete software development cycle and related processes, especially in Agile methodologies.

Ricardo has several years of experience in Java development as well as in Groovy, Perl, and Python development, with a strong background in back-end (server-side, business logic, SQL, and NoSQL databases) and front-end development. Several years ago, Ricardo added Business Process Manager (BPM) design and development to his skill set, which allowed him to assume the role of BPM consultant and developer using IBM Business Process Manager. While working at the Mobile Innovation Lab, Ricardo gained valuable skills and knowledge in the iOS and Android ecosystems.

Ricardo is now mainly focused on the adoption of the Swift language on the server and the IBM cloud, Bluemix. He has a B.S. in Computer Engineering from the University of Puerto Rico, Mayagüez Campus.

Samuel (Shmuel) Kallner is a Senior Technical Staff Member in the Smart Client Platforms group at the IBM Research Lab in Haifa, Israel. He is currently the Technical Lead of the Kitura project. Shmuel has over thirty years of experience at IBM working on a wide variety of projects including mobile apps, web-based end-user application development environments, mobile app developer tools, both sides of client-server–based applications, and more.

About the Technical Editor

Matthew Perrins is a Senior Technical Staff Member working on IBM Cloud Developer Services in Austin, Texas. Matt is one of the architects for the company's production-ready public Cloud Developer Experience on Bluemix—the IBM cloud platform. He is focused on making it very easy to develop and deploy mobile, web, and digital channel applications with the IBM cloud, and to integrate them with world-class leading runtimes for Swift, Node.js, and Java. Matt has been leading the IBM cloud teams in the evolution to true DevOps continuous delivery with cloud-native architectures, and driving that integration into the IBM Bluemix user experience.

Matt has spent a significant part of his career building systems-of-record and systems-of-engagement solutions using IBM technologies with IBM clients. He understands developers, user experiences, transactions, and cognitive solutions and how to deliver them at scale on the IBM cloud.

Credits

Acknowledgments

Many thanks to everyone at Wiley Publishing for their outstanding work on this project: to Jim Minatel for encouraging us to take this book concept forward and for yet again supporting the realization of a book that engages in deeper learning; to Adaobi Obi Tulton, the project editor, for driving this project to completion in the most efficient way possible—it was a real pleasure to work with such an accomplished and adept editor; to Marylouise Wiack, the copy editor, for translating this book into readable prose; and to Dassi Zeidel, the production editor, for bringing everything together to create a final, polished product.

Sincere thanks go to Matthew Perrins, the technical editor, for the incredible amount of work and personal time he selflessly put into ensuring that the content in this book can be utilized seamlessly by readers. Also, thanks to Steven Stansel, who was instrumental in formulating the original concept and proposal for the book. Brian White Eagle provided invaluable assistance with peering over the horizon in Chapter 9. And Shereen Ghobrial contributed the bulk of the mainframe-related content.

The biggest thank-you must, of course, go to our own families. This book was written over six months, predominantly at night and over weekends and holidays. In addition to sharing us with extremely demanding full-time jobs, our families made further sacrifices to enable us to spend time on this project.

Contents at a Glance

Contents

Introduction

Since Apple introduced the Swift programming language in 2014, it has become one of the most rapidly adopted computer programming languages in history. Programmers love the modern syntax used by Swift and the way it's fun to develop code, similar to how they felt about Java a generation ago. Programming skills and experience in Swift are in high demand in the industry, with the promise of high salaries for those who invest the time to learn and practice the language.

Apple originally introduced Swift as an alternative language to Objective-C for developing iPhone, iPad, and macOS applications. The company has now expanded Swift into the realm of solutions for the Internet of Things, with support for tvOS (Apple TV) and watchOS (Apple Watch wearable devices). As illustrated in Figure 1, Swift is now one of the most popular open source projects and Swift frameworks such as Kitura are gaining ground quickly.

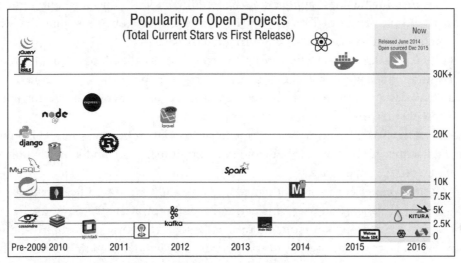

Figure 1: Popularity of the Swift programming language

At about the same time that Swift was first introduced, Apple and IBM formed a strategic partnership to produce innovative, industry-specific mobile applications for the Apple iOS ecosystem. IBM proceeded to embrace the Swift programming language and implemented over 100 mobile apps as part of this partnership. IBM engineers saw the value of Swift firsthand in these applications. The open source release of the Swift language in late 2014 began another chapter in the partnership, as IBM chose to invest in and support the cause of bringing the Swift language to the cloud as a result of the focus on server-side Swift environments.

Development of these applications highlights the critical, expanding role of server-side logic in powering these new experiences that users now take for granted. From syncing data across devices; to connecting people with friends and co-workers; to monitoring news and alerting us about new events based on our interests and activities; to providing cognitive insights into our applications; server-side logic is critical to creating truly brilliant apps. Now the ability to develop, debug, and deploy this logic in the same language used to create mobile experiences is a game changer for the development community.

This book, written by members of the development team at IBM who helped bring Swift to the cloud, covers everything you need to know about how to develop Swift programs that run in cloud environments. It combines technical information with the concepts that originally led to the development of the technology. This book provides plenty of examples of Swift language code, as well as a living website where a community consisting of the authors and other passionate Swift experts continues to discuss Swift and its future directions.

IBM, Apple, and Swift

On July 15, 2014, IBM and Apple announced what was at the time a very surprising partnership, with the goal of transforming business applications by building mobile enterprise and industry-specific solutions for the Apple platform. This partnership was unexpected by most industry watchers and radically altered the enterprise mobile computing landscape.

The IBM offering that resulted from the Apple partnership is called MobileFirst for iOS. It focuses on enterprise and industry transformation by providing users with the latest features of the Apple platform and user design, coupled with the back-end data center integration required to reinvent the next generation of enterprise applications.

Key features of the IBM offering include large-enterprise–class robustness and scalability; back-end enterprise data center integration; big data and analytics integration; and a highly polished mobile front-end user interface experience.

The user interface experience was codesigned by Apple and IBM to significantly upgrade the standards for usability, elegance, and user satisfaction beyond typical enterprise software. Since 2012, IBM has been making massive investments in IBM Design Thinking philosophy and techniques, building up several large design studios in an effort to apply good design to business software. This software design emphasis by IBM was one of the natural collaboration areas of the partnership, with the strong Apple design culture being applied to all of their own products.

As IBM MobileFirst for iOS was being developed, a choice was made to use the latest iOS platform APIs for iPhone and iPad business applications. The scope was later extended to include Apple Watch. IBM leveraged many of the extended development kits provided by Apple, such as HomeKit, CloudKit, and the connected car capabilities in various new and innovative business solutions. As of December 2015, IBM had created over 100 industry-specific mobile apps for the IBM MobileFirst for iOS collection.

While Apple has pioneered the transformation of the consumer mobile app experience, IBM and Apple consider business mobile app transformation to be an underserved market and a really great design opportunity that they can uniquely address together.

Introduction of Swift

Apple introduced the Swift language at the Apple World Wide Developers Conference (WWDC) in 2014, and IBM decided to begin using the language to build the first wave of IBM MobileFirst for iOS mobile applications. IBM assembled a team of developers with expertise in building mobile solutions. Their previous programming language skills included Java, JavaScript, and Objective-C. This team of IBM programmers quickly learned Swift and began using it to implement the mobile apps in the IBM MobileFirst for iOS collection.

Working with Apple, we at IBM learned a lot about what it takes to build amazing mobile business applications. IBM also discovered the value of Swift.

Swift was designed by Apple to be a safe, interactive, and high-performance systems language. It also blends the ease of scripting language syntax with the performance of a systems language. The IBM team found that in comparison to mobile apps developed in Java for the Android mobile platform and Objective-C for iOS, Swift apps required less code.

The IBM team appreciated everything about Swift, from its type safety—which empowered them to be agile and evolve the applications quickly while knowing that the compiler would catch any errors—to its performance and memory advantages, which are critical for application responsiveness. The concise syntax of the language also led to great developer productivity.

The IBM teams also learned to understand what is necessary to develop application-specific web services to power these business mobile applications. It significantly enhanced the overall productivity of the team to not have to switch languages away from what was used for the mobile front end (Swift) to work on the back-end services.

The developers found the Swift code easier to read, share, and evolve. What the Swift language did for legibility of the application code represented a large increase in productivity for the development team. Other languages used for mobile apps were generally more verbose. It also significantly increased code quality with Swift-based type checking. The importance of a strongly typed language in the productivity of the development team can hardly be overstated. Most of the more than 100 applications developed by IBM for various business solutions could be produced by a handful of programmers working in small teams.

Figure 2 shows a comparison of Swift with other programming languages and illustrates how Swift enables inherent application performance and developer productivity benefits through its attributes such as:

- Modern programming language constructs
- Error detection at compile time, not runtime
- Code reengineering

- Built-in performance features such as an optimized search algorithm that is up to 2.6 times faster than Objective-C and 8.4 times faster than Python 2.7
- A compiled language with the benefits of an interpreted language

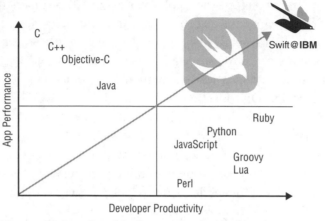

Figure 2: Benefits of Swift compared with other languages

These same benefits around ease of programming, type safety, and compiled performance are also desired on the server side of the applications. Until the release of Swift 3.0, Swift developers were forced to abandon their favorite language if they wanted to develop application logic that ran on the server. When Swift was made open source in 2015, IBM recognized the developer and business value that could be unlocked by bringing this language to the server and, by extension, to the cloud computing environment.

Swift is not just a programming language syntax, but also includes a robust compiler back-end infrastructure, based on the LLVM (originally named *Low Level Virtual Machine*) machine-independent intermediate code optimization. The compiler architecture includes debugging capability, *read-eval-print loop* (REPL) language statement interpretation, and distinct layers for binary code generation. This design of the language infrastructure is forward-looking and lends itself to flexible reuse of the basic language constructs. Swift is an up-to-date, modern programming language with support for closures, tuples, extensions, generics, type inference, custom operators, enumerations, and option types. Also, Swift execution performance is on par with modern native programming languages (that is, very fast).

Chapter 3 of this book covers the key aspects of the language in more detail, as well as information about performance and memory attributes that we found to be especially attractive relative to other languages.

Open Source Swift

The IBM team continued to be impressed with Swift as new and innovative ways to leverage it were discovered. IBM has a history of investing in programming languages for both the open technology community and enterprise business uses. We've learned that the wide adoption and enthusiastic embracing of a programming language by the open source community yields usage and success in greater orders of magnitude for a well-designed language whose time in the market is right.

The year 2015 seemed to be the right time for Swift, and the Swift programming language was released as open source in December 2015, where it continues to grow with the open source community through the *Swift evolution process* (https://swift.org/contributing/#participating-in-the-swift-evolution-process). By opening up the language to wider community support and development, Apple has ensured that Swift will enjoy robust language evolution with backwards compatibility.

With the open source release of Swift, IBM was inspired by past experiences to embrace the opportunity to bring this language to the cloud. IBM has a history of helping language communities to bring their languages to the business world. Figure 3 shows example timelines of IBM and open source community investment and evolution of the Java programming language and the Node.js JavaScript ecosystem.

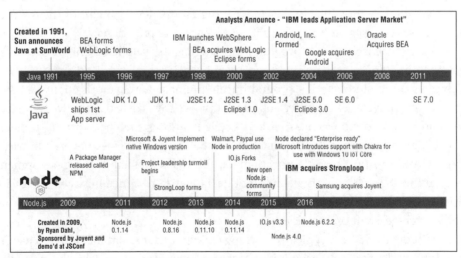

Figure 3: An overview of IBM involvement in major programming language evolution

The open source community that supports and evolves Swift is named Swift.org (http://swift.org). This organization is supported by a broad range of contributors from dozens of major technology companies—including Apple, IBM, PayPal, and Dropbox—and educational institutions. The stated goal for Swift.org is to "develop the language in the open" with "public conversations ... encouraged." As in other open community projects, this transparent approach to managed technological evolution will produce much faster enhancements and a wider range of innovation than any one company can possibly deliver, no matter how large and wealthy.

Swift.org includes all the foundational components for the language, including the Swift compiler, standard library, package manager, core libraries, REPL, and debugger.

IBM is excited to be a part of the global Swift community and to bring our company's expertise to the effort to take Swift to the cloud. Since the first day that Swift was available on the Swift.org community web pages, IBM has been releasing assets to support it. These have included the IBM Swift Sandbox, the Kitura web framework, the IBM Swift Package Catalog, IBM Cloud Tools for Swift, and over 85 new open source projects on GitHub. In this way, IBM has been working with the community to make Swift on the cloud possible on the server. This book provides an overview of these offerings and how they can be used to create amazing applications. Chapter 1 of this book provides greater details about Swift.org and the open source process that guides the development of the Swift programming language.

Bringing Swift to the Server

The release of Swift as an open source project provided developers with the possibility to run Swift code on "back-end" server machines. These are environments that IBM has focused on over many decades, and the company immediately began working on the development of the Swift ecosystem components that are necessary to support robust server-side applications.

Because Swift started as a client-side programming language, developers familiar with this language are already accustomed to the ecosystem of tools and libraries that surround Swift.

An underlying goal of supporting a programming language across both client and server environments is to enable developer mobility and productivity. Towards this end, we felt that the Swift ecosystem should be as common as possible across client and server. The Swift.org project has been supporting this goal of a common development ecosystem with the release of core libraries on Linux to match those found in Apple client environments. IBM has invested in the development of these libraries on Linux to help provide this consistent developer experience between the client and the cloud. Language support, along with availability of these core libraries, is important, but more is needed to fully leverage Swift on the cloud.

Client-side Swift developers are typically working on applications that include rich user interfaces, application data models, and network communication logic for a variety of cloud services. These client-side developers can rely on the base platform provided by Apple, along with a number of client-side packages that make it easy to do things like interacting with users, accessing local sensors and devices, client-side networking, and much more.

Likewise, server-side developers typically write applications called web services that interact with other back-end services or data sources on a network. Web service developers are typically writing code to listen for incoming network requests (from the client) and routing these requests to the appropriate back-end logic. This logic, in turn, might end up calling other network services, and finally the logic will respond to the incoming network request with a status code and optional payload. These server-side developers also require a base platform along with a rich set of packages. IBM has joined the greater Swift community to help build the server-side base platform as well as the surrounding packages needed to deploy Swift-based web services.

IBM is leading a new open source project called Kitura, which is a web application framework for Swift. Kitura leverages the core libraries of Foundation and libdispatch to provide a consistent development environment for client code programmers as well as cloud application developers. Kitura also includes a number of additional libraries needed on the server to deliver networking, security, and HTTP processing support. The Kitura platform also leverages many packages from the wider community to handle other server-side functions dealing with credentials, sessions, database communication, and much more.

With all of this included, web service developers can focus on writing great services knowing they can leverage Swift safety, performance, and tools that they learned and love from the client development ecosystem.

Figure 4 illustrates the Swift language client environment compared to the Swift environment for server and cloud hosted code. You can see from this illustration the drive towards a consistent Swift developer experience across both client and server environments.

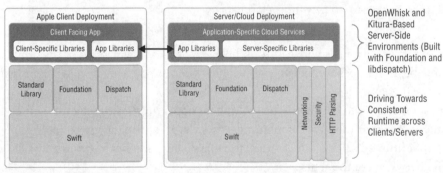

Figure 4: Comparison of client and server elements for Swift

The End-to-End Developer Experience

For developers to be successful and productive, they need to be empowered through a rich language ecosystem that can include open source projects as well as tools and platform capabilities that support and augment their workflow.

As the Swift ecosystem continues to grow, so too does the opportunity for an even more encompassing developer experience. A developer's workflow includes performing local development of both client and server code; testing code snippets and asking questions about this code with the community; discovering and pulling in packages from the community; linking applications to dependent cloud services; and, finally, deploying and monitoring server code running in the cloud.

The Swift@IBM team has been working on tools to augment this developer workflow. These tools will be covered in more detail in this book. Figure 5 shows how a use case driven design ensured simplicity in the combined, integrated end-to-end developer experience.

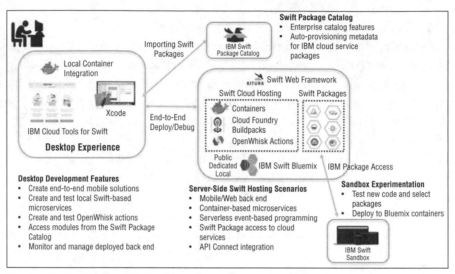

Figure 5: End-to-end Swift development

As a result of our experiences with Swift on both client and server sides of the application, we've developed some best practices for end-to-end (that is, client-to-server) development using one consistent programming language.

A crucial best practice is to constantly be looking for opportunities to refactor your code and move pieces from client to server (and back sometimes) in order to optimize your code. You need to break the back-end code into smaller chunks (microservices), but also keep in mind the need to reduce network traffic between components.

Later chapters of this book cover several options for how to organize and deploy Swift code on the server or cloud environment. Each approach for cloud deployment has advantages and shortcomings that are different from the others. One of our goals for this book is to explain the distinctions sufficiently so that you can determine which cloud deployment architecture best fits your application needs.

Scope of This Book

This book covers technical details of all aspects of creating and running Swift language applications in cloud computing environments. The techniques described here combine the concepts that motivated support for cloud-hosted Swift code with many examples of real code that the reader can run and experiment with. The book was written *by* the developers who produced the support for Swift in the cloud; it was written *for* developers as a practical guide for how to quickly create server-side applications using Swift and run them on pay-as-you-go cloud infrastructure.

The content of this book includes a historical recap of the origins of Swift and the strategic vision for the future potential of the language (this Introduction). The recent introduction of an open source project for Swift (Swift.org) will be discussed too (in Chapter 1). Before the reader can do anything with the Swift examples in this book, they need an execution environment for the language. The cloud hosted Swift Sandbox is a free environment, easy to access for experimenting with learning the language. Chapter 2 introduces the Swift Sandbox and several activities to help the reader gain familiarity with its capabilities.

Next, a brief overview of the key aspects of the Swift language for readers who have not yet experienced it is provided in Chapter 3. We discuss the original use of Swift to produce mobile apps for Apple iOS devices, and we address its role in wearable device and Internet-of-Things (IoT) software. We briefly discuss the strengths and weaknesses of the language, as well as a look at its performance compared to other programming languages.

Once we address these foundational topics, the content evolves to more specific cloud computing aspects of Swift. We cover all of the various mechanisms for running Swift code in the cloud, with plenty of background and examples: cloud-hosted Swift Sandbox, Docker container Swift runtimes, and Cloud Foundry buildpack for Swift.

We then expand the cloud-based Swift development topic more fully to address the concepts of the new web application framework for Swift and also the new Package Manager for Swift modules that make reuse of Swift code among different programmers extremely simple. As in the earlier chapters of this book, we include a lot of examples for these topics.

Finally, the book covers an entirely new programming style of event-driven or "serverless" software (similar to AWS Lambda) and how to use Swift in this context. The book focuses on OpenWhisk, an open technology system that supports event-driven software, and how to implement solutions in OpenWhisk using the Swift language. In the final chapter of the book, we peer over the horizon and speculate about the future of the Swift language, especially as it relates to cloud computing environments and advanced solutions leveraging analytics and cognitive computing technology.

Swift and the cloud are now ready to move beyond the iPhone and MacBook environments; and this team of authors at IBM, having brought Swift to the cloud, is ideally positioned to help developers master this new world of cloud opportunities. No other group of authors is currently in a position to write such a book. Other books on Swift focus entirely on the language syntax and its use in creating mobile apps or software that runs on personal computers. This book uniquely covers the use of the new language for applications that run as highly scalable "server-side" software, hosted on elastic, dynamic, pay-as-you-go cloud platforms.

Swift™
in the Cloud

## CHAPTER 1

Swift.org, the Open Source Project

On December 3, 2015, Apple made version 2.2 of the Swift programming language open source software by creating Swift.org and contributing a key set of source code repositories covering the compilers, debuggers, libraries, and more. The Swift.org site (`https://swift.org`) was set up to serve as a central hub for this new community. The site contains documentation, binary downloads, links to the open source repositories on GitHub, mailing lists, and bug reporting mechanisms, as well as continuous integration support to maintain stability across the projects. In this chapter, I will cover what is included on the site as well as some pointers about how to get involved in this exciting community.

What's Included

The Swift.org website is the focal point for the Swift language development community. Because the community supporting Swift is composed of people with diverse skill levels and different interests, the site is designed to be a single entry point from which visitors can access the information relevant to their needs. The navigation categories listed on the left-hand side of the Swift.org home page represent major topic areas into which visitors can dive, depending on whether they are developers who want to look at the source code, testers wanting to report a bug, people with general interest who want to subscribe to a mailing list, or any of the dozens of possible reasons why they are involved with the language.

There are roughly a dozen of these major navigation categories on the Swift.org home page. Visitors can learn general information about the language by following the About Swift link. They can access public blogs and documentation by clicking on those same named links. They can learn about the rules of the community and how to contribute through the Community and Contributing links. You will learn more information about community involvement later in this chapter.

For developers, one of the most important Swift.org categories is the Source Code link. All of the source code for the Swift language and related utilities is stored in GitHub repositories (a separate website from Swift.org). The SOURCE CODE navigation link from the Swift.org home page takes you to a web page where the organization of the source code is explained and links are provided to the various GitHub repos containing code for different Swift libraries.

Source Code Repositories

The open source Swift language is managed by the community as a collection of projects, each with its own source code repositories. These repositories are the core of Swift.org. Anyone can freely access the source repositories to get the code for the Swift language, build it, and run their own local version; they can even make enhancements or fix defects as long as the community rules for contributions are followed. These source code repositories include the following:

- **Swift compiler and standard library**
  - `https://github.com/apple/swift`
- **Core libraries (Foundation, `libdispatch`, and `XCTest`)**
  - `https://github.com/apple/swift-corelibs-foundation`
  - `https://github.com/apple/swift-corelibs-libdispatch`
  - `https://github.com/apple/swift-corelibs-xctest`
- **LLDB debugger and REPL**
  - `https://github.com/apple/swift-lldb`
- **Swift Package Manager**
  - `https://github.com/apple/swift-package-manager`
- **Xcode Playground Support**
  - `https://github.com/apple/swift-xcode-playground-support`
- **A variety of repositories that include support for compiler tools, tests, code samples, `protobuf` support, and much more**

These projects are published under an Apache 2 license with a runtime library extension. The importance of this kind of license is that it solves the potential problem of a schism between the compiler and runtime library by allowing both to be covered uniformly under the same license.

Figure 1-1 shows the GitHub web page for a typical Swift.org repository—in this case, for the Swift compiler and standard library project.

Swift Compiler and Standard Library

The Swift compiler and standard library provide basic language and type system support across the platforms. This support is completely equivalent for macOS and Linux, but no other operating systems are supported as of this writing. All the language features described in this chapter are delivered by the compiler and standard library.

The Swift standard library supplies a programmer with the fundamental data types such as `Int`, `Double`, and `String`, as well as more complex data structures including `Set`, `Array`, `Dictionary`, and many more. It is within this library that many common protocols are defined for the language features. Many language features have a corresponding protocol, and any type that conforms to the protocol can be used with that feature. For example, a `for-in` loop can iterate over the elements of any value whose type conforms to the `Sequence` protocol.

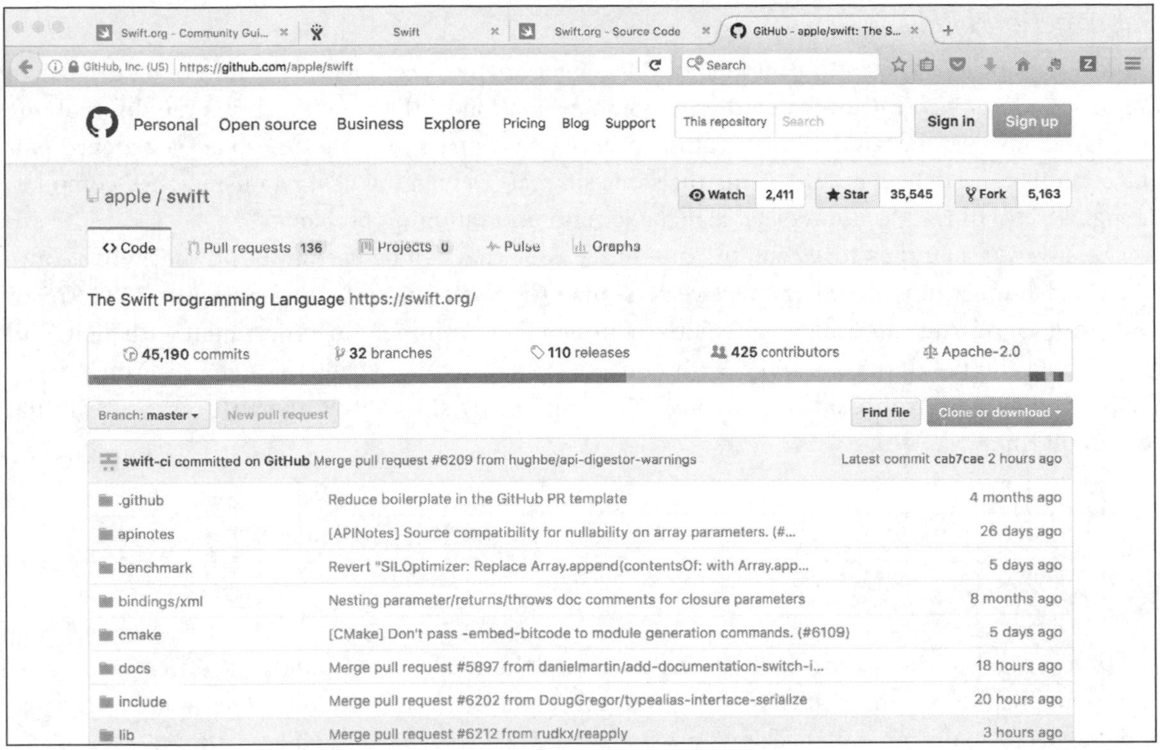

Figure 1-1: One of the Swift.org source repositories

Foundation

The Foundation library provides many core capabilities that Swift developers are accustomed to, such as `URLSession`, `JSONSerialization`, and more. On Apple platforms, this library is implemented in Objective-C. The Swift.org version of this library is being implemented in Swift. As such, there are several APIs in Foundation that are being rewritten to make Foundation support on Linux more mature. To view the latest status of Foundation, you can check the status page at `https://github .com/apple/swift-corelibs-foundation/blob/master/Docs/Status.md`.

Libdispatch (Grand Central Dispatch)

Swift developers are accustomed to using Grand Central Dispatch to leverage concurrency support in their applications running on client operating systems such as iOS. Grand Central Dispatch support is provided within the libdispatch core library. This library is provided as part of the Swift runtime. When Swift was first made open source, the libdispatch core library was included as part of Swift.org. At that time, the library had not been ported to Linux. IBM agreed that it was important to provide this same consistent concurrency support on Linux, and set about porting libdispatch to Linux. The ported version of libdispatch was included in the Swift 3.0 release in September 2016. This was an important milestone because many Foundation APIs (like `OperationQueue` and `URLSession`) also depend upon libdispatch.

Debugger and REPL

Tight integration of the Swift compiler and debugger enables accurate inspection of data types in the debugger, as well as full-featured expression evaluation in the context of this rapidly evolving language. However, because of this tight integration, developers must be sure to use a matched pair of a compiler and debugger built using the same sources. Debugging using a mismatched compiler-debugger set will lead to unpredictable behavior and programming problems.

The swift-lldb repository contains the source code that can be used to build the Swift debugger. The debugger includes an interactive version of the Swift language, known as the REPL (read-eval-print loop). You can use this interactive command environment to experiment with Swift and quickly see the results of arbitrary Swift code snippets that you write and execute. You can try the Swift REPL environment on your macOS computer by simply typing **swift** on the Terminal command line:

```
Leighs-MacBook-Pro:~ leighwilliamson$ swift
Welcome to Apple Swift version 3.0.1 (swiftlang-800.0.58.6 clang-800.0.42.1).
Type:help for assistance.
  1>
```

All you need to do is type Swift statements, and the REPL immediately executes your code. Expression results are automatically formatted and displayed along with their type, as are the results of both variable and constant declarations.

```
1> var whoami = "Leigh Williamson"

whoami: String = "Leigh Williamson"
  2> print("Hello")
Hello
  3> print("Hello, \(whoami)")
Hello, Leigh Williamson
  4>
```

The swift-lldb project wraps enhancements around the core LLDB (Low Level Debugger) open-source debugger project developed under the broader LLVM (Low Level Virtual Machine) project, located at llvm.org. Therefore, any code modifications that are contributed to swift-lldb will undergo extra scrutiny because of the potential impact outside of the Swift language ecosystem.

Swift Package Manager

Swift Package Manager is a new feature that was introduced with Swift 3.0. Although it is not yet used for building applications on other Swift platforms, it is used extensively for building applications on Linux. Projects that are compatible with Swift Package Manager are built around a Package.swift file that specifies build targets as well as other packages that the project is dependent upon. Chapter 6 is devoted to Swift Package Manager and all of its details.

Xcode Playground Support

The "playground" feature in Xcode has long been used by developers to experiment with a language, explore its standard library types, and learn high-level concepts using visualizations and practical examples. Within Xcode there are several "playgrounds" supported for different languages. For instance, a programmer can use the Xcode Swift Playground to learn how the Swift language uses protocols and generics to express powerful constraints. The playground feature is valuable for developers who are new to the language, but also very handy for those who are well versed in the behavior of the language.

The Xcode Playground Support project enables the Swift language to be integrated with the Xcode playground feature so that developers can take advantage of the playground to learn and explore the language. This same project code is used outside of Xcode for similar language learning "playground" systems such as the Bluemix Swift Sandbox (see Chapter 2).

Other Related Projects and Repositories

The Swift.org open source code builds upon other, earlier open source projects. This has the advantage of leveraging years of previous innovation and thousands of hours of hard work contributed by developers all over the world. However, this approach to building Swift comes with the price of requiring very careful cloning and merging with the source code of the open source projects on which the Swift implementation depends.

Swift.org development follows a policy of pushing any changes to the most upstream repository feasible. This means that contributions to Swift code that involve the repositories of open source projects on which Swift depends will be pushed to the code base for those other projects rather than residing in a version of the code only applicable to Swift. This, in turn, means that any such code changes will be reviewed by multiple open source project teams before being accepted, not just Swift.org.

The open source projects on which Swift.org code has dependencies include LLVM Core, Clang, and LLDB. Swift.org maintains cloned copies of those other projects' repositories and frequently updates these clones as the code evolves in the other projects.

How to Get Involved

There are many ways to work with and contribute to the open source Swift community. You do not have to be an expert developer of programming languages or compilers in order to make valuable contributions. You can start getting involved by subscribing to the mailing lists for the community and providing answers that you have to the questions that are posted there. The community encourages everyone to submit bugs that they uncover while using Swift. When reporting bugs for Swift, be sure to follow the guidelines described at `https://swift.org/contributing/#reporting-bugs` for information that you need to provide as part of the bug report. When filing a bug report, it is important to distinguish the difference between a new language feature and a defect in the existing, defined language features. New feature requests must go through the Swift evolution process, whereas bug reports are submitted to the Swift bug tracking system.

Another way to get involved in the Swift community is to take part in triaging reported bugs. Once a bug report has been submitted, someone must validate the bug by reproducing it. Additional information may be needed to augment the bug report so that Swift developers can more efficiently address it. The bug report may also be a duplicate of another already-existing bug report. Triaging bug reports for the community is an extremely valuable contribution to improving Swift.

Many members of the community are enthusiastic about contributing code changes for Swift. Full guidelines for making these code contributions are found at `https://swift.org/contributing/#contributing-code`. There are several considerations for contributing code to the project, including the following:

- **Use short-lived code branches containing small, incremental changes**—Small changes are easier to track and integrate. Longer-lived branches tend to result in messy code-merge problems and are discouraged.
- **Keep each change self-contained**—Every commit should be able to be shipped in a release without dragging along other uncommitted changes.
- **Use clear and thorough commit messages for all code changes**—Your code change will be reviewed and examined by many other developers, so it is crucial that you sufficiently describe what you changed so that others can quickly understand.
- **Use the developer email list to keep the community aware of what you are doing.**
- **Use the designated source code header when committing new source files**—This ensures that the license and copyright protections are called out at the top of every Swift.org source file.
- **Expect and actively participate in the code review for your change.** Code review is often an iterative process; it is carried out in the open through GitHub and reflected in the associated commit email list postings.
- **Provide test cases for all bug fixes and code changes**—Tests are considered a required component of any code modification, and your change will not be committed without them.
- **Be prepared to rapidly address any failures that your code change may cause in the Swift continuous integration (CI) once the code has been committed.**
- **Stay alert for potential regressions that your code change may cause, even days after it has been initially committed**—When you submit a code change to the community, your responsibility to support it is ongoing and long lasting.
- **Avoid adding new external code libraries as part of making a code change**—External libraries may not follow the same license and legal rules as the rest of the Swift.org code, and there may be issues with compatibility of the external code across all supported Swift target platforms.

As with any vibrant open source community, it is important to support communication across a wide range of interests within the community. This communication within Swift.org is handled via mailing lists, shared source repositories (such as GitHub.com and Swift.org), and bug tracking. I've already covered the shared code repositories, so let's consider mailing lists and bug tracking.

Mailing Lists

Swift.org has defined and set up several mailing lists targeting certain personas and their interests in different parts of the project. Mailing lists are considered to be the primary method of communicating among community members, and the volume of interaction is high on the main topic lists. The General Interest list is the most popular, covering most common questions related to the use of the Swift language rather than issues related to its development.

The set of Swift Developer mailing lists is used by programmers who are actively delivering contributions to the open source code-base for Swift, and the mailing lists are organized based on the Swift.org project and code repository that the users are discussing. The Swift Evolution lists focus on encouraging and reviewing proposals for new language features. Swift.org has a well-defined and open process for the evolution of the language, and these lists, along with the Swift Evolution Repository (`https://github.com/apple/swift-evolution`), support that process.

Figure 1-2 shows the web page where you can register to participate in one of the Swift email lists. For more information on these mailing lists and to sign up for any of them, go to `https://swift.org/community/#mailing-lists`.

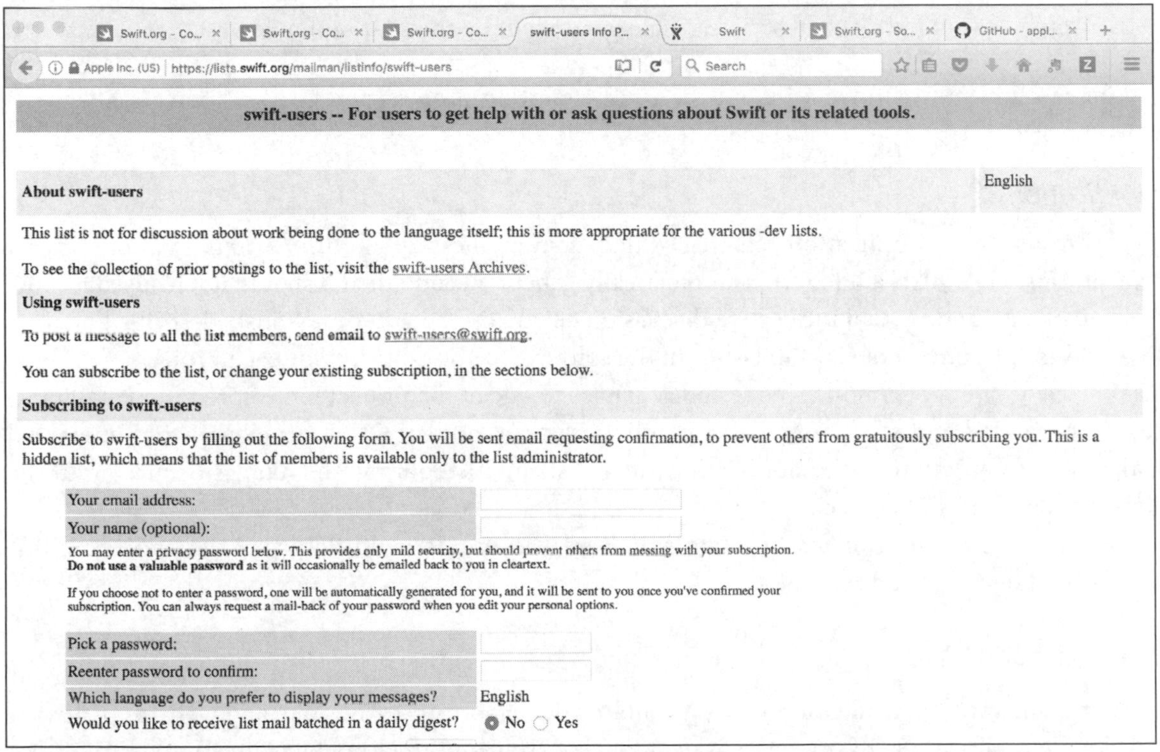

Figure 1-2: Email list signup page for the Swift General Interest group

Discussion lists

Some of the email lists for Swift.org are interactive and encourage a free flow of discussion exchange. Other lists are for one-way communication to notify subscribers about something with no expectation that they respond. The discussion email lists are further divided into categories based on the subscriber's role. These discussion categories and their associated email lists are organized as follows:

General Interest
- **swift-users**—For questions regarding Swift and its related tools

Swift Developers
- **swift-dev**—Swift compiler, low-level runtime, standard library, and **SourceKit**
- **swift-corelibs-dev**—Swift core libraries
- **swift-server-dev**—New server-focused capabilities developed by the Server APIs workgroup
- **swift-lldb-dev**—Swift REPL and Swift-specific aspects of LLDB
- **swift-build-dev**—Swift Package Manager and low-level build system (llbuild)

Swift Evolution
- **swift-evolution-announce**—Swift evolution proposal reviews and results (low volume)
- **swift-evolution**—A discussion of the evolution of Swift, its libraries, and more. This is a very active mailing list, so subscribing via digest might be the best option.

You can find more information on the Swift evolution process and current focus at `https://github.com/apple/swift-evolution`.

Notifications

There are also many notification lists that contain commit messages for the various Swift.org project repositories. These lists are fed from automatically generated content and should not be used for discussion of any kind. Actual interactive discussion occurs on the other previously described mailing lists and in the content of GitHub Issues in the source code repositories for each project.

When a developer commits source code changes to one of the project repositories, an email message is generated and sent to the corresponding notification list. Other developers and interested stakeholders can monitor the notification email lists and keep up with changes occurring to the source code for Swift.

The Swift.org notification mailing lists include swift-commits, swift-lldb-commits, swift-corelibs-commits, and swift-build-commits.

Bug Tracking

Like any software, the code for Swift.org contains defects—bugs! And, like any well-run software development project, Swift.org has a system for reporting and tracking bugs in the code. Swift.org manages bugs and code issues with a JIRA-based bug-tracking site. This site can be used to open issues to report defects and problems against any part of the Swift.org ecosystem. It can also be used to find the latest information about updates that might be included in future releases. The Swift.org bug-tracking system is maintained at `https://bugs.swift.org`.

In order to log in to the Swift bug-tracking tool, you have to create an account. It is free to create a JIRA account for the Swift.org bug-tracking tool, and it only takes a couple of minutes. Figure 1-3 shows the web page that you use to sign up for a new Swift.org JIRA account, and the information required.

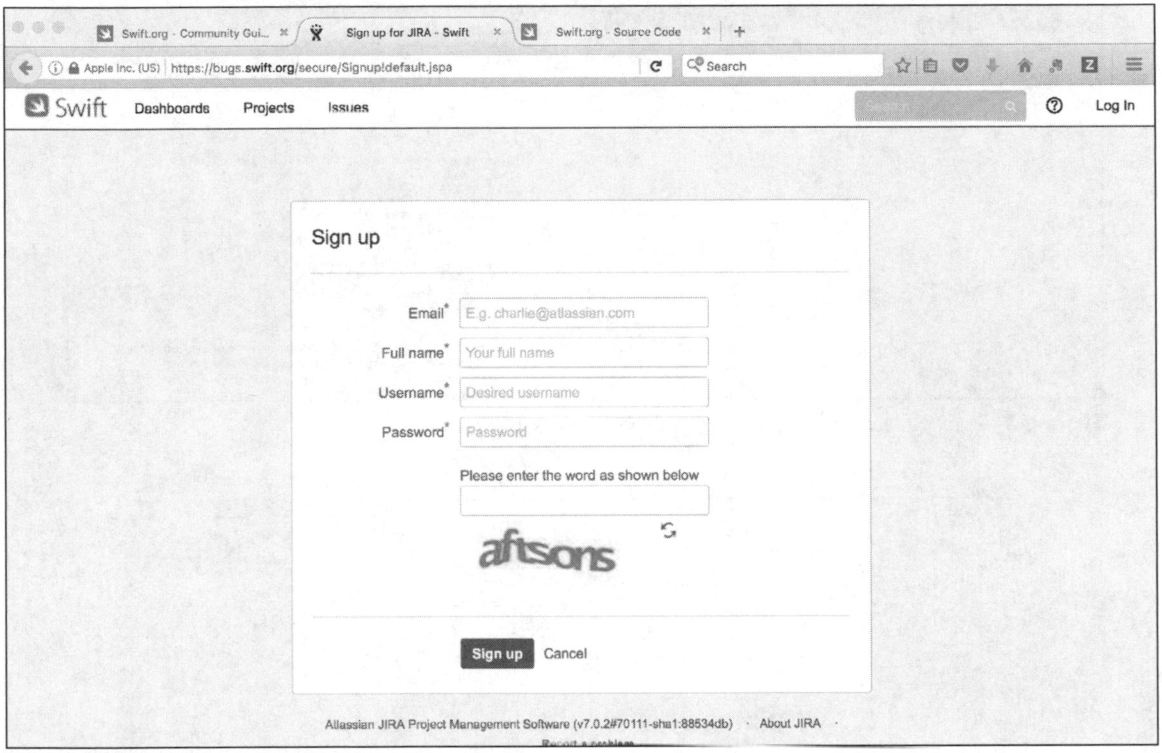

Figure 1-3: Sign-up web page for a Swift JIRA bug-tracking account

After you create a Swift.org bug-tracking system account, you can return to the login web page, which also serves as the system dashboard. On this page, you can see a feed of recent project activity and log in to your new account. Figure 1-4 shows a typical dashboard view.

When you log in to the Swift.org bug-tracking system, the first page you see gives you a choice of three activities to pursue, as shown in Figure 1-5. You can choose to begin the process of creating and submitting a new bug report about some defect in the Swift code. Or, you can search for bug reports that match some criteria that you're interested in. Perhaps someone else has already submitted a bug report for the same problem that you are experiencing and it would save you time if you didn't have to create a duplicate. The third path allows you to explore the projects and view Kanban boards of the associated work, as well as generate reports about various metrics that are measured against the activity tracked in the system.

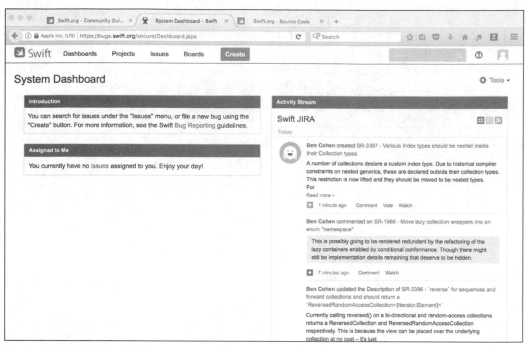

Figure 1-4: Swift.org bug-tracking dashboard and login page

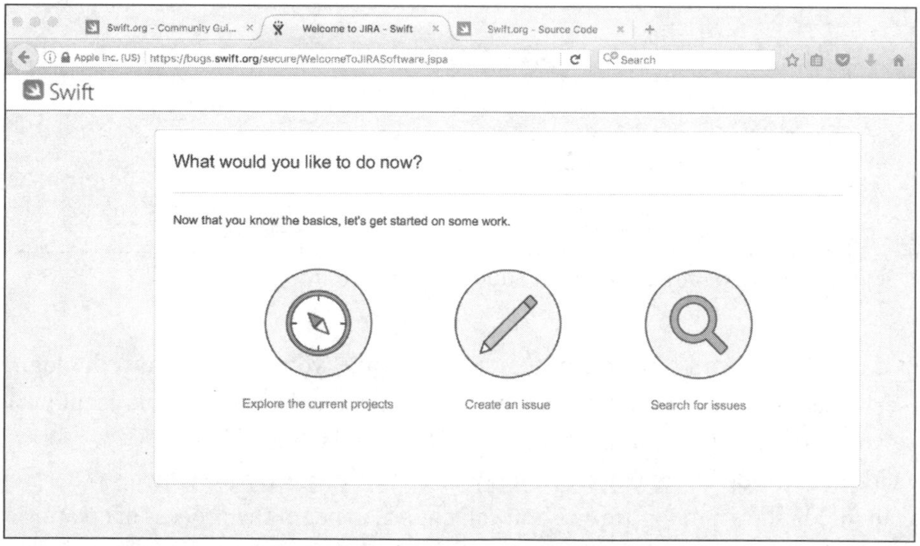

Figure 1-5: Swift.org bug tracking—what would you like to do now?

Figure 1-6 shows the web page where you can browse the list of projects to explore. The list shown in the figure only contains the main Swift.org project. By clicking the Boards tab in the main menu bar, you can access a web page that shows a list of the available Kanban boards, as shown in Figure 1-7.

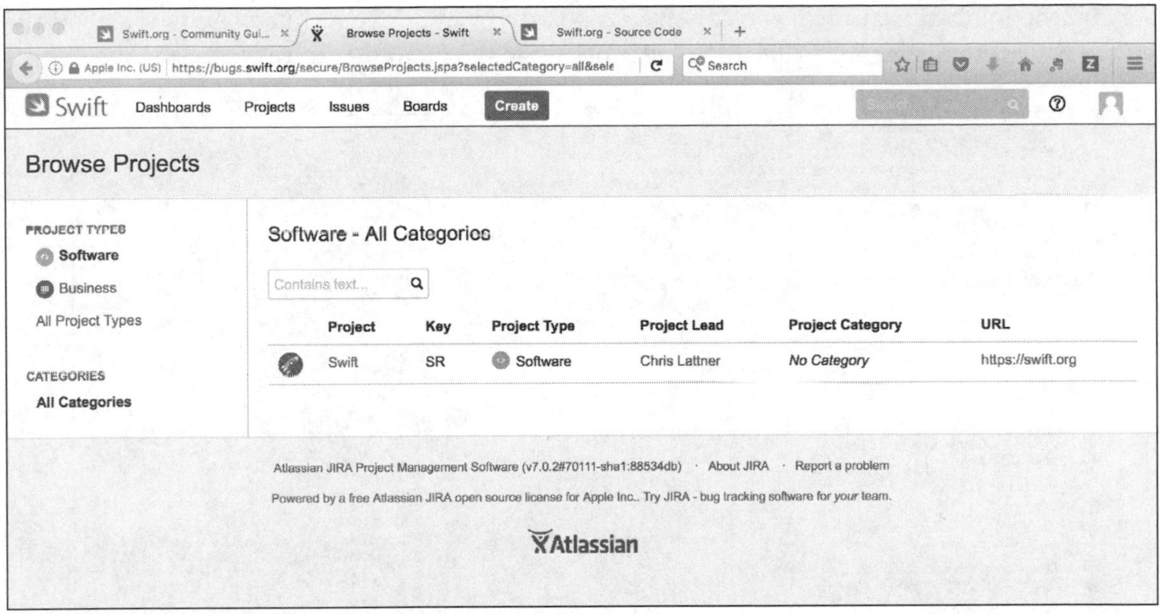

Figure 1-6: Swift.org bug-tracking Projects list

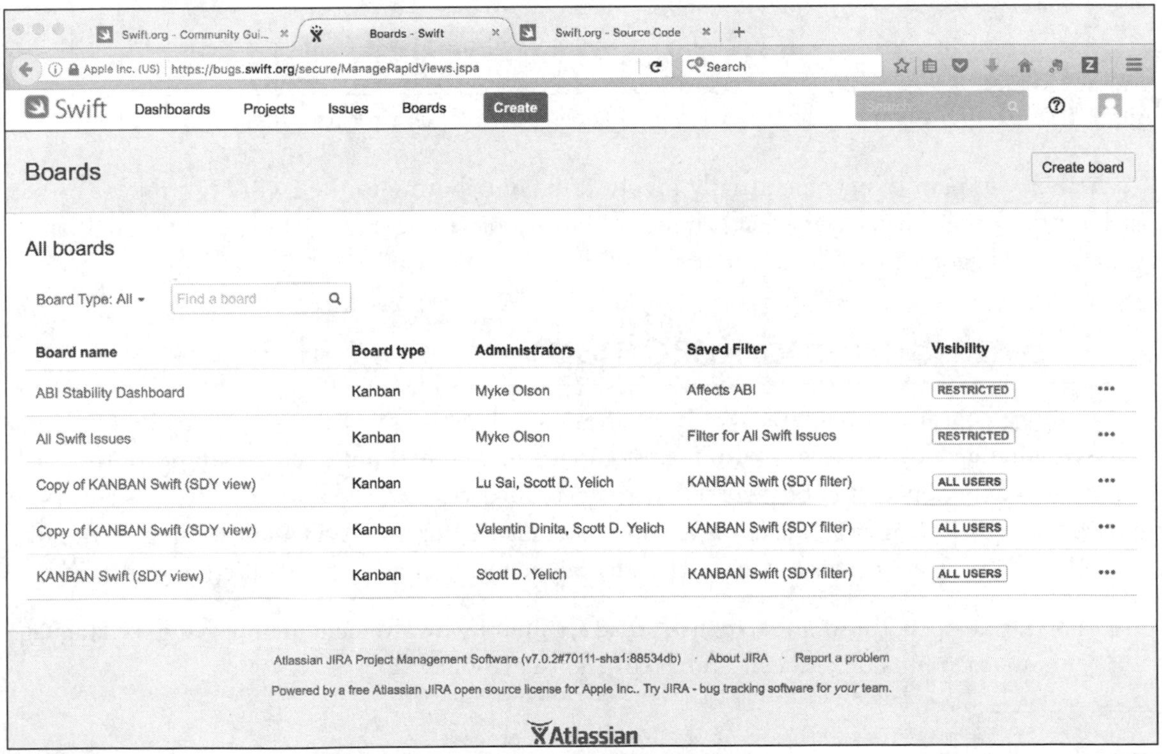

Figure 1-7: Swift.org bug tracking, showing a list of Kanban boards

From the Kanban board list, you can select a board to view, or you can choose to see all of the issue cards consolidated on one board for all projects, as shown in Figure 1-8.

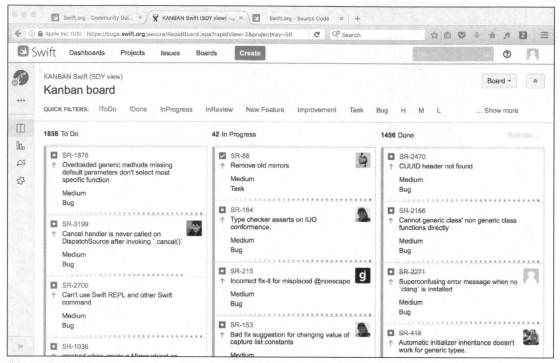

Figure 1-8: Swift.org bug tracking, showing the Kanban board for all projects

Whether you plan to become heavily involved in contributing to the Swift.org projects or you just want to explore the activity that is underway in a project, the bug-tracking tool for Swift.org is a valuable application to know how to use.

Swift Evolution and Roadmap

The Swift.org community established the *Swift evolution process* to define a consistent way for a proposed language feature to grow from a rough idea into something that can "improve the Swift development experience" and be included in an upcoming release.[1] The evolution process covers all changes to the Swift language, including any new language features or API (application programming interface) enhancements. This process strives to balance and achieve two conflicting goals:

- Provide an open, transparent, robust, broad community involvement in improving the language
- "Maintain the vision and conceptual coherence of Swift"[2]

---

[1] https://github.com/apple/swift-evolution/blob/master/process.md
[2] https://github.com/apple/swift-evolution/blob/master/process.md

Everyone is welcome to propose new ideas for improvement of the Swift language, and to engage in the review and discussion of these ideas. However, there is a *core team* that is ultimately responsible for the strategic direction of the Swift language and that has the authority to accept or reject proposed changes. The members of this core team will change over time, but the latest membership list can be found on the Swift.org Community web page at `https://swift.org/community/#community-structure`.

Every proposal for a new feature undergoes a thorough, public review and discussion before being accepted or rejected. Each proposal is considered in relation to the specific goals for the upcoming release, whether the proposal is significant enough to warrant making the change to Swift, and whether the proposal fits well with the direction of the language, especially compared with other programming languages and ecosystems.

To participate in this evolutionary process for Swift, you can follow the instructions documented at `https://github.com/apple/swift-evolution/blob/master/process.md` and submit a proposal for consideration. Once submitted, your proposal will progress through various states in the process until its ultimate status is determined. As of this writing, the states that your proposal may inhabit will be one of the following:

- **Awaiting review**—The proposal is awaiting review. Once known, the dates for the actual review are placed in the proposal document and updated in the list of proposals. When the review period begins, the review manager updates the state to *Active review*.
- **Scheduled for review (MONTH DAY. . .MONTH DAY)**—The public review of the proposal on the swift-evolution mailing list has been scheduled for the specified date range.
- **Active review (MONTH DAY. . .MONTH DAY)**—The proposal is undergoing public review on the swift-evolution mailing list. The review continues through the specified date range.
- **Returned for revision**—The proposal has been returned from review for additional revision to the current draft.
- **Withdrawn**—The proposal has been withdrawn by the original submitter.
- **Deferred**—Consideration of the proposal has been deferred because it does not meet the goals of the upcoming major Swift release. Deferred proposals are reconsidered when scoping the next major Swift release.
- **Accepted**—The proposal has been accepted and is either awaiting implementation or is actively being implemented.
- **Accepted with revisions**—The proposal has been accepted, contingent upon the inclusion of one or more revisions.
- **Rejected**—The proposal has been considered and rejected.
- **Implemented (Swift VERSION)**—The proposal has been implemented. The version number is appended in parentheses, for example, Implemented (Swift 2.2). If the proposal's implementation spans multiple version numbers, the version number is indicated for the implementation that will be complete.

Priorities for the Swift 4.0 Major Release

When Swift was first made open source on December 3, 2015, the official release number at that time was 2.2. From that point on, the Swift language evolution process was followed in order to plan for a 3.0 release in September 2016. Version 3.0 of Swift included many breaking changes in the source and in the API. However, this was done intentionally to avoid any additional breakages in subsequent releases. As of this writing, you can look forward to version 4.0 in 2017, with the Swift community focusing primarily in that release on source stability and ABI (application binary interface) compatibility.

ABI compatibility is important because it allows a developer to create a pre-built library of Swift code using one version of the compiler, and then another developer can link their application with that pre-built Swift library without having to worry about using the same version of the compiler that was used to build the library. There is no ABI compatibility for Swift release 3.0 and earlier, and so developers of application frameworks and libraries have to create multiple compiler-specific versions of their deliverable. Also, the developers who want to consume these libraries need to ensure that the compiler they use for their application matches the one used to build the linked binary libraries. With only a few versions of the Swift compiler released, this has not yet become a serious problem. However, as more versions are released, the critical need for ABI compatibility will increase.

Of course, the concern about lack of ABI compatibility can be (and is being) addressed by developers distributing their libraries in source code instead of binary format. Source-code distributed libraries will be compiled by the same compiler that is used for the main application. So, in theory, this mechanism for distributing libraries will always be "compatible." However, there are some problems with source code distributed libraries. For example, many developers want to distribute libraries in binary form so that they can protect their intellectual property contained in the library code. Commercial products offered for sale, that include libraries or frameworks, are especially concerned about preventing code piracy, and ABI compatibility is a crucial feature for them. Furthermore, even source level compatibility has not been fully realized between Swift language releases (at least up to 3.0).

You can find more information on these focus areas at `https://github.com/apple/swift-evolution/`.

Binary Downloads

Swift.org binary releases (`https://swift.org/download/`) include installable versions of Swift for Apple macOS as well as Ubuntu Linux hosts. These releases are organized as official releases, preview releases, and development snapshots.

The official releases are typically what you should use for developing applications using Swift. Preview releases are useful to test whether your existing application contains any language usage that is broken by planned upcoming language enhancements. Development snapshots are most often used by programmers who are actively working on the actual language. Having all of these binary versions of the language available for download demonstrates the openness and transparency for public scrutiny that characterizes Swift.org operating practices.

MacOS Binaries

On macOS, the most recent Xcode version includes the latest official Swift language binaries. So, if you already have Xcode installed and updated on your system, you should not need to download a binary release from Swift.org unless you are planning to work on upcoming releases of the language or to test your app against a preview release. It is very important to keep in mind that in order to submit an app to the Apple App Store, you must build your app using the version of Swift that is included within Xcode. The supported target platforms for production apps using Swift are:

- macOS 10.9.0 or later
- iOS 7.0 or later
- watchOS 2.0 or later
- tvOS 9.0 or later

There are installation instructions on the Swift.org website for how to set up a downloaded version of Swift binaries to be used by Xcode instead of the default version that ships with Xcode. Note that setting up the Xcode IDE tool to use a different version of Swift does not change what is used by the command line (`xcodebuild` and `xcrun` commands). You must either modify the `PATH` environment variable to put the new Swift release `/bin` directory ahead of other paths, or else use the explicit `-toolchain` parameter on the command line invocation:

```
$ xcodebuild -toolchain . . .
```
or

```
$ export PATH=/Library/Developer/Toolchains/swiftlatest.xctoolchain/usr/bin:"${PATH}"
```

The `.pkg` package file downloaded from Swift.org and all the binary files contained in the package are digitally signed by the developer ID of the Swift open source project so that you know you have the official version and not code that has been tampered with.

The Swift Toolchain Installer program on macOS should display a lock icon on the right side of its title bar. Clicking the lock brings up detailed information about the signature (see Figure 1-9). The signature should be produced by "Developer ID Installer: Swift Open Source (V9AUD2URP3)." If the lock is not displayed or the signature is not produced by the Swift open source developer ID, *do not proceed* with the installation. Instead, quit the installer and send an email to `swift-infrastructure@swift.org` with as much detail as possible. The importance of ensuring that you are only using binary images produced by Swift.org cannot be overstated. Images that come from other sources may contain malware or other undesirable content that you would not want to include in your application and unknowingly put into production.

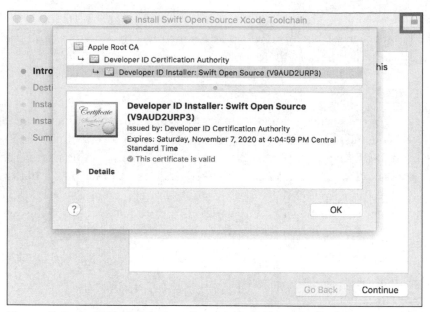

Figure 1-9: Swift Toolchain Installer showing signature detail

Linux Binaries

The Swift language packages are built and tested against the Ubuntu 14.04 and 15.10 (64-bit) Linux distributions. This does not mean that Swift only works on these distributions of Linux, only that these are the two distributions that Swift.org uses for testing and verification.

Before attempting to install a downloaded Linux binary package for Swift, you need to install some prerequisite libraries—clang and libicu-dev:

```
$ sudo apt-get install clang libicu-dev
```

You can then install the downloaded TAR archive for Swift to any location as long as the extracted /bin directory is included in your PATH environment variable.

The first time that you install Swift on a Linux host, you have to import the supplied PGP keys into your keyring. Once this is done on a given Linux system, it does not have to be repeated for subsequent binary downloads and installation.

Swift packages that are downloaded to Linux are digitally signed with keys of the Swift open source project. For the same reasons that macOS binary release packages must be checked to ensure that they haven't been tampered with, Linux binary packages must also be verified.

The Swift.org download web page includes a section about the Active Signing Keys used by the project and how to obtain them. You use the GPG command on Linux to verify the signature of the Swift.org binaries. GPG is an encryption and signing tool for Linux operating systems; it is used along with the active signing key from Swift.org to confirm that the binary download truly matches the package produced by the open source project. If you follow the verification instructions, and the gpg command fails to verify and returns a report of "BAD signature," *do not use the downloaded package*. Instead, send an email to swift-infrastructure@swift.org to report the situation along with as much detail as possible.

Swiftenv, Swift Version Manager

Due to the dynamic and rapid evolution of the Swift language, developers using Swift need to juggle multiple release levels of the language on the same workstation. Manually switching between different releases of Swift on the same system can be slow, cumbersome, and error-prone.

In order to address this issue, the community has rallied around a tool called swiftenv to help developers manage multiple versions of the Swift binaries on both macOS and Linux. This tool and the instructions for installing it can be found at https://github.com/kylef/swiftenv. You can install the tool from this GitHub project or by using the Homebrew tool, which is probably the easiest method.

The swiftenv tool allows developers to set a global version of Swift to use as the default on their system. This default language release level can be overridden by changing an environment variable, as well as configured specifically for each project implemented using Swift.

The swiftenv tool offers integration with multiple continuous-integration build tools such as Travis CI, GitLabs CI, and CircleCI. This integration helps ensure that your automated build and deploy system always uses the proper release version of the Swift language, rather than whatever may be the default version that is accessed first in the environment PATH.

Several Docker images are also available that contain swiftenv. The Docker images are based on Ubuntu Linux and include a release version of the Swift language in addition to the Swift Version Manager tool. A buildpack is also available for Heroku so that you can automatically install the local version of Swift that you've specified in that environment. Documentation for Swift Version Manager is available at https://swiftenv.fuller.li/en/latest/.

Summary

The Swift.org open source community is an active group composed of representatives from many high-tech companies, as well as passionate individuals committed to the transparent development of the language and its supporting libraries and tools. You can follow the development and evolution of Swift by getting involved in this community and contributing in one of several different ways.

The Swift.org community depends on involvement from a broad range of users—from beginning programmers to seasoned developers. You have many choices for how to, and how much to, contribute, so you can tailor your involvement to fit your needs, skill level, and available time. Of course, by finding your own way to become involved in the Swift evolution process, you may discover that you have gone through your own evolution at the same time!

CHAPTER 2

A Swift Sandbox in the Cloud

When Apple made the Swift language open source on Swift.org, they also made available an Ubuntu Linux version of the language for binary download. IBM responded by announcing the IBM Swift Sandbox (`https://swift.sandbox.bluemix.net`), which is a website that developers can visit to write Swift code in a web-based code editor. When they are ready, the developers can click the run button and their code is compiled and runs on a fresh Linux container in the IBM Bluemix Cloud.

While the Sandbox was originally intended to simply allow developers easy, one-click access to the newly released Swift language runtimes on Linux, the response from the development community was very positive. Based on feedback from the community, IBM has added a number of features, including selecting specific versions of the Swift language to be used to compile the code; creating immutable snapshots of developers' Sandbox code that returns a Sandbox URL that can be used on mailing lists, blogs, and Stack Overflow; adding personalization to allow users to save code in the Sandbox for later use; better support on mobile devices; and even the ability to embed Sandbox code and results in a user's own blog or webpage.

This chapter will cover a number of these use cases, as well as introduce a few Swift samples that you can try.

The IBM Cloud Platform

The Linux environment hosting the Swift Sandbox that we will be using for examples in the next two chapters is one of several runtime environments available for free on the IBM cloud platform, also called IBM Bluemix. Before we cover the Swift Sandbox part of Bluemix, you might find it helpful to get a brief introduction to the overall Bluemix cloud platform and environment.

There are many cloud computing environments available on the Internet. In general, a cloud computing environment usually offers a self-service approach for users to acquire various kinds of computing capabilities on an as-needed basis, and pay for these computing capabilities with a subscription model (sometimes called pay-as-you-go). Originally the computing capabilities offered by cloud environments were narrowly focused on various flavors of virtual machines—an entire computer run in virtual mode. But as time has progressed and the cloud computing market has matured, there is now a vast selection of runtimes, services, and tools available to rent from the cloud vendors.

Modern enterprise cloud platforms offer dozens or even hundreds of virtual application components and services. These cloud services are typically based on so-called "cloud native principles" to be easily provisioned, scalable, and flexible for developer needs. Some of the distinct advantages of leveraging cloud platforms for your software development and deployment include:

- **Low cost of experimentation**—Since you only pay for what you use, it can cost as little as nothing to deploy some code in a cloud environment and see how it works (or if it works!).
- **Vast scalability**—Enterprise cloud platforms have thousands of physical computers behind the virtual façade of the cloud environment. One of the main aspects of cloud platforms is: The more resources you need, the more that will be available.
- **Rapid deployment**—While deployment time is dependent on the type of code and application runtime used, in general it is faster to push code to a cloud environment and get it running. This is especially true if you employ so-called "cloud native" application architectures and runtimes.
- **Wide choice of services**—Enterprise cloud platforms offer a vast array of pre-built, pre-tested "services" that can be used as Lego blocks of software to be assembled into a full application.

There are many cloud environments that serve niche needs and a few that serve large-scale enterprise requirements. Amazon Web Services is an example of an enterprise cloud platform, and so is Microsoft Azure as well as Google cloud platform. IBM also offers an enterprise cloud platform called IBM Bluemix, and this is the cloud environment in which the Swift@IBM team built and hosts a Swift Sandbox that we'll be using several times in this book.

In order to use the Swift Sandbox in Bluemix for the examples in this book, you will have to sign up for a free Bluemix account. Start by pointing your web browser at `www.bluemix.net`. Figure 2-1 shows an image of the Bluemix login page, which changes appearance now and then, so don't be concerned if it looks slightly different when you visit it. There is a Sign up button on the Bluemix home page, so you can click on that button if you don't already have an account. Enter in the information required to establish one of the free user accounts for the IBM cloud platform.

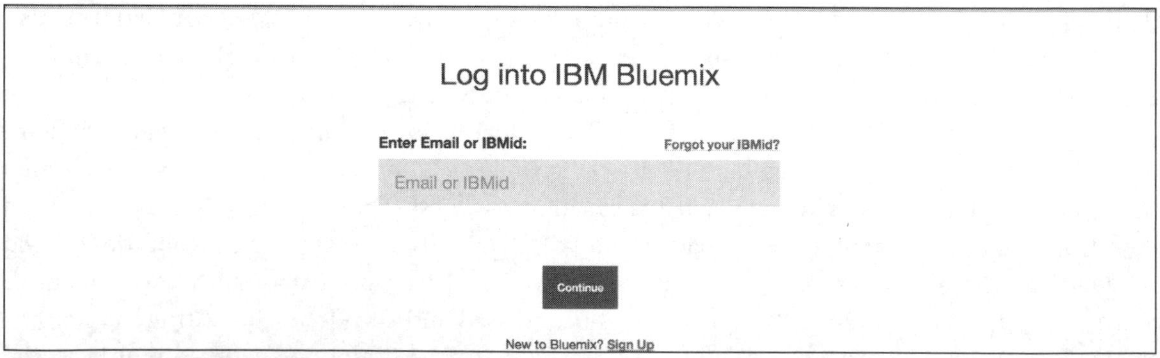

Log into IBM Bluemix

Enter Email or IBMid: Forgot your IBMid?

Email or IBMid

Continue

New to Bluemix? Sign Up

Figure 2-1: IBM Bluemix cloud platform login page

Once you have signed up for a Bluemix account (or if you already have one), you can login to the cloud platform and see your dashboard user interface (Figure 2-2) which displays any applications or services that you have deployed in your Bluemix cloud environment.

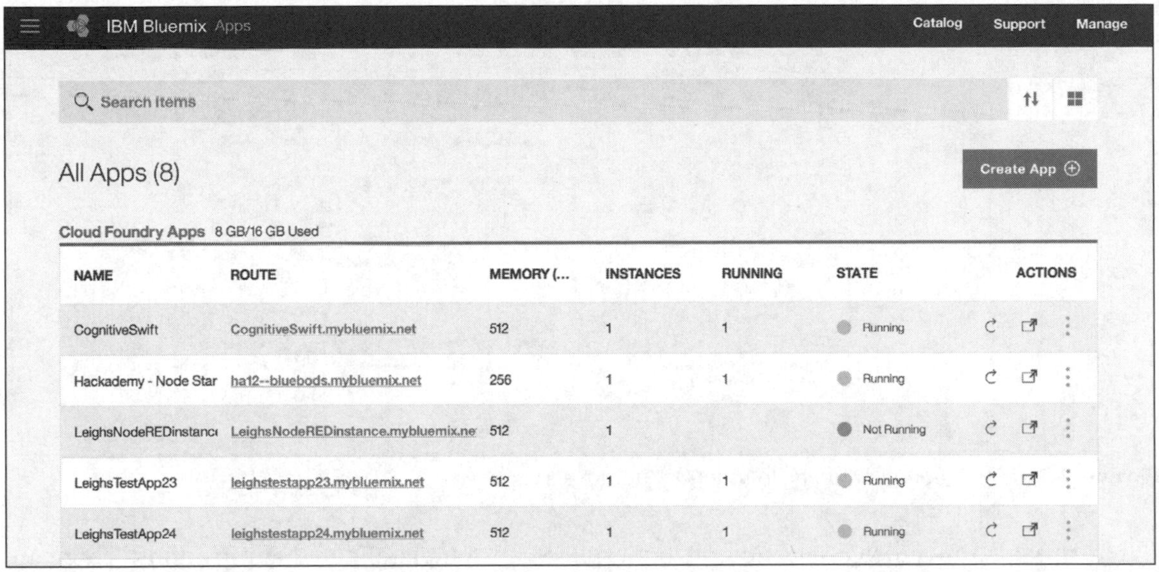

Figure 2-2: Typical Bluemix cloud platform user dashboard

IBM Bluemix is a cloud computing platform originally based on the open-source Cloud Foundry project. More recently, the IBM cloud platform includes support for Docker image applications, pure Virtual Machine (VM) images, and even "Bare metal" compute capabilities, in addition to the standard Cloud Foundry code. Beyond the runtime and compute infrastructure services, IBM has added dozens of additional enterprise-class language runtimes and application services. There are also more than 30 cloud services for code development and testing, as well as automated code deployment and monitoring (so called DevOps services). Many of the additional services in Bluemix have been developed by IBM, but there are also dozens of services from other third-party vendors besides just IBM.

Click on the Catalog tab in the upper right of your dashboard in order to explore the range of services available in Bluemix. You will see the top of the Catalog view in your web browser, as shown in Figure 2-3.

From the top of the Services Catalog in Bluemix (Figure 2-3), you can either scroll down through all of the service listings or you can click on one of the fast navigation links on the left side of the page in order to jump to a specific group of services such as Containers or Mobile application component services.

You can use the cloud services in Bluemix in many different ways to create applications. And you can link the cloud services in Bluemix with non-cloud based code to form what is called a hybrid cloud application. Given the amount of existing non-cloud IT services, data and applications, it seems reasonable to imagine that hybrid cloud applications will be very common for quite a few years. So the Bluemix platform includes lots of integration and security components that come in handy when assembling hybrid software solutions.

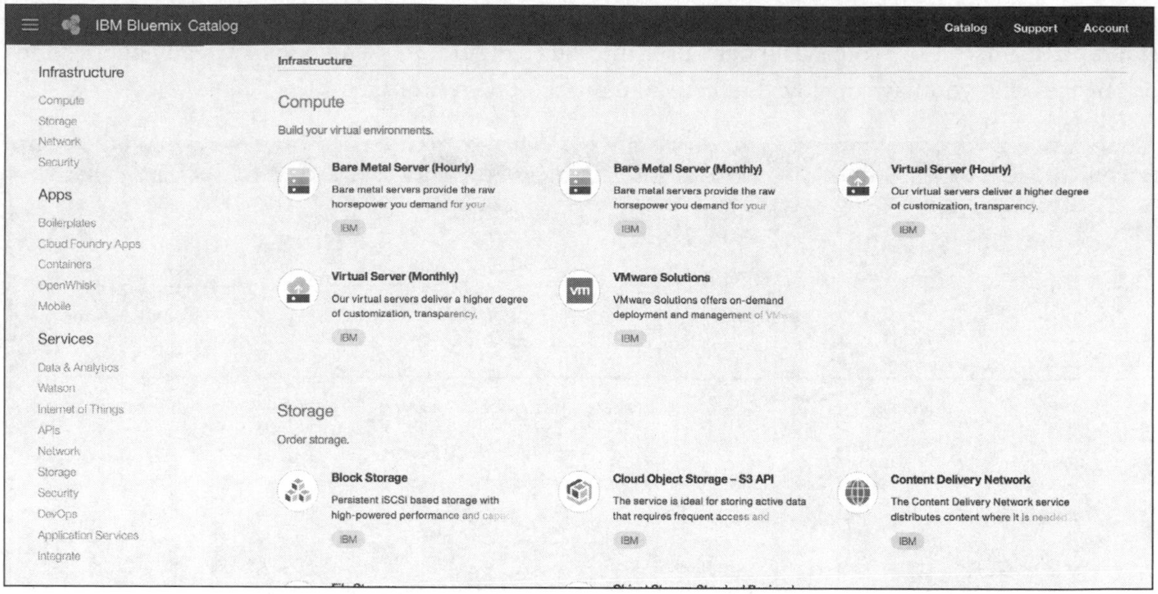

Figure 2-3: IBM Bluemix catalog cloud infrastructure services view

Bluemix also includes a selection of "boilerplate" (or template) cloud applications. These are quite useful for getting a new application running in an initial configuration, if the application that you want to build happens to match with one of the available boilerplates in the Bluemix catalog. Figure 2-4 shows a partial list of the boilerplates that you can choose in Bluemix.

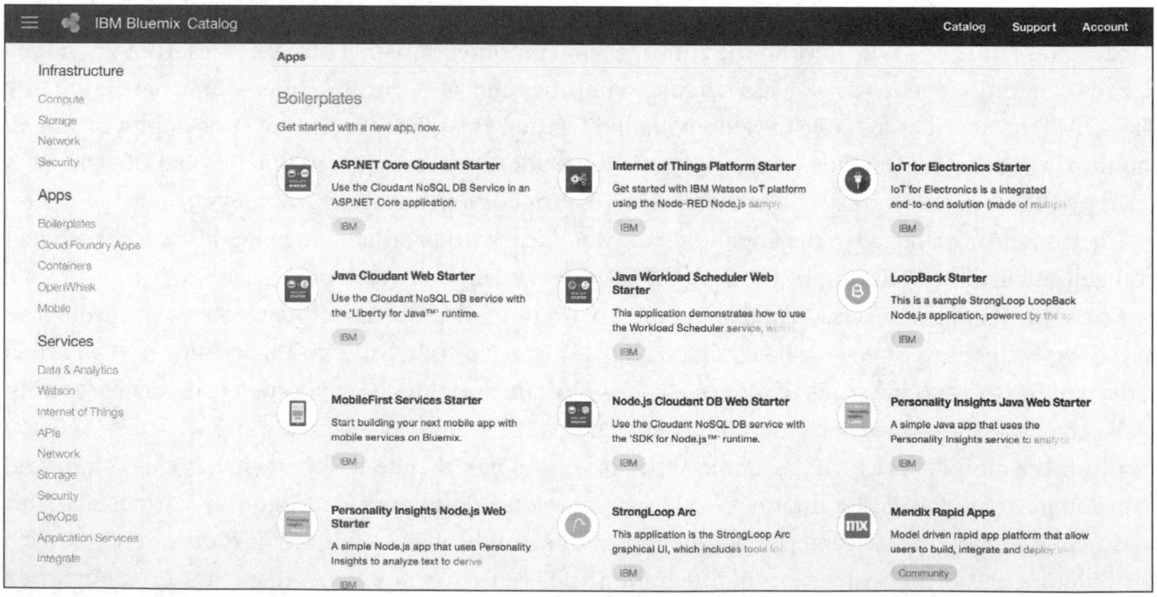

Figure 2-4: Partial list of boilerplate cloud application templates in Bluemix catalog

In addition to using boilerplates as a way to get started developing applications in Bluemix, you can select from a variety of application runtime environments in which to execute your application code. Bluemix offers runtime support for Cloud Foundry buildpacks, Docker containers, and Virtual Machine images, so it is possible to run almost any kind of application code in this cloud environment. There are more details about running applications written in Swift using Cloud Foundry buildpacks in Chapter 4 of this book. And Chapter 5 goes into detail about how to leverage containers in Bluemix to host your Swift application.

The platform includes software development tools too, so you can set up an automated continuous-integration, continuous delivery pipeline to process code changes for your application as soon as they are committed. Figure 2-5 shows a list of development tools available in Bluemix.

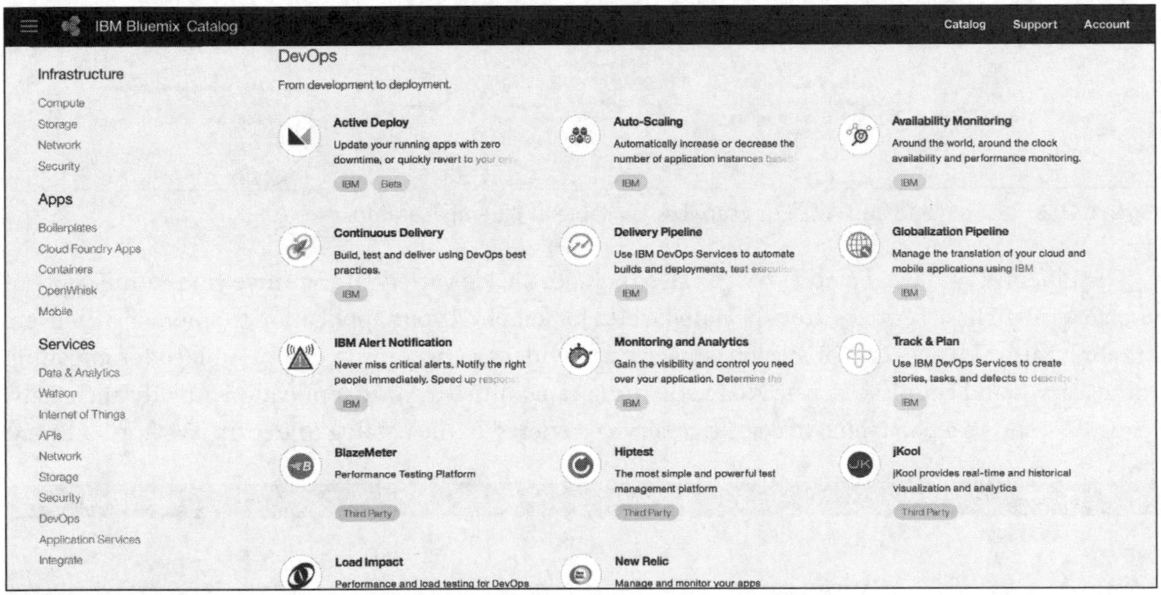

Figure 2-5: List of DevOps development tools available in Bluemix catalog

The Bluemix cloud platform also offers dozens of virtualized application components—"services" that can be bound to your application and used within it by having your application code invoke the programmatic interface (the API) for the service. These cloud services would be extremely expensive for you to develop on your own but, when incorporated into your application with a pay-as-you-go subscription cost, they are very affordable and offer a way to quickly enhance your application with scalable, tested, production-ready capabilities.

There are numerous kinds of database systems available "as-a-Service" in the Bluemix catalog, including support for both structured data and unstructured (also known as NoSQL databases). In addition to data storage and management services, there are also many kinds of data analytics services that you can use in your application. See Figure 2-6 for a partial view of the analytics available.

Figure 2-6: List of Data and Analytics services available in Bluemix catalog

The Bluemix catalog of cloud services also includes a wide variety of cognitive computing application services. These services are especially useful for enabling your application to interact with users in more natural ways. Use of speech, images, and videos is becoming commonplace for engaging applications, and cognitive services can add these capabilities to your application quickly and easily. Figure 2-7 shows a partial list of cognitive services offered in the catalog under the Watson category.

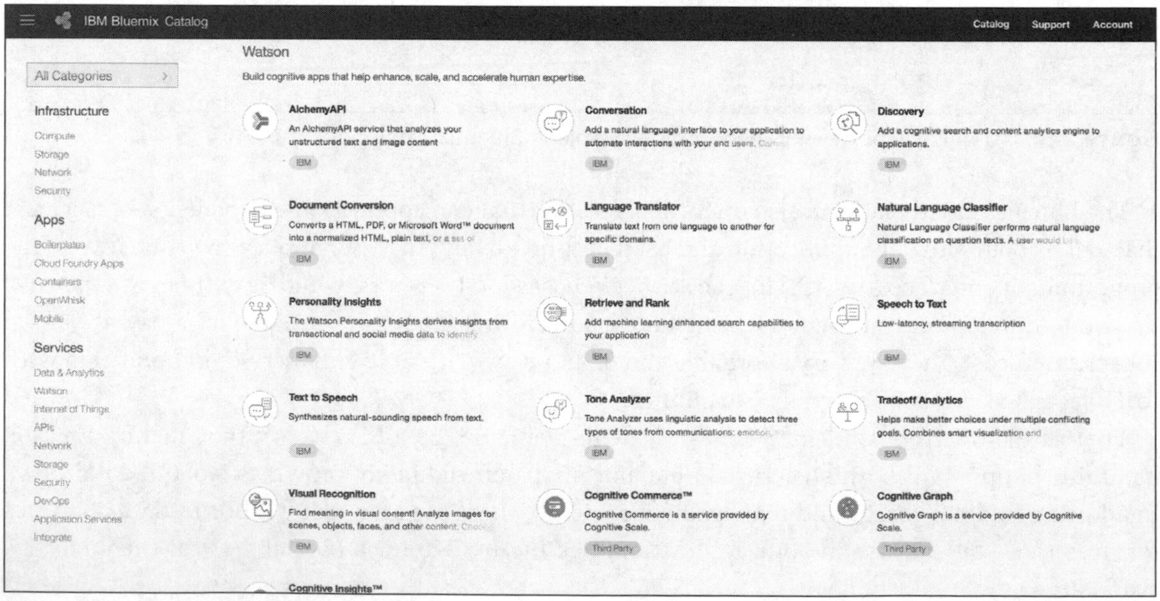

Figure 2-7: Watson Cognitive application services shown in Bluemix catalog

There are several categories of services in Bluemix, including a group called Application Services (see Figure 2-8). This group of services contains sophisticated functions such as Blockchain fabric, video services, asynchronous messaging services, and many non-IBM services offered by different companies for you to use within your application.

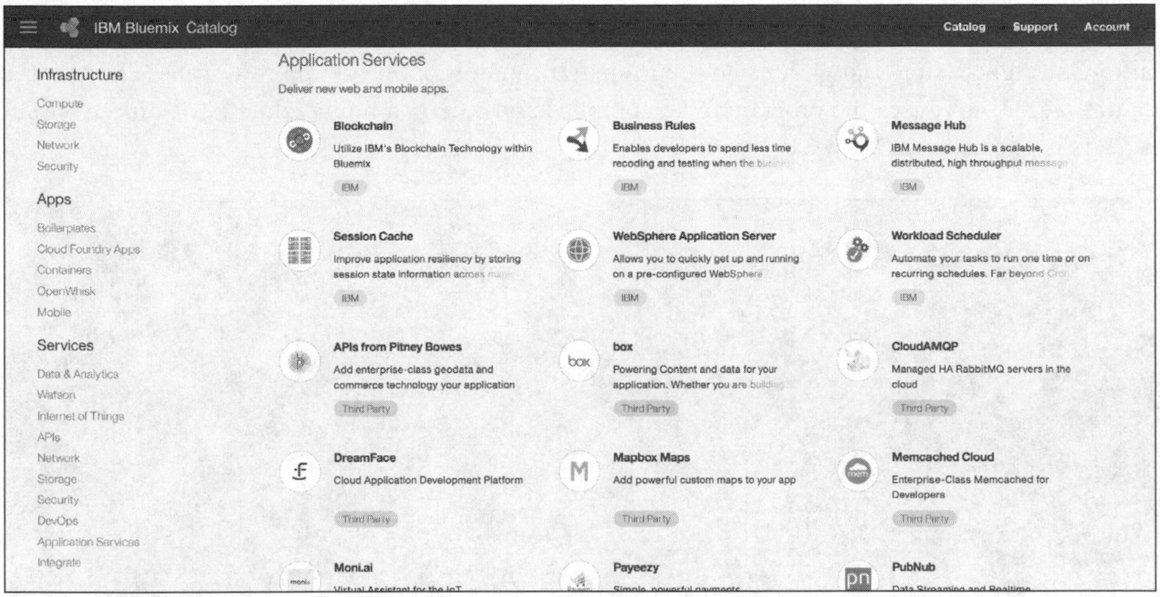

Figure 2-8: Application Services available in the Bluemix catalog

There are dozens of other kinds of application services in the Bluemix catalog. An entire book would be needed to fully address all of the virtual infrastructure services, application runtimes, data storage services, and application services in the IBM cloud platform catalog. And the list of services gets added to almost weekly, so the book would be out of date before it was printed!

Developers typically select the services from the Bluemix catalog that they want to use in their application and bind those services to their application. Binding a service to an application means that the logic in that application can easily make use of the service because it has access to the necessary service credentials and other properties needed when the API for the service is invoked. These service instance properties that are dynamically generated for each instance of a service when that service is bound to the application, are stored in the VCAP_SERVICES environment variable for the application. Other code within that application can access the information in the VCAP_SERVICES environment variable and use it to call the bound service instance. This topic of service binding will become more important in later chapters, so keep it in mind.

The Swift Sandbox is another service running in the IBM cloud platform. You can reach it directly using the web address `https://swift.sandbox.bluemix.net`. Go ahead and access that web page in your browser now and we will begin exploring the Sandbox in greater depth.

Getting Started

When you visit the Sandbox website, the default screen displays a code editor on the left side and an output window on the right. The default sample code is, of course, a small Swift program that prints "Hello world!"

To run this simple program, you click the Execute icon at the bottom of the screen. The Execute button is a right-facing triangle, or arrow, button in the middle of the bottom row of the Sandbox (see Figure 2-9). This causes the program to be compiled and run on a Linux container, and the output appears to the right, as shown in Figure 2-9.

Figure 2-9: Swift "Hello world!" program shown in the Swift Sandbox

The Sandbox also includes a number of code samples that you can load into the editor, edit, and run.

When you click the Load Code button in the bottom left-left corner, shown in Figure 2-10, a pop-up window appears where you can select either from a set of basic samples included by the Sandbox or from popular community samples that have been shared.

Sign Me Up!

While many features are available within the Sandbox while anonymous, it is often nice to be able to save code samples you are working on and retrieve them later. The Sandbox allows you to sign in with either your IBM Bluemix Cloud ID or your GitHub ID. Figure 2-11 shows a typical login prompt for the Swift Sandbox. Once you are signed in, you can save your code samples and retrieve them later from another device by signing in with the same account.

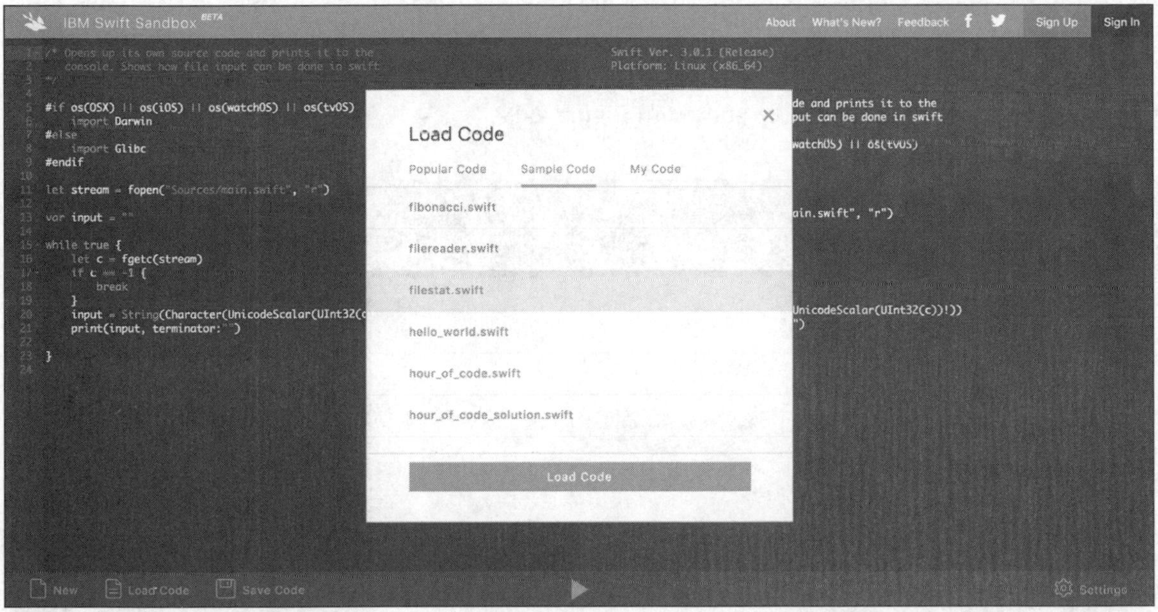

Figure 2-10: Loading sample Swift code into the Sandbox

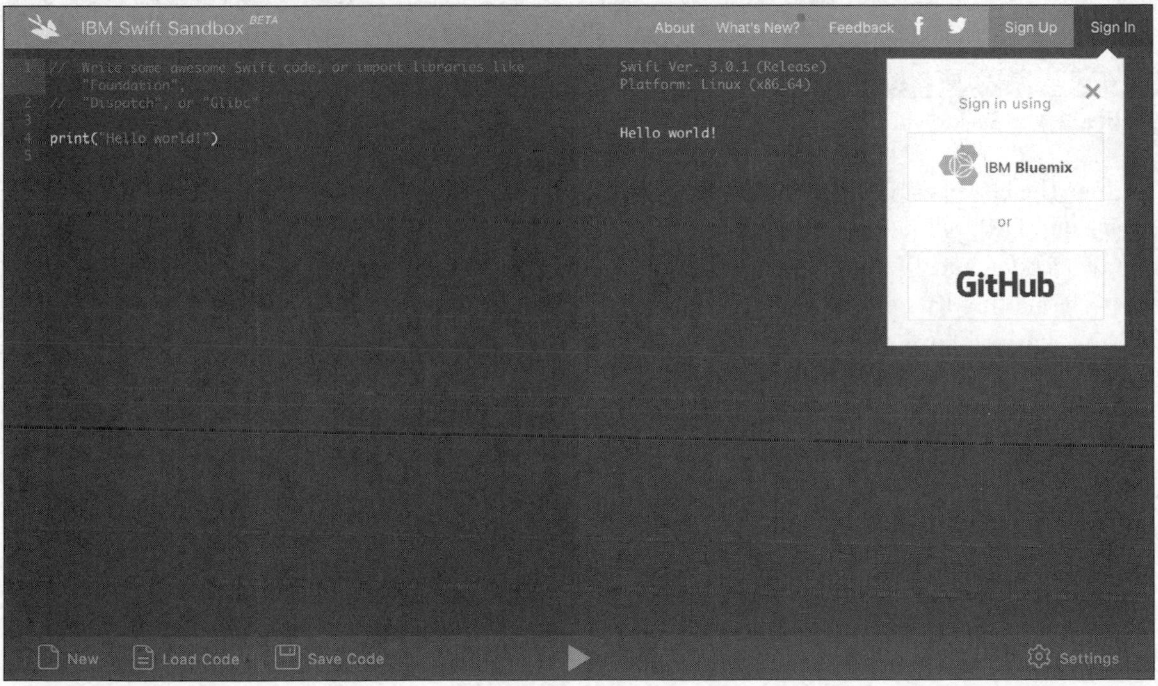

Figure 2-11: Signing in to the Swift Sandbox

Saving and Sharing Code Samples

The Sandbox is a great place to easily test your Swift code on Linux with a single click. Because the code editor is hosted in the Cloud, it is also a great place to share code samples with others. Once you have a piece of code you want to share, you can click the Save Code button at the bottom left of the screen. This brings up a window that prompts you to enter a name for your sample along with a simple description of your code, as shown in Figure 2-12.

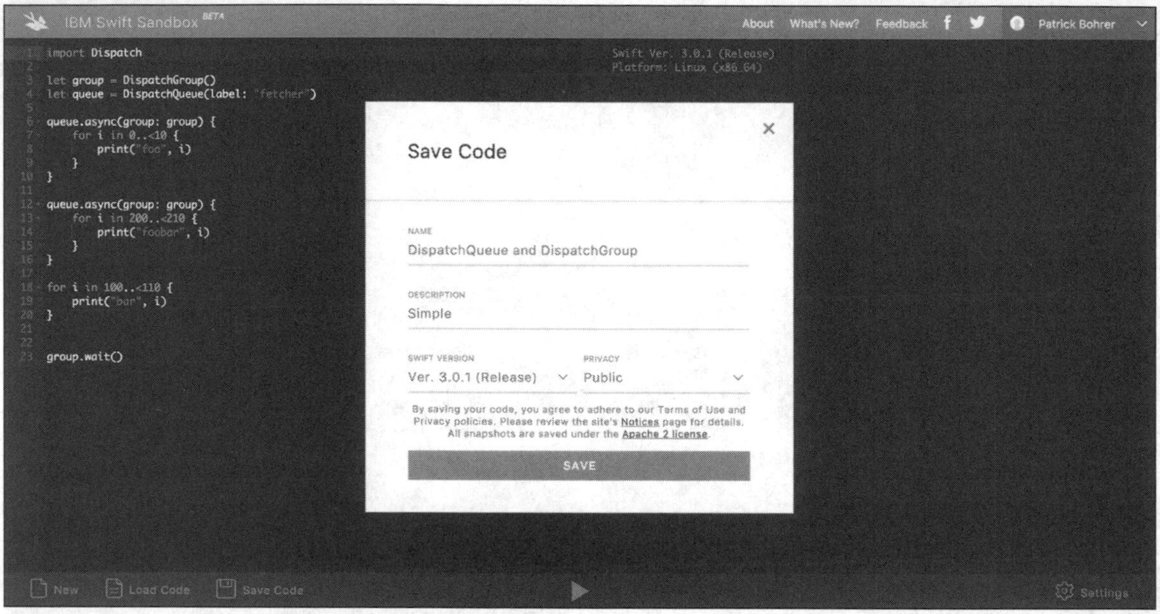

Figure 2-12: Saving your code in the Swift Sandbox

Once the code is saved, a window appears, prompting you to share your sample. You can either copy a new URL pointer to an immutable copy of your code saved in the IBM cloud, or you can share it via Facebook and Twitter, as shown in Figure 2-13. This is also a great way to ask or answer questions via mailing lists or Stack Overflow by sharing pointers to executable code.

Now that you have saved your sample, you can also click in the top-right corner on your name, as shown in Figure 2-14, and choose My Code.

This brings up a dialog box shown in Figure 2-15 with all of the code samples you have saved.

Once you select the code, you can choose to load it in the editor, share the saved code, or delete it.

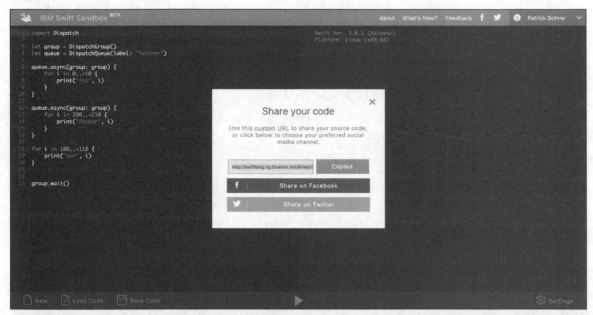

Figure 2-13: Share your code from the Swift Sandbox

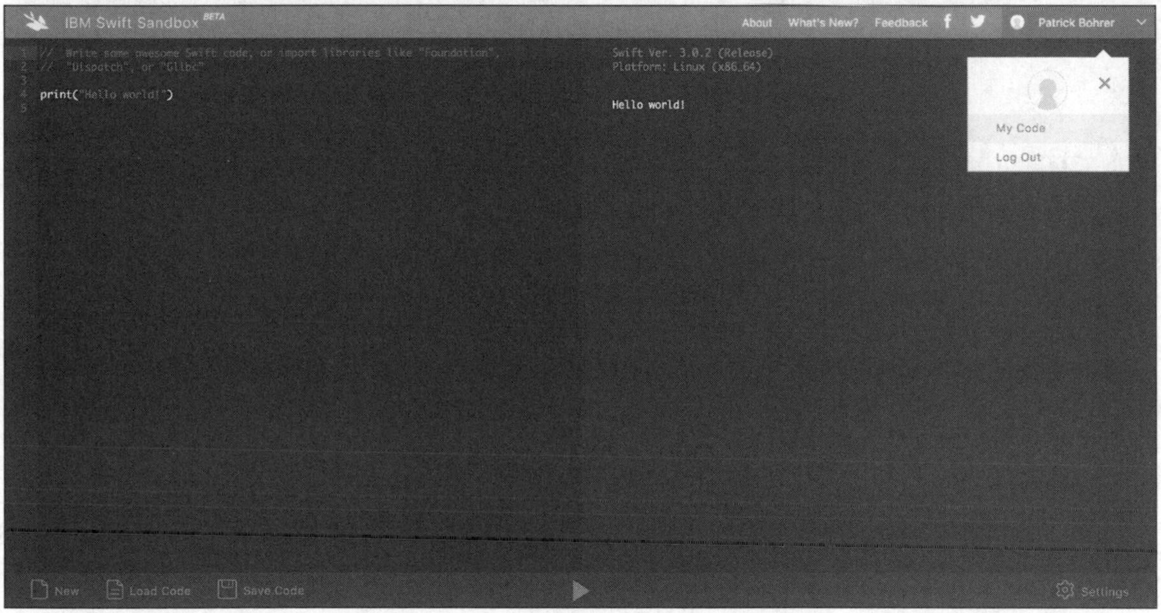

Figure 2-14: Accessing your saved code from within the Swift Sandbox

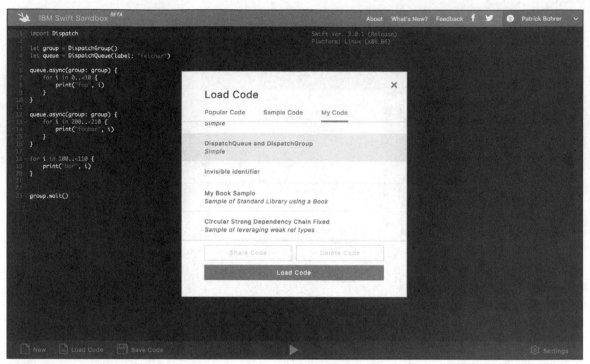

Figure 2-15: Reloading your saved code in the Swift Sandbox

Selecting Swift Versions and More

Over the past few years, Swift has undergone a number of iterations from version 1 in 2014 to version, 3, in 2016. Now that Swift is open source, a much bigger community is interested in helping the language to evolve over time by participating in the Swift Evolution process (https://github.com/apple/swift-evolution).

To help the community, IBM has extended the Sandbox to allow users to select from among a set of Swift versions in which they would like to compile and run their code (see Figure 2-16). At the time of this writing, the number of versions is limited, but based on feedback from the community, IBM will soon be releasing a version of the Sandbox that will allow for a wider selection of Swift versions.

Have You Run on a Mainframe Lately?

IBM has also worked to bring the Swift language to its mainframe systems (LinuxONE and z/OS). They have even made it possible for you to select the architecture where you would like your code to be run (see Figure 2-17). So go ahead and try to run your code on a mainframe in the Cloud—it's a brave new world.

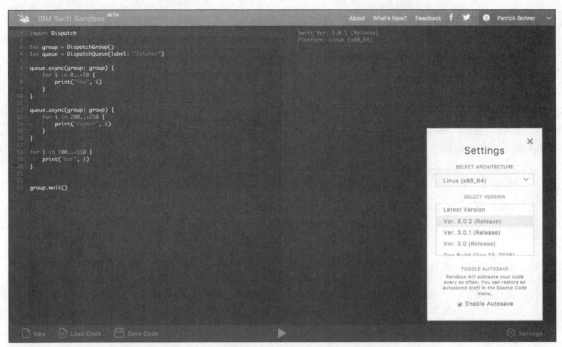

Figure 2-16: Selecting the version of Swift to use for the Sandbox

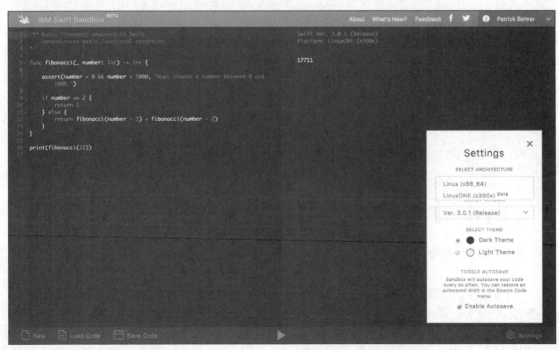

Figure 2-17: Running your Swift Sandbox code on a mainframe computer

IBM Swift Package Catalog and Sandbox

IBM Swift Package Catalog (www.packagecatalog.com) is a great resource that allows you to discover and share Swift packages with the broader community. Swift Package Manager and Swift Package Catalog are covered in greater detail in Chapter 6. You may just want to try out a package before you pull it into your project, so IBM has also made it possible for package owners to create Sandbox samples for their packages. If these packages exist, Package Catalog displays a Try in Sandbox button on that package's details page, as shown in Figure 2-18.

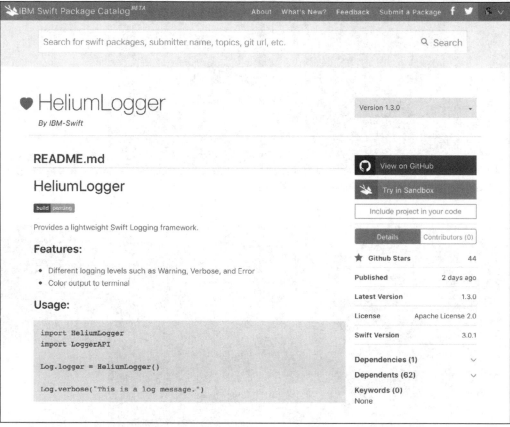

Figure 2-18: Swift Package Catalog page for the HeliumLogger package

This brings up a window displaying the samples that are available for that package, as shown in Figure 2-19.

In this case, you select the first sample, and it takes you to the Sandbox, which loads that sample along with the package as a dependency for the sample, as shown in Figure 2-20.

For more information on creating samples for your packages, you can go to the Swift@IBM devCenter blog, at https://developer.ibm.com/swift/2016/11/11/leverage-the -ibm-swift-package-catalog-to-provide-package-samples-to-your-users/.

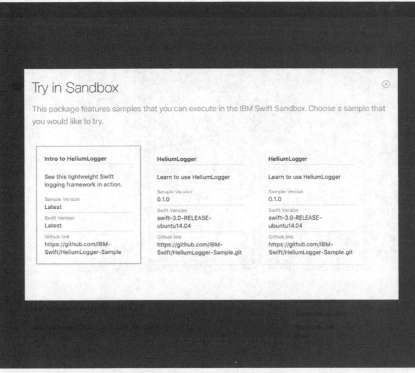

Figure 2-19: Try a Swift package in the Swift Sandbox

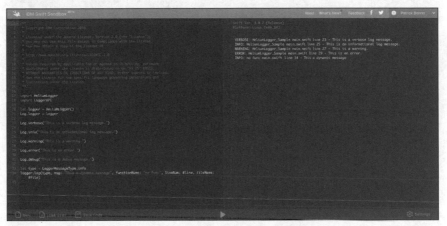

Figure 2-20: Swift package and its sample loaded into the Swift Sandbox

Summary

As IBM continues to add features to the Swift Sandbox, you may see slight differences from the figures in this book. IBM continues to listen for feedback from the community and rolls out new updates. To view some of the recent updates, you can click the What's New button, shown in Figure 2-21.

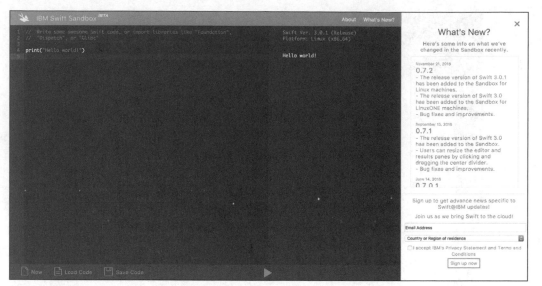

Figure 2-21: What's new in the Swift Sandbox

If you would like to report an error or perhaps a new idea for the Sandbox, you can click the Feedback button, which takes you to the dW Answers page for the Sandbox, shown in Figure 2-22.

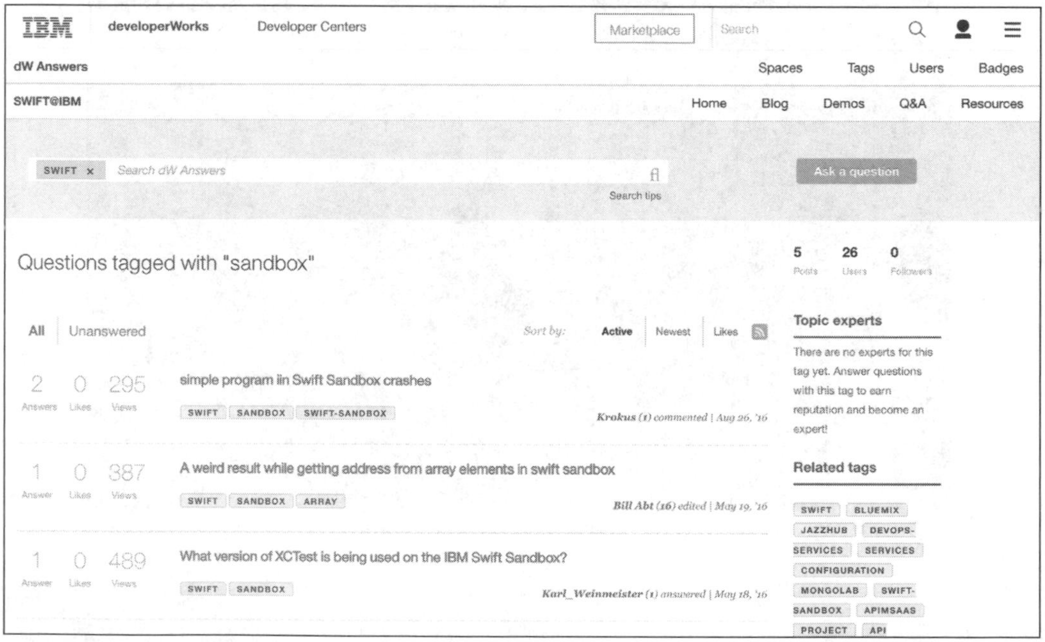

Figure 2-22: Providing feedback for the Swift Sandbox

Stay tuned, and I hope you enjoy using the Sandbox to get Swifting.

CHAPTER 3

A Basic Introduction to Swift

A number of resources are available for learning to program with Swift. While the focus of this book is primarily on the tools, libraries, and runtimes needed to create Swift applications on the server, this chapter will start off with a background and overview of the Swift language.

Background

The Swift programming language was first announced to the public by Apple at their World Wide Developers Conference in 2014. At that time, Apple developers were writing their applications solely in the Objective-C language, which was first released back in 1984. This was a big deal. Swift offered the potential for better performance and improved application security and stability, along with a host of modern language features. Swift provided easy interoperability with existing C and Objective-C libraries, while also offering fresh, modern language capabilities such as type-inference, generics, enumerated types, first-class functions, some functional language capabilities, and more. The result was a language that was fun to program with its extensibility and concise syntax (similar to some scripting languages), while also offering the safety and performance of a strongly typed, compiled language.

In the past two years since its release, Swift has gone through a number of versions as it has matured. With the release of Swift 3.0 in September 2016, the language has reached a new level of source stability. I would encourage you to learn the new language features and syntax that are available in version 3.0, as this is the first language version that is supported on Linux.

Let's Get Coding!

Enough talk; let's jump in and write some Swift code to get a feel for the language. You will be using the IBM Swift Sandbox, covered in Chapter 2, to run your code. The examples in this chapter offer only a glimpse of the language; feel free to spend some time in the Sandbox playing with Swift!

Swift Standard Library

The Swift standard library (https://swift.org/compiler-stdlib/#standard-library-design) provides support for basic data types, protocols, collections, and more. This library is made up of a number of parts that augment the Swift compiler to provide dynamic features that are fundamental to the language. These include a core library (which includes basic types, protocols, and functions), a runtime (responsible for casting, reference counting, generics, and more), and SDK overlays (used on Apple platforms to map between Swift and Objective-C).

Because the standard library is so fundamental to Swift, all of the examples in this book leverage this library in one form or another. As a simple example to start with, let's create a sample program that creates a class that also contains variables with basic data types as well as collections. You will then add to the collection, and print out the contents of this class by making the class conform to CustomDebugStringConvertible (which requires that you implement debugDescription).

```swift
class Book: CustomDebugStringConvertible {
    var title: String
    var pages: Int
    var url: String
    var tags = [String]()

    init(title:String, pages:Int, url:String) {
        self.title = title
        self.pages = pages
        self.url = url
    }

    var debugDescription: String { return "Title: \(title), Pages: \(pages), URL:
\(url), Tags: \(tags)" }
}

var book = Book(title:"The Swift Programming Language (Swift 3.0.1)", pages: 500,
url:"https://itunes.apple.com/us/book/swift-programming-language/id881256329?mt=11")

book.tags.append("Technical")
book.tags.append("Swift")

print("You should read this book: \(book)")
```

This should look very familiar if you are an object-oriented programmer. When you run this code in the Sandbox, you get the following:

```
You should read this book: Title: The Swift Programming Language (Swift 3.0.1),
Pages: 500, URL: https://itunes.apple.com/us/book/swift-programming-language/
id881256329?mt=11, Tags: ["Technical", "Swift"]
```

Figure 3-1 shows the Swift Sandbox, that was introduced in Chapter 2, with the source code for our example on the left side and the output from running the code shown on the right. As you can see, there are many things you can do with just the Swift language along with the standard library. The rest of this chapter explores additional libraries and capabilities that are a key part of the Swift ecosystem.

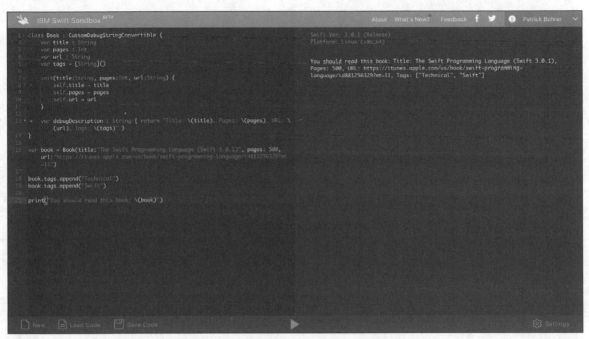

Figure 3-1: A simple Swift program in the Swift Sandbox environment

Swift Foundation Library

Swift developers are also accustomed to leveraging a library called Foundation (https://developer .apple.com/reference/foundation), which provides a basic set of functionality needed by most applications. On Apple platforms, this library is implemented, in large part, in Objective-C. As part of the Swift.org release, a new Foundation library was introduced (https://swift.org/ core-libraries/#foundation), which is being implemented as IBM continues to bring Swift to the server. As of the Swift 3.0 release, there were a number of APIs in this library that were still being implemented, so it is a great opportunity to get involved. You can find more information on the status of the Foundation implementation for Linux at https://github.com/apple/swift-corelibs-foundation/ blob/master/Docs/Status.md.

With that said, a number of features are already implemented in the new Foundation library that make it much easier to work with Swift. Because Foundation is a separate library, you need to use the import statement to gain access to symbols from that library in your sample application. You can then leverage APIs like Date, URL, URLSession, and more, which are used across many applications. In this example, you will create an instance of Date and then use the DateFormatter to format your output to handle different locales and formatting requirements.

```
import Foundation

let now = Date()
let formatter = DateFormatter()
formatter.locale = Locale(identifier: "en_US")
formatter.dateStyle = .short
formatter.timeStyle = .short

print("Date and time is \(formatter.string(from:now))")

formatter.locale = Locale(identifier: "en_GB")

print("Date and time is \(formatter.string(from:now))")

formatter.dateStyle = .none
formatter.timeStyle = .full

print("Time is \(formatter.string(from:now))")
```

From the output of this code, you can see that you are printing the date and time consistent with either the United States or Great Britain. Also, when you only want to display the time, you can turn off the date output and receive a complete time output.

```
Date and time is 12/15/16, 9:33 PM
Date and time is 15/12/2016 21:33
Time is 21:33:27 GMT
```

The Foundation library also contains support for managing URL session requests with URLSession. The following code can be run to call the GitHub URL to find the latest release of the IBM Kitura framework from Swift.

Because the Sandbox does not allow network access, this code needs to be either run in the Xcode Playgrounds application or built locally on your machine.

```
import Foundation

var config = URLSessionConfiguration.default
let session = URLSession(configuration: config)

let url = URL(string:"https://api.github.com/repos/ibm-swift/kitura/releases/latest")

if let url = url {
  let dataTask = session.dataTask(with: url, completionHandler: {
```

```
          data, response, error in

      if let data = data {
        if let jsonAny = try? JSONSerialization.jsonObject(with: data, options: [])
        {
          if let json = jsonAny as? [String:Any]
          {
            if let url = json["html_url"] as? String
            {
              print("Kitura Release URL is \(url)")
            }
          }
        }
      }
    })
    dataTask.resume()
}

// The following is needed to keep running until our URL get is completed.
// This will run forever so if you are running in Playgrounds, you will need to stop it.
let group = DispatchGroup()
group.enter()
group.wait()
```

At the time of writing, when I ran this code in Xcode Playgrounds, I got back the following output:

```
Kitura Release URL is https://github.com/IBM-Swift/Kitura/releases/tag/1.3.0
```

This highlights a small number of capabilities that are available in Foundation. I would suggest you spend some time becoming familiar with this library if you are not already.

C Library Interoperability

Unlike some other languages, Swift has very easy access to C libraries. As the Swift ecosystem continues to mature, this easy access to such a rich collection of C libraries natively will certainly prove to be a strength of the language. Some features in the server libraries directly leverage C libraries, such as URLSession leveraging libcurl (http://libcurl.org/) and the security libraries leveraging OpenSSL (https://www.openssl.org/).

Module maps are used to provide a mapping from the Swift language to the C syntax. For more information on creating and using module maps for system libraries, go to https://github.com/apple/swift-package-manager/blob/master/Documentation/Usage.md#require-system-libraries.

In the following example, you will leverage the fact that the default Swift releases include a module map for the glibc library on Linux. With this module map included in the Swift release, you can call directly into glibc and perform some actions from Swift in the Sandbox. The following is a slight variation on one of the samples in the Sandbox. In this example, you will use the glibc libraries on your Linux host to call fopen and fgetc to read the /etc/passwd file on the target Linux machine where your code is being run.

```swift
#if os(OSX) || os(iOS) || os(watchOS) || os(tvOS)
    import Darwin
#else
    import Glibc
#endif

let stream = fopen("/etc/passwd", "r")

var input = ""

while true {
    let c = fgetc(stream)
    if c == -1 {
        break
    }
    input = String(Character(UnicodeScalar(UInt32(c))!))
    print(input, terminator:"")
}
```

When you run this code in the Sandbox, you receive the following output:

```
root:x:0:0:root:/root:/bin/bash
daemon:x:1:1:daemon:/usr/sbin:/usr/sbin/nologin
bin:x:2:2:bin:/bin:/usr/sbin/nologin
sys:x:3:3:sys:/dev:/usr/sbin/nologin
sync:x:4:65534:sync:/bin:/bin/sync
games:x:5:60:games:/usr/games:/usr/sbin/nologin
man:x:6:12:man:/var/cache/man:/usr/sbin/nologin
lp:x:7:7:lp:/var/spool/lpd:/usr/sbin/nologin
mail:x:8:8:mail:/var/mail:/usr/sbin/nologin
news:x:9:9:news:/var/spool/news:/usr/sbin/nologin
uucp:x:10:10:uucp:/var/spool/uucp:/usr/sbin/nologin
proxy:x:13:13:proxy:/bin:/usr/sbin/nologin
www-data:x:33:33: www-data:/var/www:/usr/sbin/nologin
backup:x:34:34:backup:/var/backups:/usr/sbin/nologin
list:x:38:38:Mailing List Manager:/var/list:/usr/sbin/nologin
irc:x:39:39:ircd:/var/run/ircd:/usr/sbin/nologin
gnats:x:41:41:Gnats Bug-ReportingSystem (admin):/var/lib/gnats:/usr/sbin/nologin
nobody:x:65534:65534:nobody:/nonexistent:/usr/sbin/nologin
libuuid:x:100:101::/var/lib/libuuid:
syslog:x:101:104::/home/syslog:/bin/false
replrun:x:999:999::/home/replrun:
```

Figure 3-2 shows this code and the output in the Swift Sandbox. This is a powerful capability in Swift that allows server-side developers to easily leverage a wide range of libraries on a Linux system from Swift.

Figure 3-2: Swift code accessing C language libraries in the Swift Sandbox

Another example of a Swift package consisting of a module map for the OpenSSL library can be found at `https://github.com/IBM-Swift/OpenSSL`. This is an example of leveraging a high-performance, rich library with deep technical roots for use with the Swift ecosystem on Linux. The ease with which C libraries can be leveraged directly from Swift provides a wealth of server-side functionality that you can take advantage of as you bring Swift to the server.

Concurrency Library

Swift developers are accustomed to leveraging a library called Grand Central Dispatch (`https://developer.apple.com/reference/dispatch`), which provides concurrent execution support in their applications. This library has also been made available on Linux and is now included as one of the core libraries in the Swift runtime. The library is included as one of the Swift.org core libraries (`https://swift.org/core-libraries/—libdispatch`).

Although this subject is beyond the scope of this book, you'll create a sample in the Sandbox that leverages a few of the key features available in Dispatch.

It is worth noting that Dispatch library syntax had a significant update for version 3.0, so if you see samples on the web that include a different syntax, that is likely because those samples predate the 3.0 release.

To get started, because libdispatch is included in a module outside of the application you are writing, you need to issue an import statement to get access to the symbols from that module.

```
import Dispatch
```

Now you have access to all of the symbols from libdispatch. Dispatch provides support for submitting work to DispatchQueues. Work submitted to these queues is run across a number of threads managed by the system. It is also possible to associate these work items into groups so that you can wait for them all to complete. In this example, you will create a single group and a single queue.

```
let group = DispatchGroup()
let queue = DispatchQueue(label: "fetcher")
```

It is possible to submit work to these queues to be run synchronously or asynchronously. In this example, you will submit two blocks of work asynchronously, then run a similar block of code inline, and finally issue a wait command on your group.

```
queue.async(group: group) {
    for i in 0..<10 {
        print("foo", i)
    }
}

queue.async(group: group) {
    for i in 200..<210 {
        print("foobar", i)
    }
}

for i in 100..<110 {
    print("bar", i)
}

group.wait()
```

You can run this command multiple times in the simulator, as shown in Figure 3-3, and see that the output is being interleaved as it is being run concurrently in the background.

```
bar 100
bar 101
foo 0
bar 102
bar 103
bar 104
bar 105
foo 1
foo 2
bar 106
bar 107
foo 3
foo 4
bar 108
bar 109
foo 5
```

```
foo 6
foo 7
foo 8
foo 9
foobar 200
foobar 201
foobar 202
foobar 203
foobar 204
foobar 205
foobar 206
foobar 207
foobar 208
foobar 209
```

Feel free to play around in the Sandbox with this example, and try out a few more of the features that are available with the Dispatch library.

Figure 3-3: Swift concurrency demonstration in the Swift Sandbox

Memory Management

Memory management for Swift is handled with Automatic Reference Counting (ARC). You can find more information on ARC at https://developer.apple.com/library/content/documentation/Swift/Conceptual/Swift_Programming_Language/AutomaticReferenceCounting.html. As you will see, ARC accounts for Swift programs maintaining a very low memory footprint compared to other interpreted or JVM-based languages. ARC keeps track of memory used by class instances and frees up that memory when those instances are no longer being referenced. The memory is freed at the moment the last reference to that memory is released. To demonstrate this, let's run a sample again in the Sandbox.

First, create a class called MyClass that has an init method as well as a deinit method. Both methods print out to the console when they are run.

```
class MyClass {
    var message: String

    init() {
        message = "Hello"
        print("I am a new instance")
    }

    deinit { print("Goodbye world... it was fun while it lasted") }
}
```

Next, print out a statement when you start, create an instance of MyClass, free it, and finally print a statement at the end.

```
print("Here we go")

var mc: MyClass? = MyClass()

mc = nil

print("We are done here")
```

When you run this code in the Sandbox, you see the following output. As you can see, the output of your class being de-initialized comes immediately after you remove your only reference to the class instance.

```
Here we go
I am a new instance
Goodbye world... it was fun while it lasted
We are done here
```

Circular Dependencies

While the ARC approach means that you don't usually need to think about memory management, there are certain situations where you need to ensure that you don't create what are called circular strong retain cycles. This means that two or more instances are pointing to each other, but no other instances are pointing to them. When this occurs, these instances will never be freed and your application footprint can grow over time. To help resolve this, ARC supports different reference types that can be used to break this cycle. These types are strong, weak, and unowned. Weak and unowned references do not interfere with the target instance being cleaned up. You use weak references when the target instance will likely have a shorter lifetime than the host instance. Weak references are converted to nil when the object they are referencing is freed. You use unowned references when both instances have the same lifetime. An example of this might be a class that creates another class instance that points back to itself.

Before you create a strong circular dependency, let's create a new sample that is slightly more complex. You will start with two classes, where the second class contains a reference to the first.

```
class MyClass {
    init() {
        print("MyClass: new instance")
    }

    deinit { print("MyClass: Goodbye") }
}

class MyOtherClass {
    var otherClass: MyClass?

    init(other:MyClass?) {
        otherClass = other
        print("MyOtherClass: new instance")
    }

    deinit { print("MyOtherClass: Goodbye") }
}

print("Here we go")

var mc: MyClass? = MyClass()

var moc: MyOtherClass? = MyOtherClass(other:mc)

mc = nil

print("mc is now nil")

moc = nil

print("We are done here")
```

Now when you run this sample in the Sandbox, you see the messages when each class is created; then you see the message after you set "mc" to nil (note that MyClass was not cleaned up at this point because the MyOtherClass instance is still pointing to it); next you see the message that MyOtherClass is going away; and, finally, you see that your MyClass is being cleaned up immediately afterwards.

```
Here we go
MyClass: new instance
MyOtherClass: new instance
mc is now nil
MyOtherClass: Goodbye
MyClass: Goodbye
We are done here
```

Now let's cause some trouble by making a couple more changes to your sample and adding another reference from MyClass back to MyOtherClass.

```
class MyClass {
    var otherClass: MyOtherClass?

    init() {
        print("MyClass: new instance")
    }

    deinit { print("MyClass: Goodbye") }
}

class MyOtherClass {
    var otherClass: MyClass?

    init(other:MyClass?) {
        otherClass = other
        print("MyOtherClass: new instance")
    }

    deinit { print("MyOtherClass: Goodbye") }
}

print("Here we go")

var mc: MyClass? = MyClass()

var moc: MyOtherClass? = MyOtherClass(other:mc)

mc!.otherClass = moc

mc = nil

print("mc is now nil")

moc = nil

print("We are done here")
```

When you run this example, you see the following output where your de-initialization routines were never called, even though you dropped both references to mc and moc from your program. This is an example of a strong circular dependency chain.

```
Here we go
MyClass: new instance
MyOtherClass: new instance
mc is now nil
We are done here
```

You can now fix your example to break this chain by adding one word. You will change the line where you reference MyOtherClass in MyClass and add the word *weak* before the declaration.

```
weak var otherClass: MyOtherClass?
```

Now, when you run the sample, you see the following; note that your instances are cleaned up:

```
Here we go
MyClass: new instance
MyOtherClass: new instance
mc is now nil
MyOtherClass: Goodbye
MyClass: Goodbye
We are done here
```

This section gave you a glimpse into the world of memory management in Swift. I would suggest that you read more about the topic and play around with it in the Sandbox, as illustrated in Figure 3-4.

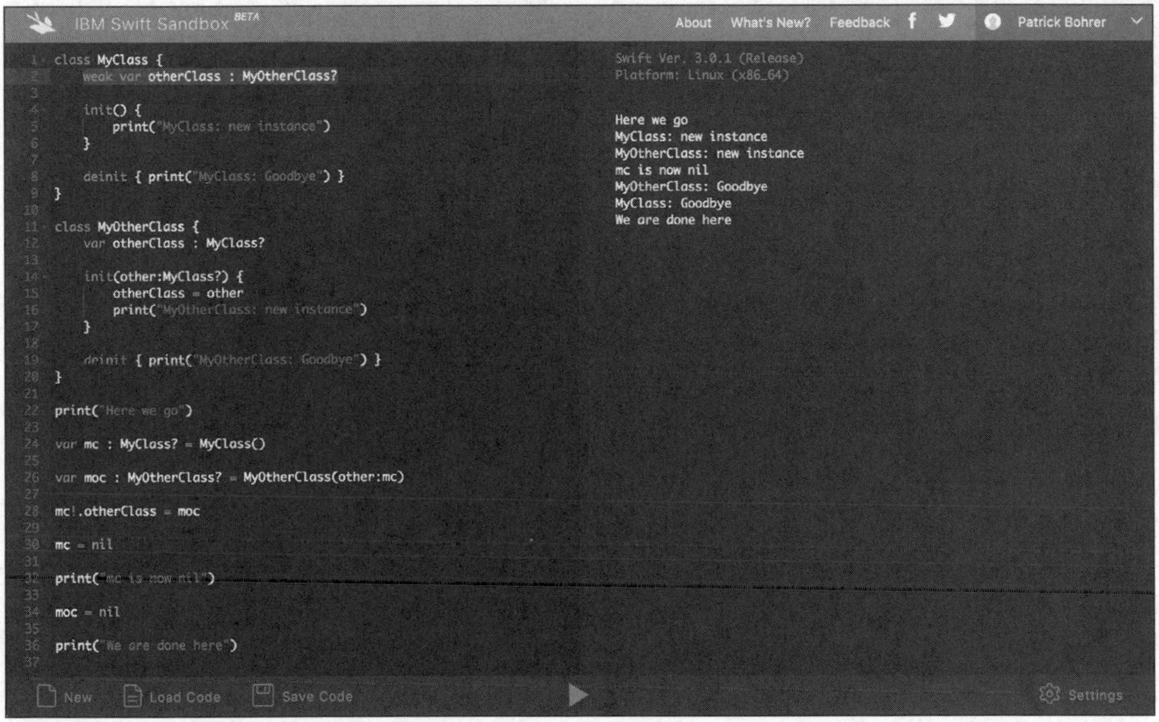

Figure 3-4: Swift memory management example shown in the Swift Sandbox

The Language Landscape

There are a large number of programming languages to choose from, depending upon the task at hand. Languages often become specialized in a given domain based on collateral libraries, tools, and solutions that are built with a given language for a given task. Due to its background as a mobile development language, you naturally see a number of frameworks, libraries, and solutions being built that target a back-end for front-end type of role for Swift in the cloud. However, beyond this domain specialization, in this section you will step back and look at the landscape of languages that are available on both clients and the server, and provide a rough characterization of their performance and memory consumption.

Language Groupings

You can generally group computer programming languages into four categories: C/C++, JVM-based, scripting, and "modern native."

Both the C and C++ languages are over 30 years old. They are compiled languages that are transformed from source code into executable machine code. They provide a baseline for many other languages, they function at a much lower level, and they generally perform better than other languages.

Java virtual machine (JVM)–based languages like Java, Scala, and Clojure can be grouped together as running within the JVM. Instead of the compilers for these languages producing low-level, directly executable machine code, the compilers produce Java bytecode which runs in the JVM (which itself runs on the machine operating system). An advantage of using a JVM-based programming language is that the compiler output (Java bytecode) can generally run anywhere that a Java virtual machine is available, without needing to recompile the program. However, the JVM does introduce a "layer of abstraction" between the operating system and the application code, which imposes overhead beyond a pure object code compiled language such as C/C++.

Scripting languages like JavaScript, Ruby, PHP, Python, and Erlang are interpreted at runtime instead of being compiled to machine code. The benefits of scripting languages are that they tend to be easy to learn and use; they offer very rapid code edit/run/debug development cycles because you don't have to wait for them to be compiled; and they are relatively high level languages that allow complex functions to be expressed in a few simple statements. The disadvantage of scripting languages is that they are slower than compiled languages, as can be seen in Figure 3-5.

Modern native languages such as Swift offer the ease of programming advantages of scripting languages, along with the performance advantages of compiled code. Swift is easy to learn quickly and has a simple, clean syntax free of obscure special characters or rigid formatting rules. But it compiles directly to native machine code, so memory overhead and performance are very good when compared to other languages besides C/C++.

Performance Comparisons

The graphs shown in Figure 3-5 through 3-7 highlight the performance and memory consumption characteristics of a number of languages for an N-body benchmark. While the importance of performance and memory consumption is often dependent upon the benchmark, it is good to see that Swift offers solid performance results as well as lower memory consumption than many languages.

While good performance density is beneficial for mobile devices, in the age of microservices, compute density is also valued in the cloud.

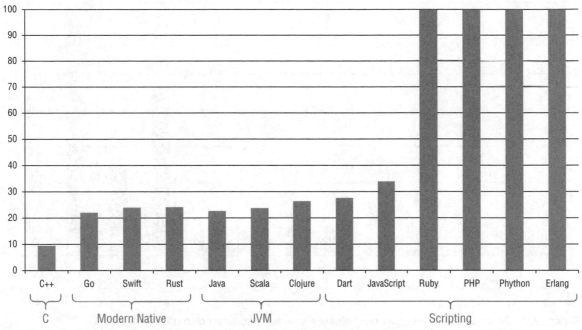

Figure 3-5: Swift language performance compared with other languages
Source: http://benchmarksgame.alioth.debian.org/u64q/swift.html

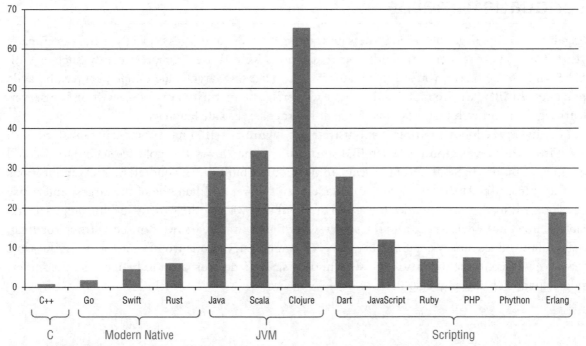

Figure 3-6: Swift memory usage measurement compared with other languages

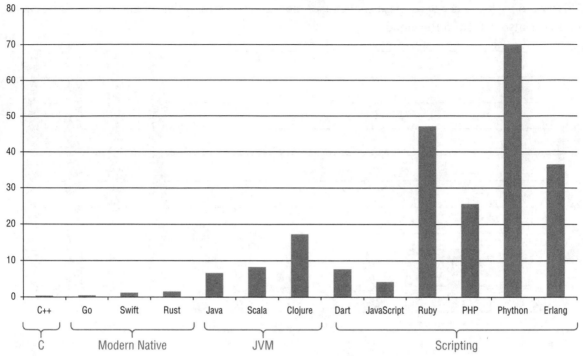

Figure 3-7: Swift language memory performance over time compared to other languages

Language Timeline

As with other languages before it, Swift is just getting started. Languages typically mature over many years, and their ecosystems are built over that time as well. However, more recently, such as with JavaScript on the server, you see this maturity rate increasing largely due to open source and agile practices. At IBM, we are motivated to help accelerate the maturity curve for Swift on the server, learning from our rich history of involvement in other server-side languages.

Looking at the following timeline, illustrated in Figure 3-8, IBM has been deeply involved with Swift from the very beginning. When IBM started its partnership with Apple, we set out to build all of our applications in Swift. Over the years, IBM and Apple built over a hundred rich iOS applications for the enterprise. At the time Swift was made open source, IBM had one of the largest enterprise development teams in the world. It was only natural that we saw the benefits of this language and have jumped in to help bring it to the server. Over the coming years, we can see a strong roadmap that will introduce binary compatibility and even language-level concurrency into Swift. At the same time, we will continue to mature the surrounding server-side ecosystem to better meet the server-side demands of the language.

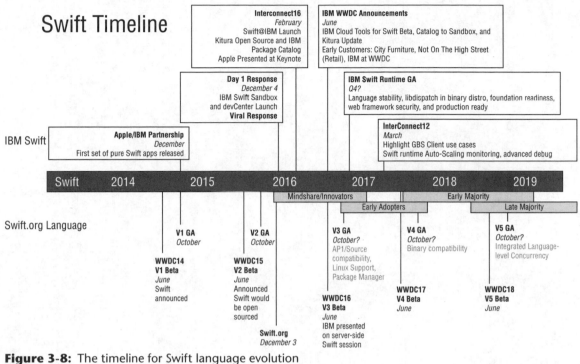

Figure 3-8: The timeline for Swift language evolution

Summary

This chapter has provided a very basic overview of the Swift language, as well as a rough comparison of its performance and memory consumption to other languages. However, all of this just provides a foundation to build upon as you bring this language to the server.

Throughout the rest of this book, you will learn about the additional work being done by IBM to build out an ecosystem of libraries, runtimes, integrations into monitoring and logging, Auto Scaling, and much more. All of this is necessary as you complete the picture around server-side Swift.

CHAPTER 4

The IBM Bluemix Buildpack for Swift

Bluemix supports Cloud Foundry (http://docs.cloudfoundry.org), which is a popular open source Platform as a service (PaaS) for creating and deploying applications on the Cloud. Because of this, as a developer on Bluemix, you have access to artifacts and resources that are first-class citizens in the Cloud Foundry platform, such as buildpacks.

Buildpacks (http://docs.cloudfoundry.org/buildpacks/) provide the runtime required to execute your applications on the cloud when leveraging Cloud Foundry on Bluemix. Many Cloud Foundry buildpacks are available (including java_buildpack, ruby_buildpack, and nodejs_buildpack) on Bluemix. One of the new additions to the family of buildpacks on Bluemix is the IBM Bluemix buildpack for Swift. This buildpack allows developers to provision Swift applications on Bluemix that follow the structure and conventions required by Swift Package Manager (https://swift.org/package-manager). This is very exciting because it is now entirely feasible to implement back-end components and microservices in the Swift language that execute on the Bluemix cloud.

IBM provides and maintains this buildpack for Swift on Bluemix. This makes it possible for developers to implement and deploy many different types of Swift applications to Bluemix.

Cloud Foundry Buildpacks

A buildpack is a software artifact implemented in Ruby or Bash, which cloud administrators install into Cloud Foundry, which is one of the supported cloud environments on Bluemix. Once a buildpack is installed, its capabilities and functionality are immediately available to developers wanting to leverage the new language and runtime (for example, Java/Liberty, Java/Tomcat, Swift, and so on) that it supports.

Cloud Foundry buildpacks are an integral component of the Bluemix platform for allowing developers to deploy and run their applications on the cloud without having to deal with the complexities commonly associated with configuring systems and required dependencies. Buildpacks are key enablers for a seamless deployment of applications to the Bluemix cloud. They free developers from having to find and install (on the cloud) libraries, frameworks, compilers, and other dependencies in order to provision and execute their applications.

In order to use buildpacks to deploy and modify applications on Bluemix, you need to install the Bluemix command line tool (`http://clis.ng.bluemix.net/ui/home.html`) on your development system. This command line tool provides access to commands for deploying, starting, stopping, deleting, and managing applications on the cloud. For instance, once a developer is ready to provision their application on the Bluemix cloud, they can simply navigate to the root folder of their project and execute the `bx app push` command. Later in this chapter, I will go over some of the basic commands available in the Bluemix command line that you should become familiar with.

Buildpack Phases

When an application is pushed to Bluemix, buildpacks are responsible for the execution of three main phases: detection, compilation, and release.

Detection Phase

When you push an application to Bluemix using the Cloud Foundry `bx app push` command, Bluemix automatically detects which buildpack should be used for your application. This is known as the detection phase. During this phase, the Bluemix platform checks whether a buildpack can be used for staging and starting the application. The platform does this by going through the list of installed buildpacks and "asking" each buildpack if it is suited for provisioning the application.

The IBM Bluemix buildpack for Swift lets the platform know that it can provision the application if it finds a `Package.swift` file at the root folder level of the application.

Compilation Phase

The compilation phase is where most of the work occurs. For the IBM Bluemix buildpack for Swift, the source code of the Swift application (as opposed to the binaries) is pushed to the cloud, and it is the buildpack's responsibility to compile and link the application. To do so, the IBM Bluemix buildpack for Swift parses the `.swift-version` file contained in the application to determine which snapshot of the Swift binaries (`https://swift.org/download`) should be used for compiling and building your application's code. If the version of the Swift binaries required for your application isn't already cached in the installed buildpack package, then it is downloaded. Note that the Swift binaries include Swift Package Manager, which is the tool responsible for downloading and compiling any other Swift packages that your application depends on.

Also, during the compilation phase, required system-level dependencies are installed and environment variables are updated. For example, any binaries built from your Swift source code will be placed in the `$PATH` environment variable.

By the end of this phase, the buildpack ensures that you have all the necessary components for executing the app.

Release Phase

During the release phase, buildpacks can provide predefined metadata to Bluemix on how the application should be executed. This metadata is useful when an application runs in a prescribed, containerized environment such as the Java EE platform. In such environments, the executable is always the same (for example, Liberty server, Tomcat server, and so on) regardless of the application being provisioned. Such buildpacks can simply contain a predefined script that states the name or command that should be executed to start the application.

However, for Swift applications, things are a little different. The IBM Bluemix buildpack for Swift does not include a predefined command that could be used to start all Swift applications that are pushed to Bluemix. Instead, the name of the executable file to start the application is entirely dependent on the source code that was pushed to Bluemix. Therefore, for Swift apps, you need a custom command to start the application, which should be specified in the `Procfile` or the `command` attribute in the application's `manifest.yml` file. (See the section, "File Artifacts Required for Provisioning Your Application on Bluemix," for further details.)

Working with the IBM Bluemix Buildpack for Swift

The IBM Bluemix buildpack for Swift applications is powered by Swift Package Manager, which is the tool responsible for compiling your application and its dependencies. Although we developed this buildpack mainly for Bluemix, it can be used on any Cloud Foundry environment. Keep in mind that this buildpack may require access to the Internet for downloading and installing several system-level dependencies.

Where Is the Source Code Hosted?

The source code for the IBM Bluemix buildpack for Swift is hosted on GitHub at `https://github.com/IBM-Swift/swift-buildpack` (see Figure 4-1). The `master` branch contains the code currently deployed to Bluemix, while the `develop` branch contains enhancements and bug fixes that our team is currently working on. You can find the list of releases for the IBM Bluemix buildpack for Swift at `https://github.com/IBM-Swift/swift-buildpack/releases`.

Although it is not necessary to understand the inner workings of the buildpack code in order to use the buildpack, you are more than welcome to check out our GitHub repository and become acquainted with the different files that make up the buildpack.

To see a list of the current issues and defects, you can visit the Issues page at `https://github.com/IBM-Swift/swift-buildpack/issues`.

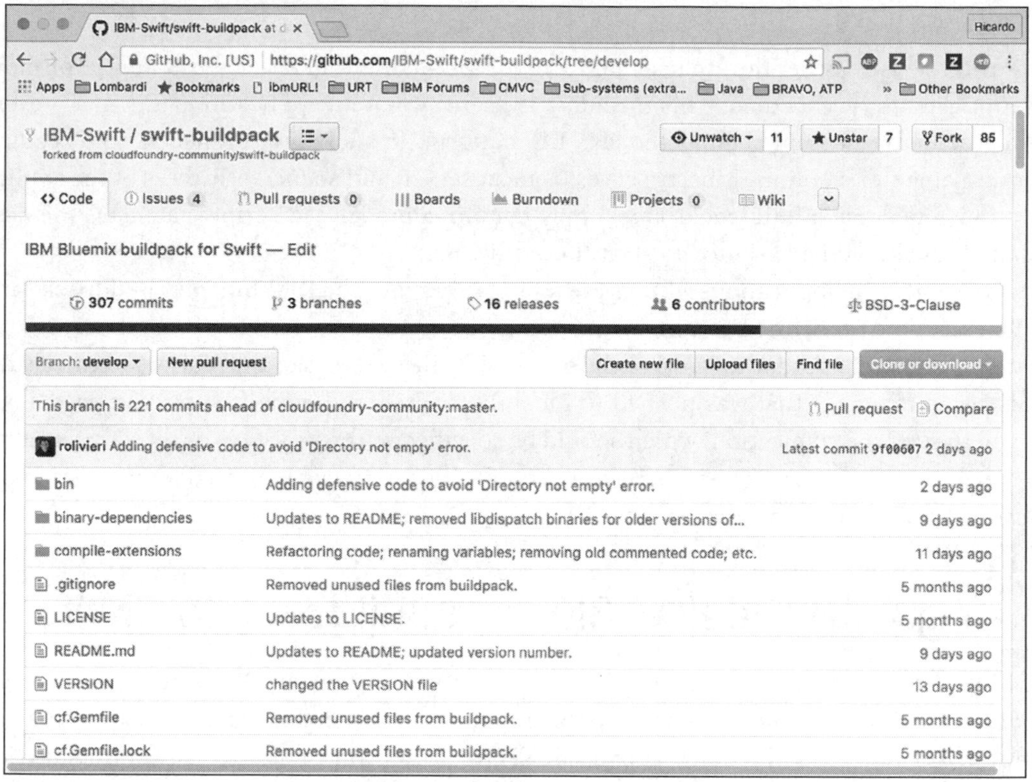

Figure 4-1: GitHub repository for the IBM Bluemix buildpack for Swift

What Version of the Buildpack Is Currently Installed?

At the time of writing, the latest version of the IBM Bluemix buildpack for Swift installed on Bluemix was 2.0.5. To verify which version of the buildpack for Swift is currently installed on Bluemix, you should install the Bluemix command line (`http://clis.ng.bluemix.net/ui/home.html`) and point to the Bluemix region you use for the deployment of your app:

- **US South**—`api.ng.bluemix.net`
- **United Kingdom**—`api.eu-gb.bluemix.net`
- **Sydney**—`api.au-syd.bluemix.net`
- **Germany**—`api.eu-de.bluemix.net`

Additional regions may be added to Bluemix at any time. To get a list of the Bluemix regions, you can execute the `bx regions` command:

```
$ bx regions
Listing Bluemix regions...

Name        Geolocation     Customer   Deployment   Domain              CF API Endpoint                    Type
eu-de       Germany         IBM        Production   eu-de.bluemix.net   https://api.eu-de.bluemix.net      public
au-syd      Sydney          IBM        Production   au-syd.bluemix.net  https://api.au-syd.bluemix.net     public
us-south    US South        IBM        Production   ng.bluemix.net      https://api.ng.bluemix.net         public
eu-gb       United Kingdom  IBM        Production   eu-gb.bluemix.net   https://api.eu-gb.bluemix.net      public
```

For this example, you will point to the US South region (api.ng.bluemix.net):

```
$ bx api api.ng.bluemix.net
Setting api endpoint to api.ng.bluemix.net...
OK

API endpoint: https://api.ng.bluemix.net (API version: 2.54.0)
Not logged in. Use 'bx login' to log in.
```

Once you are pointing to the corresponding Bluemix region, you need to authenticate using the bx login command. Authenticating is required before you can issue any other commands:

```
$ bx login
API endpoint: https://api.ng.bluemix.net

Email> roliv@us.ibm.com

Password>
Authenticating...
OK

Select an account (or press enter to skip):
1. Ricardo Olivieri's Account (86657373910894828945dd81b01281e3)
2. Swift DevOps functionalid's Account (629e1d16217c8ad85ccb31f33bd6cd37)
Enter a number> 1
Targeted account Ricardo Olivieri's Account (86657373910894828945dd81b01281e3)

Targeted org roliv@us.ibm.com

Select a space (or press enter to skip):
1. dev
2. test
Enter a number> 1
Targeted space dev


API endpoint:     https://api.ng.bluemix.net (API version: 2.54.0)
Region:           us-south
User:             roliv@us.ibm.com
Account:          Ricardo Olivieri's Account (86657373910894828945dd81b01281e3)
Org:              roliv@us.ibm.com
Space:            dev
```

Let's now use the `bx cf buildpacks` command to get a list of the buildpacks (along with their versions) that are installed on Bluemix:

```
$ bx cf buildpacks
Invoking 'cf buildpacks'...

Getting buildpacks...

buildpack                    position   enabled   locked   filename
liberty-for-java             1          true      false    buildpack_liberty-for-java_v3.8-20170308-1507.zip
sdk-for-nodejs               2          true      false    buildpack_sdk-for-nodejs_v3.11-20170303-1144.zip
dotnet-core                  3          true      false    buildpack_dotnet-core_v1.0.10-20170124-1145.zip
swift_buildpack              4          true      false    buildpack_swift_v2.0.5-20170328-1639.zip

...
```

Looking at the output, you can find an entry named `swift_buildpack`, along with its corresponding filename, which states the version of the installed buildpack for Swift (in this case, version 2.0.5).

Having the buildpack for Swift installed on Bluemix allows you to write applications in the Swift language and deploy them to Bluemix without having to import an external or custom buildpack. As we will show soon, executing the `bx app push` command from the root folder of your Swift application's repository will leverage the installed buildpack for Swift on Bluemix.

File Artifacts Required for Provisioning Your Application on Bluemix

To provision a Swift application on Bluemix, the file artifacts described in this section should exist at the root level of the project. Please note that these files are not required for running a Swift application locally on a macOS or Linux system. Instead, these files are only needed for provisioning the Swift application on the Bluemix cloud.

The .swift-version File

The `.swift-version` file specifies the version of the Swift binaries that should be used for compilation and linking of your Swift application. This file should be included in the root folder of your repository to specify a *release*, *preview*, or *development* version of the Swift binaries.

```
$ cat .swift-version
3.1
```

If you do not include a `.swift-version` file in your project, the IBM Bluemix buildpack for Swift uses the default version of the Swift binaries to compile and link your application. Because the default version of Swift may change from release to release of the buildpack, it is recommended that you always include a `.swift-version` file in your project. At the time of writing, Swift 3.1 is the default version used by the current version of the IBM Bluemix buildpack for Swift installed on Bluemix. This version (2.0.5) of the buildpack caches versions 3.1 and 3.0.2 of the Swift binaries. You can check the contents of the manifest.yml file (of the buildpack) found at https://github.com/IBM-Swift/ swift-buildpack/blob/master/manifest.yml to see the complete list of the Swift versions that are cached in the installed buildpack on Bluemix. If you'd like to use a different version of Swift (that is not cached) on Bluemix, you can specify it in the .swift-version file of your application. You should know that using a Swift version that is not cached increases the provisioning time of your application on Bluemix.

Because there are frequent Swift language releases, it's a good idea to pin your application to a specific Swift version. Once you have tested and migrated your code to a newer version of Swift, you can then update the .swift-version file with the appropriate Swift version.

The manifest.yml File

The manifest.yml file describes the configuration for your Swift application. In it, you specify the application name, memory, disk quota, and other configuration parameters. The following is the contents of the manifest.yml file for one of the Swift demo applications our team developed:

```
applications:
- name: swift-helloworld
  random-route: true
  memory: 128M
  instances: 1
  buildpack: swift_buildpack
```

The simplest manifest.yml file should contain the name attribute. As its name implies, this attribute simply states the name that should be given to the application. Keep in mind that the application name will uniquely identify your application.

The random-route attribute ensures that a unique hostname is auto-generated for your application when it is initially provisioned on Bluemix (hostnames must be unique). You may at some point want to have a formal hostname for provisioning your application instead of using an auto-generated one. However, having an auto-generated hostname that you can use throughout the development and testing phases of your app allows you to focus on writing software and to decide later what the hostname for your app should be.

The memory attribute is used to specify the memory limit for your application. Although this is an optional attribute, it is recommended that you include it in your manifest.yml file. If you don't, a default memory limit of 1GB is assigned to your application (many applications will require less memory than this).

The instances attribute states how many instances of your application should be started when provisioned on the Bluemix cloud. To minimize the possibility of service disruption to your users due to failures, it is recommended that you have at least two instances of your application.

Note that the manifest.yml file shown above also contains the optional buildpack attribute. If this attribute is not specified, then during the detection phase, buildpacks installed on Bluemix are "interrogated" to see if they can provision the application. As described earlier, the IBM Bluemix buildpack for Swift will state that it can provision the application if it finds a `Package.swift` file in your application. Therefore, the advantage of including the optional `buildpack` attribute in the `manifest.yml` file is that it speeds up the provisioning of your Swift application because you are letting the platform know up front which buildpack should be used.

For in-depth details about the different attributes that are supported in the application's `manifest.yml` file, you should check out the Cloud Foundry documentation found at `https://docs.cloudfoundry .org/devguide/deploy-apps/manifest.html`.

The Procfile File

In the `Procfile` file, you specify the name of the executable process to run for your web server application. Remember that any binaries built from your Swift source will be placed in the `$PATH` environment variable. Note that you can also specify any runtime parameters for your process in the `Procfile`. The following code snippet shows the content of a `Procfile`, where the name of the executable program is `Server` and the runtime arguments are—`bind 0.0.0.0:$PORT`:

```
web: Server -bind 0.0.0.0:$PORT
```

In this example, you can see that a predefined binding IP address and a `PORT` variable are provided in the runtime arguments. `PORT` is an environment variable populated by the cloud platform and available to your program executable. This variable specifies the port number that your Swift server application should bind to for it to serve incoming requests from clients.

You should know that there is an alternative to specifying IP address and port values in the `Procfile`. Instead, you can use the Swift-cfenv package (`https://github.com/IBM-Swift/Swift-cfenv`) in your Swift application to obtain these values at runtime. The Swift-cfenv package provides structures and methods for parsing Cloud Foundry–provided environment variables, such as the port number, IP address, and URL of the application. It also provides default values when running the application locally. For details on how to leverage this library in your Swift application, see the README file for this package. If you use the Swift-cfenv package in your application, your `Procfile` becomes very simple:

```
web: <executable_name>
```

Alternative to Procfile   Instead of using the `Procfile`, you can use the `command` attribute in the `manifest.yml` file of your application to specify the name of your executable and any runtime parameters. The following snippet of code shows how to use the `command` attribute to specify the same executable and parameter values used in the previous `Procfile` example:

```
command: Server -bind 0.0.0.0:$PORT
```

When you specify a value for the `command` attribute in the `manifest.yml` file, the platform will use the Linux `bash` command to start the execution of your application. For the value assigned to the `command` attribute in the previous example, the `bash` command execution would look like this:

```
bash -c Server -bind 0.0.0.0:$PORT
```

For further details on the `command` attribute, see the Cloud Foundry documentation.

The .cfignore File

The `.cfignore` file is used to specify those files or folders that the `bx app push` command should not upload to Bluemix for provisioning an application. Although this file is optional, it is a best practice to always include it at the root folder of the repository as a peer to the other files described in this section. At time of writing, the `.build` folder should not be pushed to the cloud. Therefore, the contents of the `.cfignore` file for Swift applications should include at least the following entry:

```
.build/*
```

Installing Additional System-Level Dependencies

One of the main tasks of the IBM Bluemix buildpack for Swift is to create an execution environment that contains the common dependencies, frameworks, and libraries (for example, Clang, Swift, and so on) that are required for provisioning and running a Swift application.

Many Swift applications do not require the installation of any additional libraries. It is very common for today's applications to have dependencies only on services that provide REST interfaces to interact with them (for example, Cloudant, AlchemyAPI, Personality Insights, and so on). For such applications, there is no need to install any additional libraries or frameworks.

However, because dependencies vary from application to application, there could be cases when additional system packages are required to compile or execute a Swift application. To address this need, the IBM Bluemix buildpack for Swift supports the installation of Ubuntu trusty packages using the `apt-get` utility. Although downloading and installing system packages increases the provisioning time of your Swift application, it does not impact the execution time of the application.

You can specify the Ubuntu packages that should be installed by including an `Aptfile` in the root directory of your Swift application (the same folder location where the `.swift-version` file resides). Each line in the `Aptfile` should contain a valid Ubuntu package name. For instance, if your Swift application had a dependency on the `jsonbot` Ubuntu trusty package, you can have the buildpack install this package during the provisioning of the application to the Bluemix cloud. To accomplish this, you should include an `Aptfile` that looks like this:

```
$ cat Aptfile
jsonbot
```

When you use the IBM Bluemix buildpack for Swift to provision a Swift application that includes an `Aptfile` with an entry for installing `jsonbot`, it generates output like this:

```
...
—-·> Aptfile found.

—-·> Entry found in Aptfile for jsonbot.
—-·> Fetching .debs for: jsonbot
      Ign http://archive.ubuntu.com trusty InRelease
      Get:1 http://archive.ubuntu.com trusty-updates InRelease [65.9 kB]
      Get:2 http://archive.ubuntu.com trusty-security InRelease [65.9 kB]
      Get:3 http://archive.ubuntu.com trusty Release.gpg [933 B]
      Get:4 http://archive.ubuntu.com trusty-updates/main amd64 Packages [1,219 kB]
      Get:5 http://archive.ubuntu.com trusty-updates/universe amd64 Packages [520 kB]
      Get:6 http://archive.ubuntu.com trusty-updates/multiverse amd64 Packages [15.6 kB]

...

2017-04-07T13:20:57.18-0400 [STG/0]      OUT—-·> Downloaded DEB files...
2017-04-07T13:20:57.21-0400 [STG/0]      OUT—-·> Getting swift-3.1

...

2017-04-07T13:22:12.80-0400 [STG/0]      OUT—-·> Installing system level dependencies...
2017-04-07T13:22:12.82-0400 [STG/0]      OUT—-·> Installing jsonbot_0.84.4-1_all.deb
2017-04-07T13:22:13.04-0400 [STG/0]      OUT—-·> Installing libpython2.7-minimal_2.7.6-8ubuntu0.3_amd64.deb
2017-04-07T13:22:13.08-0400 [STG/0]      OUT—-·> Installing libpython2.7-stdlib_2.7.6-8ubuntu0.3_amd64.deb
2017-04-07T13:22:13.36-0400 [STG/0]      OUT—-·> Installing libtidy-0.99-0_20091223cvs-1.2ubuntu1.1_amd64.deb
2017-04-07T13:22:13.38-0400 [STG/0]      OUT—-·> Installing mysql-common_5.5.54-0ubuntu0.14.04.1_all.deb

...

2017-04-07T13:22:13.88-0400 [STG/0]      OUT—-·> Building Package...
2017-04-07T13:22:13.88-0400 [STG/0]      OUT—-·> Build config: release

...

2017-04-07T13:23:21.37-0400 [STG/0]      OUT      Compile Swift Module 'Kitura_Starter' (2 sources)
2017-04-07T13:23:22.43-0400 [STG/0]      OUT      Linking ./.build/release/Kitura-Starter

...

2017-04-07T13:23:49.10-0400 [CELL/0]     OUT Creating container
2017-04-07T13:23:59.71-0400 [CELL/0]     OUT Successfully created container
2017-04-07T13:24:05.23-0400 [CELL/0]     OUT Starting health monitoring of container
2017-04-07T13:24:05.53-0400 [APP/0]      OUT [2017-04-07T17:24:05.527Z] [INFO] [main.swift:28 Kitura_Starter] Server
will be started on 'https://kitura-starter-nonselling-prereverse.mybluemix.net'.
2017-04-07T13:24:07.35-0400 [CELL/0]     OUT Container became healthy

...
```

Looking at the output, you can see the buildpack parses the `Aptfile` and finds an entry for the `jsonbot` Ubuntu package. The buildpack then proceeds to download the corresponding DEB files and installs them before it builds the application.

Although you only need to add an `Aptfile` in order to have the buildpack install the corresponding Ubuntu packages, it is not uncommon to also need to provide additional information for a successful compilation of your Swift application. For example, say your Swift application has a dependency on the Vapor MySQL for Swift package, which in turn, depends on the libmysqlclient-dev system package. If no additional information is provided to the buildpack other than the contents of the Aptfile, you will see errors like the following while provisioning the application:

```
...

--> Building Package...
      Compile Swift Module 'Jay' (21 sources)
      Compile Swift Module 'Polymorphic' (2 sources)
      Compile Swift Module 'PathIndexable' (2 sources)
      Compile Swift Module 'libc' (1 sources)
      Compile Swift Module 'Core' (28 sources)
      Compile Swift Module 'Node' (22 sources)
      Compile Swift Module 'CloudFoundryEnv' (7 sources)
      Compile Swift Module 'JSON' (8 sources)
      Compile Swift Module 'MySQL' (10 sources)
      /tmp/staged/app/Packages/MySQL-1.0.2/Sources/MySQL/Field+Variant.swift:26:24:
error: use of unresolved identifier 'MYSQL_TYPE_JSON'
                      if self == MYSQL_TYPE_JSON {
                                 ^~~~~~~~~~~~~~~
      public var MYSQL_TYPE_BLOB: enum_field_types { get }
                 ^
      CMySQLLinux.MYSQL_TYPE_LONG:1:12: note: did you mean 'MYSQL_TYPE_LONG'?
                 ^
      CMySQLLinux.MYSQL_TYPE_SET:1:12: note: did you mean 'MYSQL_TYPE_SET'?
                 ^
      CMySQLLinux.MYSQL_TYPE_BLOB:1:12: note: did you mean 'MYSQL_TYPE_BLOB'?
      public var MYSQL_TYPE_LONG: enum_field_types { get }
      public var MYSQL_TYPE_SET: enum_field_types { get }
      /tmp/staged/app/Packages/MySQL-1.0.2/Sources/MySQL/Bind+Node.swift:44:31:
error: use of unresolved identifier 'MYSQL_TYPE_JSON'
                             ^~~~~~~~~~~~~~~
      CMySQLLinux.MYSQL_TYPE_BLOB:1:12: note: did you mean 'MYSQL_TYPE_BLOB'?
      public var MYSQL_TYPE_BLOB: enum_field_types { get }
      public var MYSQL_TYPE_LONG: enum_field_types { get }
                 ^
                      if variant == MYSQL_TYPE_JSON {
                 ^
      CMySQLLinux.MYSQL_TYPE_LONG:1:12: note: did you mean 'MYSQL_TYPE_LONG'?
      CMySQLLinux.MYSQL_TYPE_SET:1:12: note: did you mean 'MYSQL_TYPE_SET'?
      public var MYSQL_TYPE_SET: enum_field_types { get }
                 ^
<unknown>:0: error: build had 1 command failures
swift-build: error: exit(1): /tmp/cache/swift-3.0.1/swift-3.0.1-RELEASE-ubuntu14.04/
usr/bin/swift-build-tool -f /tmp/staged/app/.build/release.yaml

...
```

To address the compilation errors shown here, you need to provide custom compilation flags. Before we cover how to do this using the IBM Bluemix buildpack for Swift, let's go over another example of installing a system package while provisioning a Swift application on the Bluemix cloud.

Let's say that you also have a Swift application that needs to connect to a PostgreSQL database. The libpq-dev Ubuntu system package contains a static library and header files that allow programs to communicate with PostgreSQL databases. To have the buildpack install this package, you can include an Aptfile in your project:

```
$ cat Aptfile
libpq-dev
```

Provisioning a Swift application that requires the libpq-dev package using the IBM Bluemix buildpack for Swift generates output like the following:

```
...
—-> Aptfile found.

—-> Entry found in Aptfile for libpq-dev.
—-> Fetching .debs for: libpq-dev
Ign http://archive.ubuntu.com trusty InRelease
Get:1 http://archive.ubuntu.com trusty-updates InRelease [65.9 kB]
Get:2 http://archive.ubuntu.com trusty-security InRelease [65.9 kB]
Get:3 http://archive.ubuntu.com trusty Release.gpg [933 B]
Get:4 http://archive.ubuntu.com trusty-updates/main amd64 Packages [1,147 kB]
Get:5 http://archive.ubuntu.com trusty-updates/universe amd64 Packages [502 kB]
Get:6 http://archive.ubuntu.com trusty-updates/multiverse amd64 Packages [15.2 kB]
Get:7 http://archive.ubuntu.com trusty-security/main amd64 Packages [688 kB]
Get:8 http://archive.ubuntu.com trusty-security/universe amd64 Packages [188 kB]
Get:9 http://archive.ubuntu.com trusty-security/multiverse amd64 Packages [4,015 B]
Get:10 http://archive.ubuntu.com trusty Release [58.5 kB]
Get:11 http://archive.ubuntu.com trusty/main amd64 Packages [1,743 kB]
Get:12 http://archive.ubuntu.com trusty/universe amd64 Packages [7,589 kB]
Get:13 http://archive.ubuntu.com trusty/multiverse amd64 Packages [169 kB]
Fetched 12.2 MB in 9s (1,341 kB/s)
Reading package lists...
        Reading package lists...
        Building dependency tree...
        The following extra packages will be installed:
          libpq5
        Suggested packages:
          postgresql-doc-9.3
        The following packages will be upgraded:
          libpq-dev libpq5
        2 upgraded, 0 newly installed, 0 to remove and 45 not upgraded.
        After this operation, 0 B of additional disk space will be used.
        Get:1 http://archive.ubuntu.com/ubuntu/ trusty-updates/main libpq-dev amd64
9.3.15-0ubuntu0.14.04 [140 kB]
```

```
        Need to get 219 kB of archives.
        Get:2 http://archive.ubuntu.com/ubuntu/ trusty-updates/main libpq5 amd64
9.3.15-0ubuntu0.14.04 [78.7 kB]
        Download complete and in download only mode
—-> Downloaded DEB files...
        Fetched 219 kB in 0s (221 kB/s)

...

—-> Installing system level dependencies...
—-> Installing libpq5_9.3.15-0ubuntu0.14.04_amd64.deb
—-> Installing libpq-dev_9.3.15-0ubuntu0.14.04_amd64.deb
—-> Installing libssl1.0.0_1.0.1f-1ubuntu2.21_amd64.deb
—-> Installing libssl-dev_1.0.1f-1ubuntu2.21_amd64.deb
—-> Installing openssl_1.0.1f-1ubuntu2.21_amd64.deb
—-> Building Package...

...
```

If you look at the output, you'll notice that the buildpack parses the Aptfile and finds an entry for the libpq-dev package. Just as you saw in the previous example, the buildpack downloads the corresponding DEB files (that is, libpq-dev and libpq5) and installs them before it builds the Swift application.

As you saw with the libmysqlclient-dev package, to successfully compile a Swift application that depends on the libpq-dev package, you need to provide additional information to the buildpack. For example, say your Swift application has a dependency on the Zewo PostgreSQL package, found at https://github.com/Zewo/PostgreSQL, which depends on the libpq-dev package. If you do not provide the corresponding custom compilation flags, you will see errors like the following while provisioning the Swift application:

```
        ...
        Compile Swift Module 'SQL' (21 sources)

        Compile Swift Module 'PostgreSQL' (5 sources)
        #include "libpq.h"
               ^
        #import <libpq-fe.h>
                ^
        /tmp/staged/app/Packages/PostgreSQL-0.14.3/Sources/PostgreSQL/Result.swift:1:8:
error: could not build Objective-C module 'CLibpq'
        import CLibpq
               ^
<unknown>:0: error: build had 1 command failures
        <module-includes>:1:10: note: in file included from <module-includes>:1:
        /tmp/staged/app/Packages/CLibpq-0.13.0/libpq.h:1:9: error: 'libpq-fe.h' file
not found
```

```
swift-build: error: exit(1): /tmp/cache/swift-3.0.1/swift-3.0.1-RELEASE-ubuntu14.04/
usr/bin/swift-build-tool -f /tmp/staged/app/.build/release.yaml
```

...

To address these errors, you need to let the compiler know where the necessary header files are located. In the next section, we will learn how to do this.

Additional Compiler Flags

As I mentioned in the previous section, compilation of Swift applications that depend on system-level packages may require additional compilation flags. To specify the custom flags that the `swift build` command should use, you can include a `.swift-build-options-linux` file in the root folder of your project. For example, to leverage the `libmysqlclient-dev` Ubuntu trusty package in a Swift application, you need the following custom compilation flag:

```
$ cat .swift-build-options-linux
-Xswiftc -DNOJSON
```

Including the `.swift-build-options-linux` file in your project with the contents shown here generates the following output while provisioning a Swift application that depends on the Vapor MySQL for Swift package found at `https://github.com/vapor/mysql` (which has a dependency on the `libmysqlclient-dev` package):

```
...

---> Building Package...
---> Using custom swift build options: -Xswiftc -DNOJSON
        Compile Swift Module 'Jay' (21 sources)
        Compile Swift Module 'Polymorphic' (2 sources)
        Compile Swift Module 'PathIndexable' (2 sources)
        Compile Swift Module 'Socket' (3 sources)
        Compile Swift Module 'SwiftyJSON' (2 sources)
        Compile Swift Module 'libc' (1 sources)
        Compile Swift Module 'Core' (28 sources)
        Compile Swift Module 'Node' (22 sources)
        Compile Swift Module 'CloudFoundryEnv' (7 sources)
        Compile Swift Module 'JSON' (8 sources)
        Compile Swift Module 'MySQL' (10 sources)
        Compile Swift Module 'Utils' (3 sources)
        Compile Swift Module 'Server' (1 sources)
        Linking ./.build/release/Server
---> Copying dynamic libraries
---> Copying binaries to 'bin'
---> Cleaning up build files
---> Clearing previous swift cache
---> Saving cache (default):
--->Packages
```

```
—-> Optimizing contents of cache folder...

—-> Uploading droplet (38M)

1 of 1 instances running

App started

...
```

Another system library that also requires custom flags for a successful compilation when integrating with a Swift application is libpq-dev:

```
$ cat .swift-build-options-linux
-Xcc -I$BUILD_DIR/.apt/usr/include/postgresql
```

Using these compilation options when provisioning a Swift application that references the Zewo PostgreSQL package (which depends on the libpq-dev package) generates output like the following:

```
...
—-> Building Package...

—-> Using custom swift build options: -Xcc -I/tmp/staged/app/.apt/usr/include/
postgresql
        Compile CPOSIX posix.c
        Compile CYAJL yajl_gen.c
        Compile CYAJL yajl_version.c
        Compile CYAJL yajl.c
        Compile CYAJL yajl_buf.c
        Compile CYAJL yajl_tree.c
        Compile CYAJL yajl_parser.c
        Compile CYAJL yajl_encode.c
        Compile CYAJL yajl_alloc.c
        Compile CYAJL yajl_lex.c
        Compile Swift Module 'Reflection' (24 sources)
        Linking CPOSIX
        Compile Swift Module 'POSIX' (11 sources)
        Linking CYAJL
        Compile Swift Module 'Axis' (22 sources)
        Compile Swift Module 'SQL' (21 sources)
        Compile Swift Module 'PostgreSQL' (5 sources)

...

—-> Copying dynamic libraries
—-> Copying binaries to 'bin'
—-> Cleaning up build files
—-> Clearing previous swift cache
```

```
—-> Saving cache (default):
—->—Packages
—-> Optimizing contents of cache folder...

—-> Uploading droplet (27M)

1 of 1 instances running

App started

...
```

In this output, you no longer see the 'libpq-fe.h' file not found error that you saw earlier when you did not have a .swift-build-options-linux file with the right compilation flags. The -Xcc -I$BUILD_DIR/.apt/usr/include/postgresql flag lets the compiler know where the necessary header files are located. By default, the buildpack expects header files of system packages to be found in the $BUILD_DIR/.apt/usr/include folder. However, the header files for the libpq-dev package are installed in a different folder, $BUILD_DIR/.apt/usr/include/postgresql. And in case you are wondering, BUILD_DIR is a variable that contains the path to the build folder for the Swift application. This variable is available to the buildpack while it provisions your Swift application on the Bluemix cloud.

Downloading Closed Source Dependencies

Developers who leverage closed source Git repositories (e.g., GitHub Enterprise, Git private repos, etc.) for storing package dependencies intend to keep unauthorized users from accessing those repositories. However, the buildpack will need access to these package repositories in order to provision the corresponding Swift application on the cloud. The IBM Bluemix buildpack for Swift supports downloading such package dependencies using SSH authentication.

To make use of this capability, developers provide account SSH keys or deployment SSH keys to authenticate with the corresponding repositories. For instance, if you plan to use account SSH keys, you should add a .ssh folder to the root directory of the Swift application and include in it the corresponding key files for accessing the dependency repositories. You should also include in this folder a config file, which binds the keys to the corresponding hostname of the repository:

```
$ cat config
# GitHub.IBM.com—Enterprise Host, Account Key
Host github.ibm.com
    HostName github.ibm.com
    User git
    IdentityFile ~/.ssh/ssh_key

# GitHub.com—Private Repo, Account Key
Host github.com
    HostName github.com
    User git
    IdentityFile ~/.ssh/ssh_key
```

Finally, you should use the git protocol in your Package.swift for those dependencies that are private or stored in an enterprise solution (e.g. GitHub Enterprise) as follows:

```
$ cat Package.swift
...
dependencies: [
    ...
    .Package(url: "git@github.ibm.com:Org1/package1.git", majorVersion: 2, minor: 6),
    .Package(url: "git@github.ibm.com:Org1/package2.git", majorVersion: 1, minor: 4),
    .Package(url: "git@github.com:Org2/package3.git", majorVersion: 1, minor: 6),
    ...
  ]
...
```

It is worth mentioning that teams using this feature should follow their organization's SSH key guidelines and standard best practices (e.g., not storing these keys along with the code in the application's GitHub repository). For instance, for deployment activities, it is common for teams to use SSH keys associated with a functional account instead of SSH keys bound to an individual user's account. For further details (such as using deployment keys), we invite you to check out the README file of the buildpack repository on GitHub.

Examples of Using the IBM Bluemix Buildpack for Swift

In this section, you will learn how to provision three Swift applications on Bluemix using the IBM Bluemix buildpack for Swift.

Swift HelloWorld

Swift HelloWorld, which you can download from `https://github.com/IBM-Bluemix/swift-helloworld`, is a very simple Swift application that you can deploy to Bluemix or run locally on your macOS or Ubuntu Linux system. This sample application creates a basic server that returns an HTML page that lists the different environment variables that are available to it. The Swift HelloWorld app was created for educational purposes to teach users about the types of applications that can be developed using the Swift programming language.

The Swift HelloWorld sample application is hosted on GitHub and follows the structure and conventions required by Swift Package Manager. Therefore, the IBM Bluemix buildpack for Swift can be used to provision this application on Bluemix.

Remember that before you can use the IBM Bluemix buildpack for Swift to provision an instance of Swift HelloWorld on Bluemix, you should install the Bluemix command line tool on your system. You should also be pointing to the Bluemix region you use for hosting your applications, and you should be authenticated (see the section, "Working with the IBM Bluemix Buildpack for Swift," for details). You should also be familiar with Git and its command line.

Let's now start by cloning the Swift HelloWorld project to your local development system:

```
$ git clone https://github.com/IBM-Bluemix/swift-helloworld.git
```

After cloning the repository, navigate to its root folder and execute the bx app push command:

```
$ bx app push
Invoking 'cf push'...

Using manifest file /Users/olivieri/git/swift-helloworld/manifest.yml

...

Uploading swift-helloworld...
Uploading app files from: /Users/olivieri/git/swift-helloworld
Uploading 36.6K, 16 files
Done uploading
OK

Starting app swift-helloworld in org roliv@us.ibm.com / space dev as roliv@us.ibm.com...
Downloaded swift_buildpack
Downloading swift_buildpack...
Creating container
Successfully created container
Downloading app package...
Downloaded app package (14.5K)
Staging...
—-> Buildpack version 2.0.5
—-> Default supported Swift version is 3.1

...


App started


OK

App swift-helloworld was started using this command 'Server'

Showing health and status for app swift-helloworld in org roliv@us.ibm.com / space
dev as roliv@us.ibm.com...
OK

requested state: started
instances: 1/1
usage: 128M x 1 instances
urls: swift-helloworld-uncapacious-inception.mybluemix.net
last uploaded: Mon Apr 3 18:36:43 UTC 2017
```

```
stack: unknown
buildpack: swift_buildpack

       state     since                    cpu     memory          disk          details
#0     running   2017-04-03 01:38:33 PM   0.0%    11.1M of 128M   224M of 1G
```

The `bx app push` command uses the IBM Bluemix buildpack for Swift to provision the Swift HelloWorld application on Bluemix. If you look closely at this output, you will see that version 2.0.5 of the buildpack and version 3.1 of Swift were used during the execution of the command. You will also notice that the source code of the application was uploaded to Bluemix and that the buildpack was responsible for compiling and linking it using Swift Package Manager. Finally, you should also notice that a URL was assigned to the application. The string value (in this case, `swift-helloworld-uncapacious-inception.mybluemix.net`) shown next to the `urls` field contains the value for this URL (this URL is also known as the application's route).

Once the application is running on Bluemix, you can access the application's URL to see an HTML page that lists the different environment variables that are available, such as `VCAP_APPLICATION`, `PORT`, and `USER`. (See Figure 4-2.)

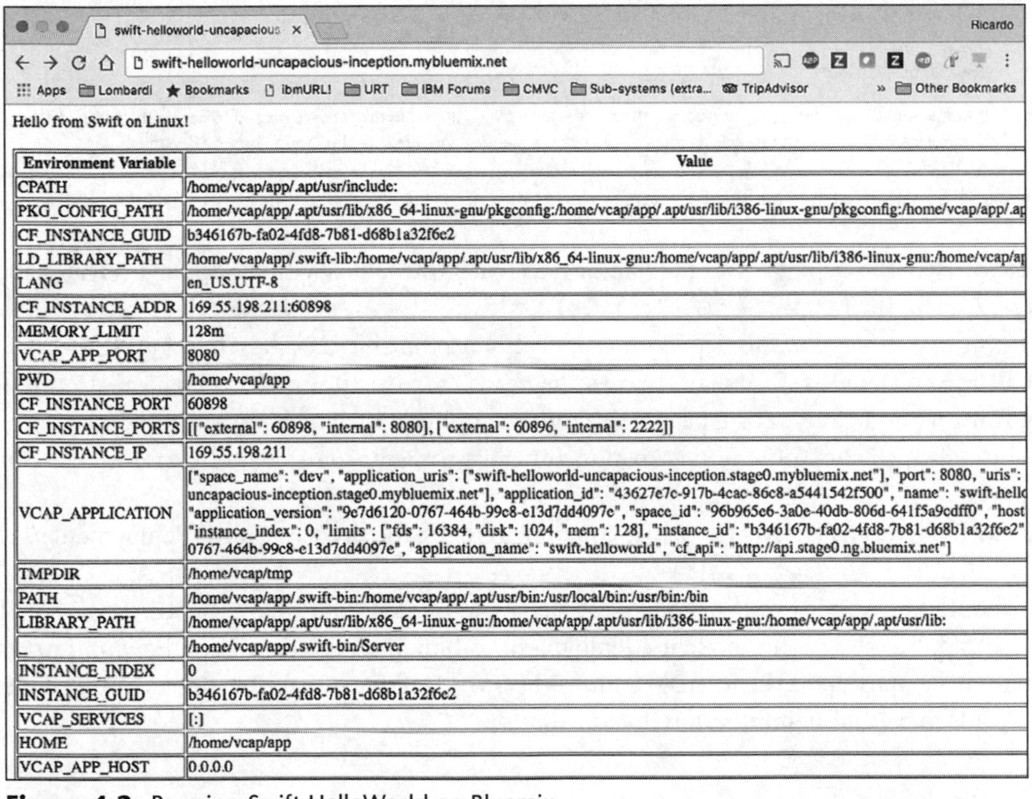

Figure 4-2: Running Swift HelloWorld on Bluemix

If you followed these steps, you should have now successfully provisioned your first Swift application on the Bluemix cloud!

If you make changes to the source code of the Swift HelloWorld application and want to see those changes on Bluemix, you just need to execute the `bx app push` command again from the root folder of the repository. This action restages the instance of the application on Bluemix. Once restaged, the application is reachable on the same URL that was initially assigned to it.

The Deploy to Bluemix Button

You can also deploy the Swift HelloWorld sample application to Bluemix by simply navigating to the project's GitHub README page and clicking the Deploy to Bluemix button found under the Running the App on Bluemix section, as shown in Figure 4-3.

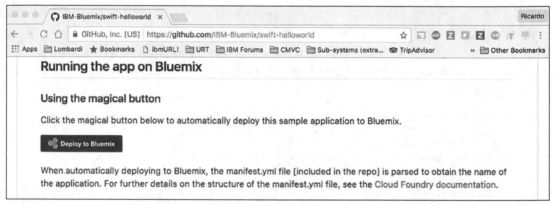

Figure 4-3: The Deploy to Bluemix button on the Swift HelloWorld application README file

After you click the Deploy to Bluemix button, you will be presented with the option to create a Bluemix DevOps Toolchain (`https://console.ng.bluemix.net/docs/services/ContinuousDelivery/toolchains_working.html`) to deploy the application to the cloud as shown in Figure 4-4.

Creating the DevOps Toolchain parses the `manifest.yml` file in the repository to obtain the configuration and provisioning properties for the application. The Delivery Pipeline component (see Figure 4-5) in the Toolchain is responsible for provisioning the application to the Bluemix cloud.

You can click on the Delivery Pipeline component to see the progress of the deployment as shown in Figure 4-6.

You should know that you can include the Deploy to Bluemix button on the README file of your own Swift application to automate its deployment to Bluemix. For details on how to do this, you can inspect the markup of the README file of the Swift HelloWorld application or you can view the Creating a Deploy to Bluemix button documentation.

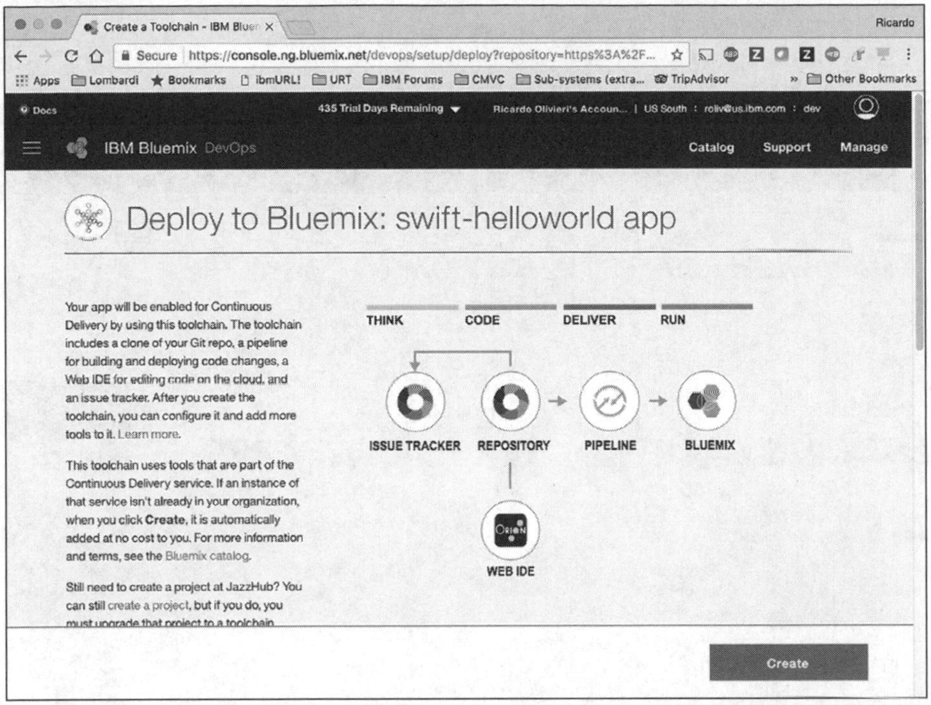

Figure 4-4: Deploying the Swift HelloWorld app using the Deploy to Bluemix button

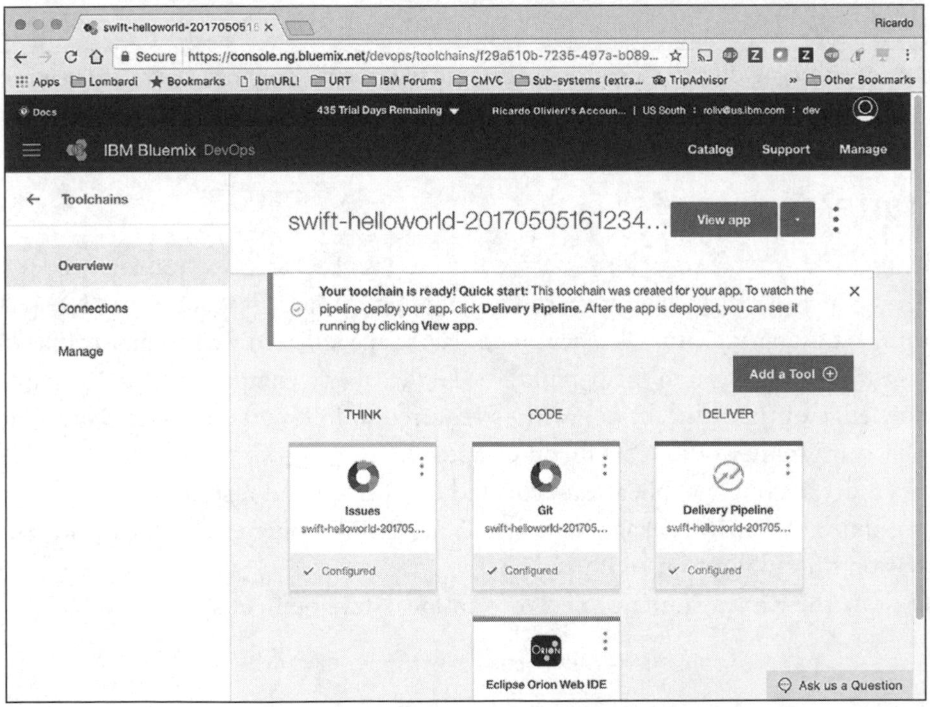

Figure 4-5: Bluemix DevOps Toolchain for the Swift HelloWorld app

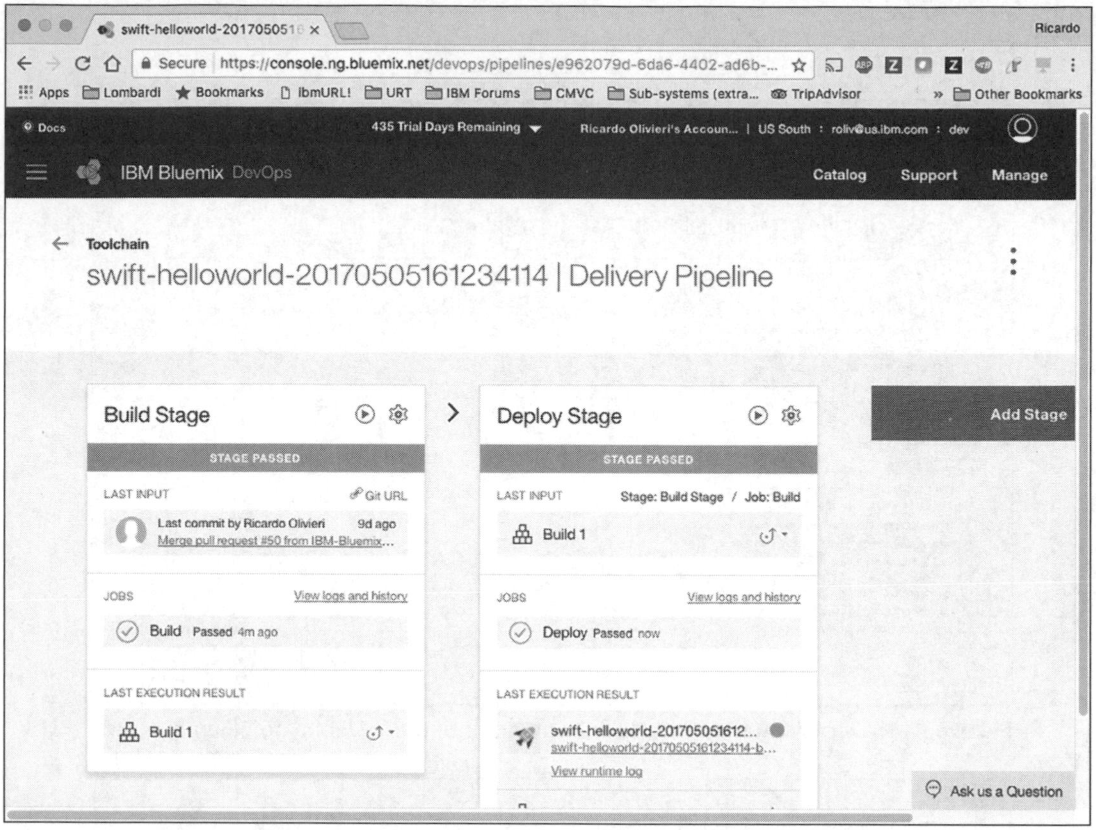

Figure 4-6: Swift HelloWorld app successfully deployed to Bluemix using the Deploy to Bluemix button

Kitura Starter

Kitura Starter (`https://github.com/IBM-Bluemix/Kitura-Starter`) is an application that developers can use as a starting point to get their own Kitura-based application (`https://github.com/IBM-Swift/Kitura`) up and running on Bluemix. Kitura is a new, modular, package-based web framework written in the Swift language, that allows you to easily build web services with complex routes. Keep in mind that no prior knowledge of the Kitura framework is required to follow the materials presented in this section. (The Kitura framework is covered in Chapter 7.)

The Kitura Starter sample application is hosted on GitHub and also follows the structure and conventions required by Swift Package Manager. Thus, the IBM Bluemix buildpack for Swift can be used to provision this application on Bluemix.

Let's now clone the Kitura Starter project to your local development system:

```
$ git clone https://github.com/IBM-Bluemix/Kitura-Starter.git
```

After cloning the repository, navigate to its root folder and execute the Cloud Foundry `bx app push` command:

```
$ bx app push
Invoking 'cf push'...

Using manifest file /Users/olivieri/git/Kitura-Starter/manifest.yml

...

Uploading Kitura-Starter...
Uploading app files from: /Users/olivieri/git/Kitura-Starter
Uploading 61K, 17 files
Done uploading
OK

Starting app Kitura-Starter in org roliv@us.ibm.com / space dev as roliv@us.ibm.com...
Downloading swift_buildpack...
Downloaded swift_buildpack
Creating container
Successfully created container
Downloading app package...
Downloaded app package (27.1K)
Staging...
—-> Buildpack version 2.0.5
—-> Default supported Swift version is 3.1

...

—-> Building Package...
—-> Build config: release

...

App started

OK

App Kitura-Starter was started using this command 'Kitura-Starter'

Showing health and status for app Kitura-Starter in org roliv@us.ibm.com / space dev
as roliv@us.ibm.com...
OK

requested state: started
instances: 1/1
usage: 256M x 1 instances
urls: kitura-starter-bluemix-cartographical-ornithopod.mybluemix.net
```

```
last uploaded: Mon Apr 3 20:44:56 UTC 2017
stack: unknown
buildpack: swift_buildpack

     state    since                     cpu    memory        disk          details
#0   running  2017-04-03 03:47:36 PM    1.0%   4.7M of 256M  225.9M of 1G
```

Just as you saw with the Swift HelloWorld application, the `bx app push` command uses the IBM Bluemix buildpack for Swift to provision the Kitura Starter application on Bluemix. The source code of the starter application is uploaded to Bluemix, and the buildpack compiles and links it using Swift Package Manager. Once the application is provisioned, a URL (that is, the application's route) is assigned to it. Looking at this output, you can find this value (for example, `kitura-starter-bluemix-cartographical-ornithopod.mybluemix.net`) next to the `urls` field.

Once the application is up and running on Bluemix, you can use the browser of your choice to access the application's URL and see the welcome page for the Kitura Starter application (see Figure 4-7). This page displays static HTML content served from the Kitura-based server.

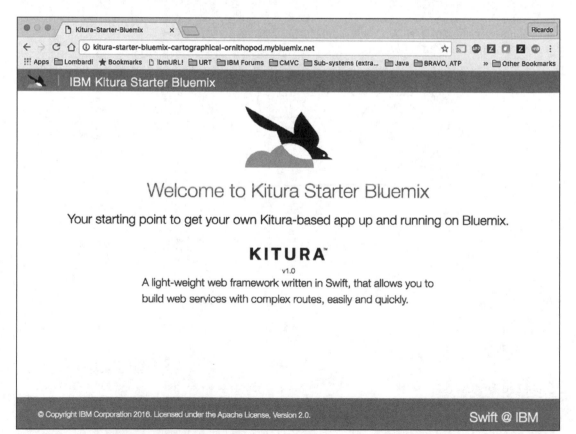

Figure 4-7: Running Kitura Starter on Bluemix

You have now successfully provisioned the Kitura Starter application on the Bluemix cloud! For more information about the different endpoints that you can access on the Kitura Starter sample application, refer to its README file on GitHub.

The Deploy to Bluemix Button

You can also deploy the Kitura Starter application to Bluemix by simply navigating to the project's GitHub README page and clicking the Deploy to Bluemix button found under the Pushing the Application to Bluemix section, as shown in Figure 4-8.

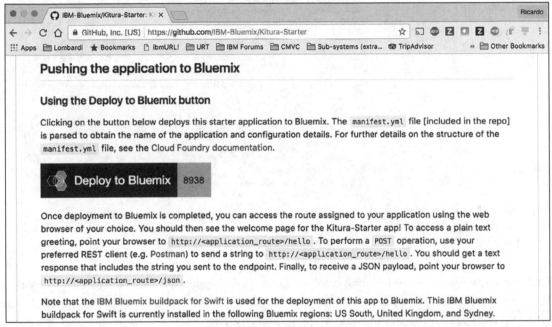

Figure 4-8: The Deploy to Bluemix button on the Kitura Starter application README file

Just as you saw with the Swift HelloWorld application, clicking the Deploy to Bluemix button will give you the option to create a Bluemix DevOps Toolchain that parses the manifest.yml file in the repository to obtain the configuration and provisioning details. Once the Toolchain is created, you can click on the Delivery Pipeline component to see the progress of the deployment. (See Figure 4-9.)

BluePic

More than likely, your Swift applications will use one or more Bluemix services to provide the functionality and experiences your users expect. To provision an application that depends on Bluemix services, you *first* need to create those services and *then* update your manifest.yml file to let Bluemix know that it should bind your application to those services.

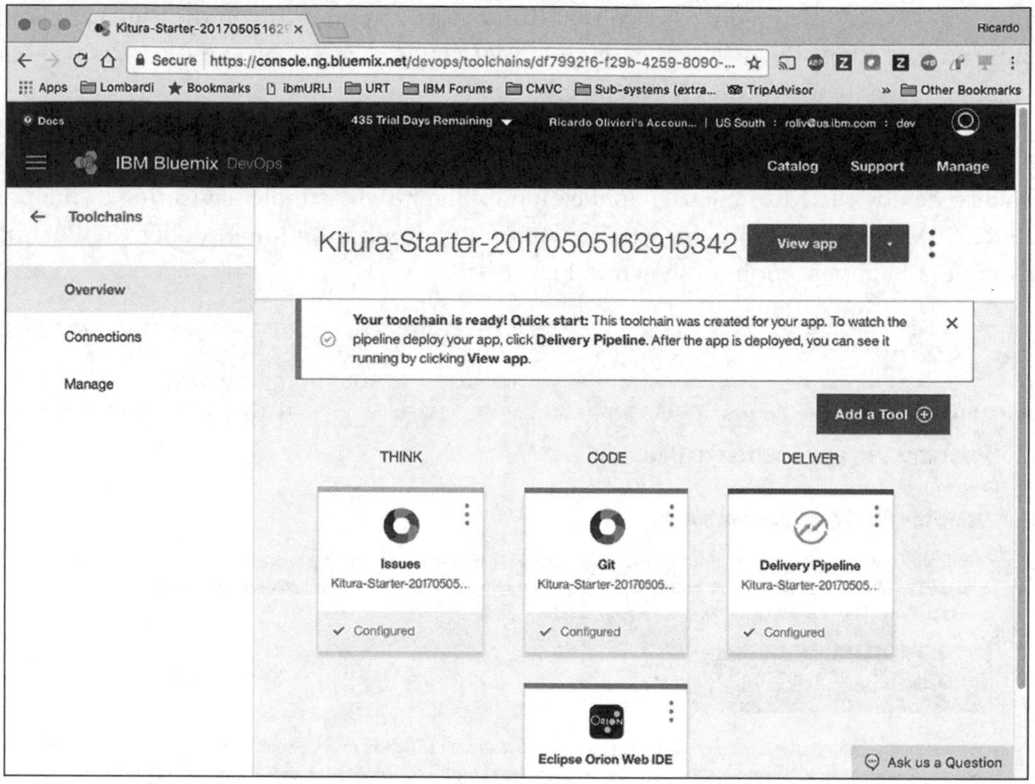

Figure 4-9: Deploying Kitura Starter using the Deploy to Bluemix button

To demonstrate how to bind Bluemix services to a Swift application that is provisioned using the buildpack, the following example will use the BluePic (`https://github.com/IBM/BluePic`) application. BluePic is a photo- and image-sharing sample application written in Swift that allows users to take pictures and share them with other users. The BluePic sample application uses the following Bluemix services:

- **Cloudant NoSQL DB** (`https://console.ng.bluemix.net/docs/services/Cloudant/index.html`)—For storing user and image metadata
- **Object Storage** (`https://console.ng.bluemix.net/docs/services/ObjectStorage/index.html`)—For storing uploaded image binaries
- **Visual Recognition** (`https://www.ibm.com/watson/developercloud/visual-recognition.html`)—For analyzing uploaded images and generating cognitive data
- **Weather Company Data** (`https://console.ng.bluemix.net/docs/services/Weather/index.html`)—For collecting weather data for a given location
- **Push Notifications** (`https://console.ng.bluemix.net/docs/services/mobilepush/index.html`)—For sending push notifications to corresponding iOS clients once an uploaded image has been augmented (with weather and cognitive data) by the back-end components
- **App ID** (`https://console.ng.bluemix.net/docs/services/appid/index.html`)—For security and authentication

Let's start by cloning the BluePic repository to your local development system using the following command:

```
$ git clone https://github.com/IBM/BluePic
```

After cloning the repository, navigate to the Cloud-Script/cloud-foundry folder in the project. For instance, because we cloned the BluePic repository into the /Users/olivieri/git folder, to get to the Cloud-Script/cloud-foundry folder, we executed the following command:

```
$ cd /Users/olivieri/git/BluePic/Cloud-Scripts/cloud-foundry
$ ls -la
total 8
drwxr-xr-x    3 olivieri   staff    102 Apr 10 12:25 .
drwxr-xr-x   11 olivieri   staff    374 Apr 10 12:25 ..
-rwxr-xr-x    1 olivieri   staff   1481 Apr 10 12:25 services.sh
```

The services.sh script found in the Cloud-Script/cloud-foundry folder is responsible for the creation of the Bluemix services that BluePic requires. As a reference, here are the contents of the services.sh file:

```
$ cat services.sh
#!/bin/bash

##
# Copyright IBM Corporation 2016
#
...

##

# If any commands fail, we want the shell script to exit immediately.
set -e

# Delete services first
echo "Deleting services..."
bx service delete -f "BluePic-Cloudant"
bx service delete -f "BluePic-Object-Storage"
bx service delete -f "BluePic-App-ID"
bx service delete -f "BluePic-IBM-Push"
bx service delete -f "BluePic-Weather-Company-Data"
bx service delete -f "BluePic-Visual-Recognition"
echo "Services deleted."

# Create services
echo "Creating services..."
bx service create cloudantNoSQLDB Lite "BluePic-Cloudant"
bx service create Object-Storage Free "BluePic-Object-Storage"
bx service create AdvancedMobileAccess "Graduated tier" "BluePic-App-ID"
bx service create imfpush Basic "BluePic-IBM-Push"
bx service create weatherinsights Free-v2 "BluePic-Weather-Company-Data"
bx service create watson_vision_combined free "BluePic-Visual-Recognition"
echo "Services created."
```

As you can see, the `services.sh` script relies on the Bluemix command line to execute the `service-create` command for the creation of each one of the services that BluePic depends on:

```
bx service create <service_type> <service_plan> <service_name>
```

The `service_type` and `service_plan` are values you can obtain from Bluemix, while the `service_name` is a value assigned by the developer of the application (for example, BluePic-Cloudant, BluePic-Object-Storage, and so on). To obtain the *type* and *plan* values for the services available on Bluemix, you can use the Cloud Foundry command line to execute the `bx service offerings` command, as shown in Figure 4-10.

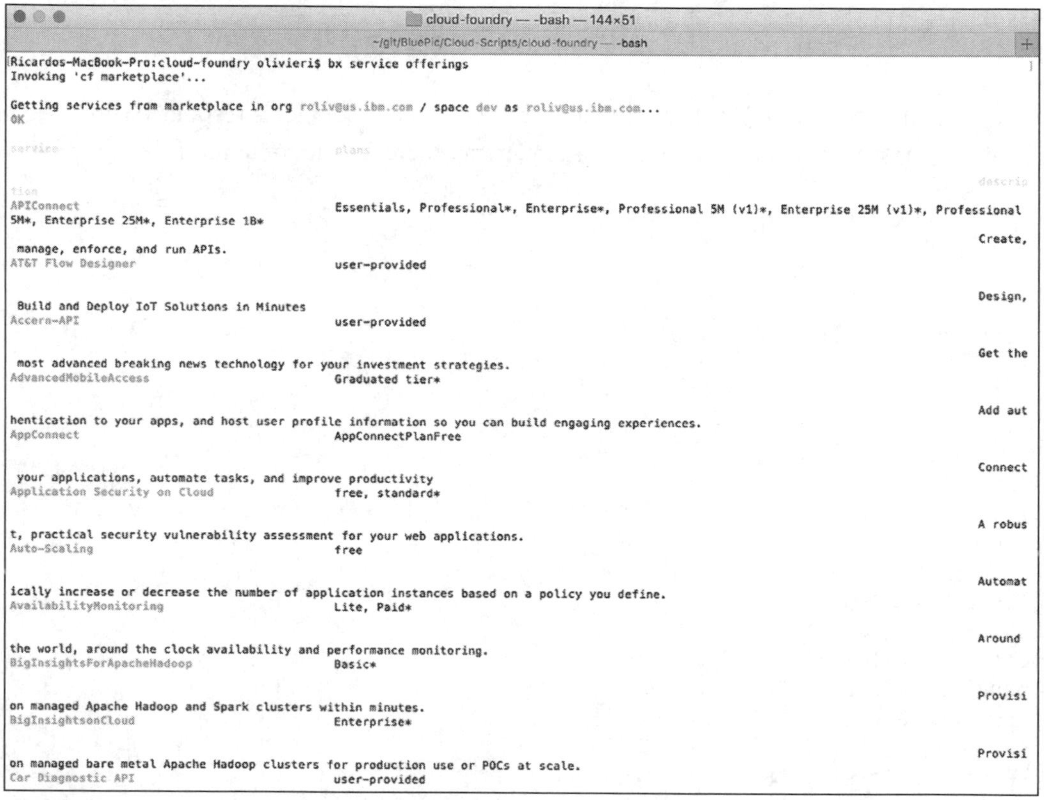

Figure 4-10: List of service offerings in Bluemix

As shown in the figure, executing the `bx service offerings` command returns a list with the following information for each available service:

■ Service type (for example, cloudantNoSQLDB, Object Storage, weatherinsights)
■ Plans (for example, Free-v2, Free, Lite)
■ Description

Let's now execute the `services.sh` script to create the Bluemix services for BluePic:

```
$ ./services.sh
Deleting services...
Invoking 'cf delete-service -f BluePic-Cloudant'...

Deleting service BluePic-Cloudant in org roliv@us.ibm.com / space dev as roliv@
us.ibm.com...
OK
Service BluePic-Cloudant does not exist.

...

Services deleted.
Creating services...
Invoking 'cf create-service cloudantNoSQLDB Lite BluePic-Cloudant'...

Creating service instance BluePic-Cloudant in org roliv@us.ibm.com / space dev as
roliv@us.ibm.com...
OK
Invoking 'cf create-service Object-Storage Free BluePic-Object-Storage'...

Creating service instance BluePic-Object-Storage in org roliv@us.ibm.com / space dev
as roliv@us.ibm.com...
OK

Create in progress. Use 'cf services' or 'cf service BluePic-Object-Storage' to
check operation status.
Invoking 'cf create-service AdvancedMobileAccess Graduated tier BluePic-App-ID'...

...

Invoking 'cf create-service watson_vision_combined free BluePic-Visual-Recognition'...

Creating service instance BluePic-Visual Recognition in org roliv@us.ibm.com / space
dev as roliv@us.ibm.com...
OK
Services created.
```

Once the services for BluePic are created on Bluemix, you can push the application using the Bluemix command line. To do so, you should navigate to the root folder of the BluePic repository on your local system and execute the `bx app push` command. This action parses the contents of the `manifest.yml` file:

```
$ pwd
/Users/olivieri/git/BluePic
$ ls -la
total 96
drwxr-xr-x   15 olivieri   staff     510 Apr 10 12:25 .
```

```
drwxr-xr-x  121 olivieri  staff    4114 Apr 10 12:23 ..
drwxr-xr-x   13 olivieri  staff     442 Apr 10 12:25 .git
-rw-r--r--    1 olivieri  staff     551 Apr 10 12:25 .gitignore
-rw-r--r--    1 olivieri  staff       0 Apr 10 12:25 .gitmodules
-rw-r--r--    1 olivieri  staff     751 Apr 10 12:25 .travis.yml
drwxr-xr-x    6 olivieri  staff     204 Apr 10 12:25 BluePic-OpenWhisk
drwxr-xr-x   14 olivieri  staff     476 Apr 10 12:25 BluePic-Server
drwxr-xr-x   10 olivieri  staff     340 Apr 10 12:25 BluePic-iOS
drwxr-xr-x   11 olivieri  staff     374 Apr 10 12:25 Cloud-Scripts
drwxr-xr-x    7 olivieri  staff     238 Apr 10 12:25 Docs
drwxr-xr-x   20 olivieri  staff     680 Apr 10 12:25 Imgs
-rw-r--r--    1 olivieri  staff   10173 Apr 10 12:25 LICENSE
-rw-r--r--    1 olivieri  staff   23714 Apr 10 12:25 README.md
-rw-r--r--    1 olivieri  staff     784 Apr 10 12:25 manifest.yml
$ cat manifest.yml
---
declared-services:
  BluePic-Cloudant:
    label: cloudantNoSQLDB
    plan: Lite
  BluePic-Object-Storage:
    label: Object-Storage
    plan: Free
  BluePic-App-ID:
    label: AdvancedMobileAccess
    plan: "Graduated tier"
  BluePic-IBM-Push:
    label: imfpush
    plan: Basic
  BluePic-Weather-Company-Data:
    label: weatherinsights
    plan: Free-v2
  BluePic-Visual-Recognition:
    label: watson_vision_combined
    plan: free
applications:
- name: BluePic
  path: ./BluePic-Server
  command: BluePicServer
  random-route: true
  memory: 512M
  disk_quota: 1024M
  instances: 1
  buildpack: swift_buildpack
  services:
  -BluePic-Cloudant
  -BluePic-Object-Storage
  -BluePic-App-ID
  -BluePic-IBM-Push
  -BluePic-Weather-Company-Data
  -BluePic-Visual-Recognition
```

Looking at the `manifest.yml` file for BluePic, notice that towards the end of the file, it lists the required services for the application. When the BluePic application is pushed to Bluemix, that information is used to bind those services to the application. Here's an excerpt from the output from the execution of the `bx app push` command:

```
$ bx app push
Invoking 'cf push'...

Using manifest file /Users/olivieri/git/BluePic/manifest.yml

Creating app BluePic in org roliv@us.ibm.com / space dev as roliv@us.ibm.com...
OK


...

Binding service BluePic-Cloudant to app BluePic in org roliv@us.ibm.com / space dev
as roliv@us.ibm.com...
OK
Binding service BluePic-Object-Storage to app BluePic in org roliv@us.ibm.com /
space dev as roliv@us.ibm.com...
OK
Binding service BluePic-App-ID to app BluePic in org roliv@us.ibm.com / space dev as
roliv@us.ibm.com...
OK
Binding service BluePic-IBM-Push to app BluePic in org roliv@us.ibm.com / space dev
as roliv@us.ibm.com...
OK


...

Compile Swift Module 'BluePicApp' (8 sources)
        Linking ./.build/release/BluePicServer
        Compile Swift Module 'BluePicServer' (1 sources)
—-> Copying dynamic libraries
—-> Copying binaries to 'bin'
—-> Clearing previous swift cache
—-> Saving cache (default):
—->—Packages (nothing to cache)
—-> Optimizing contents of cache folder...


...

App started


OK

App BluePic was started using this command 'BluePicServer'

Showing health and status for app BluePic in org roliv@us.ibm.com / space dev as
roliv@us.ibm.com...
```

```
OK

requested state: started
instances: 1/1
usage: 512M x 1 instances
urls: bluepic-eatable-dragonet.eu-gb.mybluemix.net
last uploaded: Mon Apr 10 17:46:08 UTC 2017
stack: unknown
buildpack: swift_buildpack

      state    since                 cpu     memory     disk      details
#0    running  2017-04-10 12:51:14 PM  0.0%    0 of 512M  0 of 1G
```

After the Bluemix services are bound to the application, the buildpack compiles and links the source code of the Kitura-based server component for BluePic using Swift Package Manager. Once BluePic is provisioned, a URL (that is, the application's route) is assigned to it. Looking at the output, you can find this value (in this example, `bluepic-eatable-dragonet.eu-gb.mybluemix.net`) next to the `urls` field.

After the application is up and running on Bluemix, you can use the browser of your choice to access the application's URL and see the welcome page for the BluePic application, as shown in Figure 4-11.

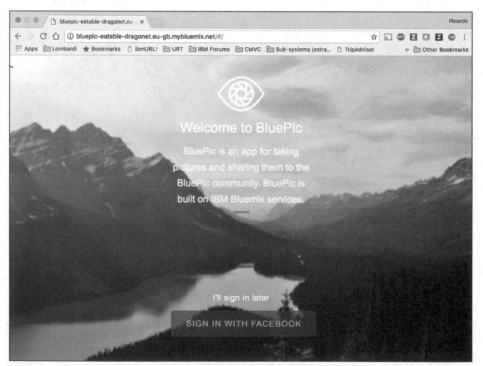

Figure 4-11: Landing page for the BluePic application

You have now successfully provisioned the BluePic application on the Bluemix cloud! If you are interested in learning more about the functionality and capabilities of BluePic, you can check out the README file of the application on GitHub. There, you will also find details on the architecture of the application and the steps required for the configuration of the different Bluemix services.

The Deploy to Bluemix Button

You can also deploy the BluePic application to Bluemix by just navigating to the project's GitHub README page and clicking the Deploy to Bluemix button found under the Create BluePic Application on Bluemix section, as shown in Figure 4-12.

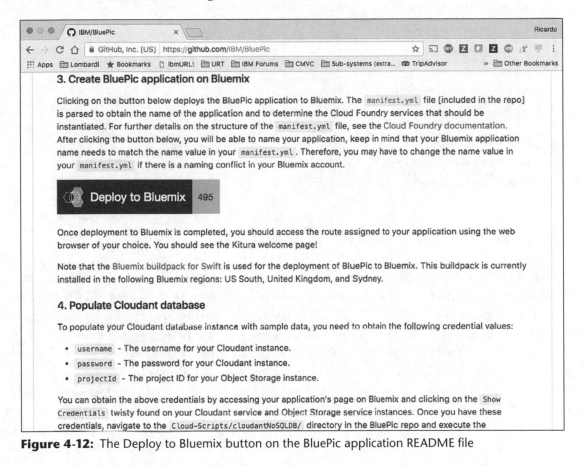

Figure 4-12: The Deploy to Bluemix button on the BluePic application README file

Clicking the Deploy to Bluemix button results in the creation of a Bluemix DevOps Toolchain (see Figure 4-13 and Figure 4-14) and the parsing of the manifest.yml file of the application to obtain the configuration and provisioning details. This includes parsing the type, plan, and name of the Bluemix services that should be created and bound to the application.

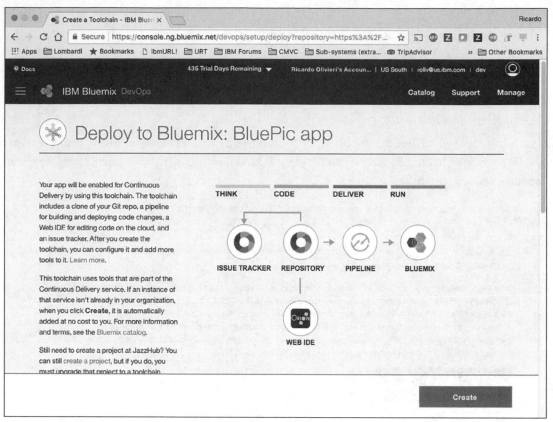

Figure 4-13: Deploying BluePic using the Deploy to Bluemix button

The logic behind the Deploy to Bluemix button first takes care of the creation of the required Bluemix services; it then creates the application and binds it to the services; finally, it provisions the application on the Bluemix cloud. If you are wondering how the logic that supports the Deploy to Bluemix button knows which services it should create, you should look at the top section of the `manifest.yml` file for the BluePic application. There, you will find a section labeled `declared-services`, which is a manifest *extension* that allows for the creation of services before an application is provisioned. The `declared-services` section lists the name for each required service along with its *type* and *plan*. The metadata contained in this manifest extension is also found in the `Cloud-Script/cloud-foundry/services.sh` file that you used to create the Bluemix services leveraging the Bluemix command line. For more details, refer to the Deploy to Bluemix button documentation found at `https://console.ng.bluemix.net/docs/develop/deploy_button.html`.

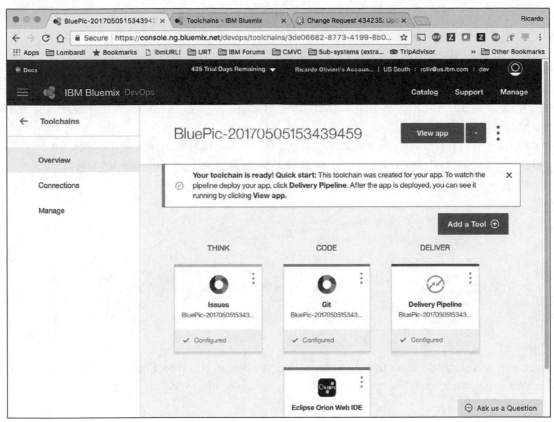

Figure 4-14: Bluemix DevOps Toolchain for BluePic

Using the Latest Code of the IBM Bluemix Buildpack for Swift

As enhancements and fixes are added to the code base of the IBM Bluemix buildpack for Swift, it is possible that the latest code available on GitHub isn't yet deployed to Bluemix. As I mentioned earlier in this chapter, the master branch should always reflect the code that is currently deployed to Bluemix, while the develop branch should contain any new enhancements or bug fixes that haven't been deployed yet.

If you'd like to leverage functionality found in the develop branch, you can do so by adding the -b https://github.com/IBM-Swift/swift-buildpack#develop parameter to the bx app push command, as shown here:

```
$ bx app push -b https://github.com/IBM-Swift/swift-buildpack#develop
```

Although using the `develop` branch of the buildpack does not affect the performance of your application, the provisioning phase will take a little longer than usual. This is because when the `-b` parameter is specified, the installed buildpack on Bluemix is not used to provision your application. Instead, the `bx app push` command uses the source code of the specified branch of the buildpack to compile and link your Swift application on Bluemix. In this case, the binaries for Swift and Clang are not pre-cached and are downloaded at runtime, which increases the length of the provisioning phase.

If you find that you often use the `develop` branch of the IBM Bluemix buildpack for Swift and would prefer to just type **bx app push** to provision your application, you can update the `buildpack` attribute in your `manifest.yml` file:

```
$ cat manifest.yml

...

# buildpack: swift_buildpack
buildpack: https://github.com/IBM-Swift/swift-buildpack#develop

...
```

Once you are ready to start using the installed version of the IBM Bluemix buildpack for Swift again, you can switch back the value of the `buildpack` attribute to `swift_buildpack`:

```
$ cat manifest.yml

...

buildpack: swift_buildpack

...
```

Summary

In this chapter, we introduced the IBM Bluemix buildpack for Swift, which is a new addition to the family of buildpacks on Bluemix. At the beginning of this chapter, we covered the different phases that a buildpack goes through when provisioning an application on the cloud. We also demonstrated how to leverage the IBM Bluemix buildpack for Swift to provision your Swift applications on Bluemix and then discussed several of the extension points the buildpack provides. Depending on the type of application you intend to run on the cloud, you may find some or all of these very useful. For instance, there are extension points for installing additional system packages, for providing custom compilation flags, and for cloning Git repositories using SSH keys. We also demonstrated how to use the Deploy to Bluemix button for provisioning Swift applications on the Bluemix cloud with just the click of a button.

This buildpack provides the runtime required to execute, on the Bluemix cloud, Swift applications that follow the structure dictated by Swift Package Manager. Therefore, the deployment to Bluemix of server back-end components written in the Swift language is entirely possible today. Our team at IBM is very excited to see the different types of Swift applications that developers will design, implement, and then deploy to Bluemix.

CHAPTER 5

Using Containers on Bluemix to Run Swift Code

The IBM Bluemix Container Service brings Docker and Kubernetes together for enabling rapid delivery of applications. Using Docker, developers can easily include all the components and dependencies an application requires to execute. If you are familiar with Docker, then you have probably seen the benefits it provides, such as portability and resource isolation. Kubernetes is an open source platform for managing containerized applications and, among other tasks, for facilitating self-healing actions in case of errors.

In this chapter, you learn what Docker is and how it can be used as a development tool and get a brief introduction to the Kubernetes platform. You will then learn how to create a Kubernetes cluster on Bluemix to host a Swift application and, finally, you will see a demonstration on how to bind Bluemix services to a Kubernetes cluster.

What Are Docker Containers?

Docker, Inc. (`https://www.docker.com`) is behind the development of the Docker software stack (`https://www.docker.com/get-docker`), an open source tool that developers can use to create a deployable unit that encapsulates an application and all the dependencies, frameworks, and libraries it needs. This deployable unit is commonly referred to as a *container*. Because containers are self-contained environments, they can be deployed to different host systems regardless of the configuration those hosts may have.

Although Docker containers may seem like virtual machines, they are different. Containers share the kernel of the host operating system, making them lightweight. Thus, containers require less processing power than virtual machines to execute on the host environment. For example, the start-up overhead commonly experienced when using virtual machines is not seen with containers.

Before you can create your own Docker container, you first need to create a Docker image. A Docker image is a binary artifact that contains the specification for the container. Thinking in object-oriented programming terms, a class is to an object instance what a Docker image is to a container. Therefore, a Docker container is simply a concretization of a Docker image.

To specify the contents of a Docker image, you use a Dockerfile (`https://docs.docker.com/engine/reference/builder`), which is a human-readable text document with a set of commands for assembling the image. The commands in this file can, among other tasks, install system-level packages, define environment variables, clone and compile Git repositories, and add scripts or binary files to the image. For example, the Dockerfile for the ibmcom/swift-ubuntu image (`https://github.com/IBM-Swift/swift-ubuntu-docker`) does the following: installs the system-level dependencies that Swift requires; downloads and installs the Swift release binaries, which includes Swift Package Manager; hardens the image to enforce common security requirements; and, for convenience, installs the Vim text editor (`http://www.vim.org`).

As part of the Docker software stack, Docker provides a command line tool (`https://docs.docker.com/engine/reference/commandline/cli`) that developers can use to create a Docker image on their system based on the contents of a Dockerfile. After creating a Docker image, you can make it available to other users by publishing it to a public or a private registry. For example, Docker, Inc. manages a cloud-based registry known as Docker Hub (`https://hub.docker.com`), while the Bluemix cloud provides a private registry that your developers can leverage for storing and sharing images with other members of your organization. These registries allow developers to download and start using an image right away without having to obtain a copy of the corresponding Dockerfile and building the image themselves.

Docker Images for Swift

IBM maintains three Docker images that you can use for development and deployment of applications and for educational purposes. These images are available at no cost on Docker Hub under the IBM organization:

- **ibmcom/swift-ubuntu** (`https://hub.docker.com/r/ibmcom/swift-ubuntu`)—An Ubuntu (v14.04 Long Term Support) image with the Swift binaries and its dependencies. At IBM, we use this image for the development and testing of Swift applications on the Linux operating system.
- **ibmcom/swift-ubuntu-runtime** (`https://hub.docker.com/r/ibmcom/swift-ubuntu-runtime/`)—An Ubuntu (v14.04 Long Term Support) image that contains only those libraries (`.so` files) from the Swift toolchain that are required for running Swift applications. This image does not contain Swift Package Manager or any of the build tools required for compiling and linking Swift applications. The `ibmcom/swift-ubuntu-runtime` image is ideal for creating your own custom images and packaging your Swift applications so they can be provisioned inside a Kubernetes cluster on Bluemix.
- **ibmcom/kitura-ubuntu** (`https://hub.docker.com/r/ibmcom/kitura-ubuntu/`)—A sample and educational image for running the Kitura Starter application; this image extends the `ibmcom/swift-ubuntu` image. Kitura Starter is a sample application that developers can use to become familiar with the Kitura web framework. Keep in mind that no prior knowledge

of the Kitura framework is required to follow the materials presented in this chapter. (The Kitura framework is covered in Chapter 7.)

You should know that the `ibmcom/swift-ubuntu` and `ibmcom/swift-ubuntu-runtime` images are tagged according to the Swift version they support. For instance, the version of the `ibmcom/swift-ubuntu` image that supports Swift 3.1 uses `3.1` as its tag name (i.e., `ibmcom/swift-ubuntu:3.1`). You can always get the most recent version of these images by using `latest` as the tag name (e.g., `ibmcom/swift-ubuntu:latest`). The most recent version of these two images should always support the most recent version of the Swift language that is available. For a list of the tags available for these images see the following links:

■ `https://hub.docker.com/r/ibmcom/swift-ubuntu/tags/`
■ `https://hub.docker.com/r/ibmcom/swift-ubuntu-runtime/tags/`

It is worth mentioning that if you use the `ibmcom/swift-ubuntu-runtime` image as the base for any of your own images, your containers will inherit the security hardening configuration we have put in place for this image, thus making your applications less vulnerable to attacks. (For example, the image has no telnet or FTP server installed and sets as a policy that the minimum password length is eight characters long.)

Installing Docker

To make the most of this chapter, you should install Docker on your development system. You can find the Docker installation guide at `https://docs.docker.com/engine/installation/`. If working on macOS, you will be installing Docker for Mac, which uses native capabilities on macOS to virtualize the Docker Engine environment. You can go to `https://docs.docker.com/docker-for-mac/install/` to find the Docker for Mac installation guide. (At the time of writing, the latest version of Docker for Mac is 1.13.)

Once Docker is installed on your system, you should be able to issue Docker commands from your terminal window. You can execute the following command to validate that your Docker installation was indeed successful:

```
$ docker run hello-world
Unable to find image 'hello-world:latest' locally
latest: Pulling from library/hello-world

c04b14da8d14: Pull complete
Digest: sha256:0256e8a36e2070f7bf2d0b0763dbabdd67798512411de4cdcf9431a1feb60fd9
Status: Downloaded newer image for hello-world:latest

Hello from Docker!
```

```
This message shows that your installation appears to be working correctly.

To generate this message, Docker took the following steps:
 1. The Docker client contacted the Docker daemon.
 2. The Docker daemon pulled the "hello-world" image from the Docker Hub.
 3. The Docker daemon created a new container from that image which runs the
    executable that produces the output you are currently reading.
 4. The Docker daemon streamed that output to the Docker client, which sent it
    to your terminal.

To try something more ambitious, you can run an Ubuntu container with:
 $ docker run -it ubuntu bash

Share images, automate workflows, and more with a free Docker Hub account:
 https://hub.docker.com

For more examples and ideas, visit:
 https://docs.docker.com/engine/userguide/
```

Using Docker as a Development Tool

In addition to using Docker for packaging your Swift application and its dependencies, you can also use it as a development tool. If you are developing a Swift package, more than likely you are developing your code on a development workstation that runs macOS. However, your code will probably need to run properly on macOS and Linux (for example, Ubuntu 14.04). This means you'll need access to both platforms to verify that your code compiles and runs without any errors.

You can use Docker to easily get access to a Linux environment that runs on your macOS system, for building, executing, and testing your Swift code. For example, say you pull down the `ibmcom/swift-ubuntu` image from Docker Hub:

```
$ docker pull ibmcom/swift-ubuntu:latest
```

You can then create a Docker container that uses the `ibmcom/swift-ubuntu` image and mount (to the container) the folder on your macOS system that contains the Swift application or library that you are working on. Doing so will give you access in the Docker container to the same source code files that reside on the macOS system. Thus, you can compile and test your code on macOS and on Linux with minimal effort. Not only this, but you can continue to use your favorite code editor that runs on macOS (Xcode, Atom, Sublime, and so on) while using the Linux environment in the Docker container for building and executing the code on that platform. For example, let's clone the Swift HelloWorld sample application, which can be found at `https://github.com/IBM-Bluemix/swift-helloworld`:

```
$ git clone https://github.com/IBM-Bluemix/swift-helloworld
```

To demonstrate how valuable Docker is for development, let's start a new Docker container that uses the `ibmcom/swift-ubuntu` image as its specification. Change to the folder that contains the `swift-helloworld` project that you just cloned, and execute the following command:

```
$ docker run -i -t -v $PWD:/root/swift-helloworld ibmcom/swift-ubuntu:latest
root@ca14d6d1eb9a:~# ls -la
total 28
drwx──── 1 root root 4096 Mar 30 20:52 .
drwxr-xr-x  1 root root 4096 Mar 30 20:52 ..
-rw-r—r— 1 root root 3116 Mar 29 15:36 .bashrc
-rw-r—r— 1 root root  140 Feb 20  2014 .profile
drwxr-xr-x  6 root root 4096 Mar 29 15:36 .vim
 rw-rw-r— 1 root root   84 Mar 29 15:33 .vimrc
drwxr-xr-x  3 root root 4096 Mar 29 15:36 swift-3.1-RELEASE-ubuntu14.04
drwxr-xr-x 19 root root  646 Mar 29 16:06 swift-helloworld
```

If you navigate to the `swift-helloworld` folder (this is the folder you mounted to the Docker container), you will find the contents of the Swift HelloWorld repository. From that folder, you can build and run the sample application:

```
root@ca14d6d1eb9a:~# cd swift-helloworld/
root@3b69eaf8613a:~/swift-helloworld# swift build
Fetching https://github.com/IBM-Swift/CloudConfiguration.git
Fetching https://github.com/IBM-Swift/BlueSocket.git
Fetching https://github.com/IBM-Swift/HeliumLogger.git
Fetching https://github.com/IBM-Swift/Swift-cfenv.git
Fetching https://github.com/IBM-Swift/LoggerAPI.git
Fetching https://github.com/IBM-Swift/Configuration.git
Cloning https://github.com/IBM-Swift/CloudConfiguration.git


...


Compile Swift Module 'Utils' (3 sources)
Compile Swift Module 'Server' (1 sources)
Linking ./.build/debug/Server
root@3b69eaf8613a:~/swift-helloworld# ./.build/debug/Server
[2017-03-30T21:16:17.799Z] [INFO] [main.swift:50 Server] Server is starting on
http://localhost:8080.
[2017-03-30T21:16:17.833Z] [INFO] [main.swift:51 Server] Server is listening on
port: 8080.
```

As a reference, here is the format of the command for creating an interactive container [that uses the `ibmcom/swift-ubuntu image`] and mounting your Swift project folder to it:

```
docker run -i -t -v <absolute path to the swift package>:/root/<swift package name>
ibmcom/swift-ubuntu:latest
```

It is worth mentioning that you can follow the same steps described here on a Windows system that has the Docker software on it so you can build, execute, and test Swift applications on a Linux environment.

Exposing Your Swift Application's Port to the Host System

If you are running your Swift application inside a Docker container on your local system, you will probably want to access your application from the host system (for example, macOS or Windows). You can easily do this by exposing the port in your Docker container to your host environment using the following command to instantiate the container:

```
$ docker run -p <host port>:<container port> <image name>
```

Using this command, you can specify the port number on the host machine that should be mapped to the port number on the Docker container. For the host port, you should choose any port value that is not currently being used on your system, while the container port is specified by your Swift application. For instance, let's create a Docker container that uses the ibmcom/kitura-ubuntu image to run the Kitura Starter sample:

```
$ docker pull ibmcom/kitura-ubuntu:latest
latest: Pulling from ibmcom/kitura-ubuntu
Digest: sha256:8efe67e4164da57f33b0b713fe438b37f09c7221a3c972ef17c4ea42c14e7ea2
Status: Image is up to date for ibmcom/kitura-ubuntu:latest

$ docker run -p 9000:8080 ibmcom/kitura-ubuntu:latest

[2017-03-30T21:39:33.250Z] [INFO] [main.swift:28 Kitura_Starter] Server will be
started on 'http://localhost:8080'.
[2017-03-30T21:39:33.254Z] [INFO] [HTTPServer.swift:104 listen(on:)] Listening on
port 8080
```

This command will instantiate the container and map port 9000 on the host system to port 8080 in the Docker container, which is the default port used by the Kitura Starter application. As shown in Figure 5-1, you can then use a browser running on the host system to access the Swift application running inside the Docker container by pointing to port 9000!

Using docker-compose

A Docker tool that you will find extremely useful for quickly building and running your Swift code in a Linux environment is docker-compose. This tool can be used to create a Docker container and execute a command in it. To leverage docker-compose in this way, you first need to create a docker-compose.yml file. In it, you specify, among other values, the name of the Docker image that should be used for creating the container and the command to be executed. Let's look at the contents of the docker-compose.yml file found in the repository for the Kitura Starter sample

application (https://github.com/IBM-Bluemix/Kitura-Starter) so that you can become familiar
with its structure: Let's first clone the repo that contains this project:

```
$ git clone https://github.com/IBM-Bluemix/Kitura-Starter
Cloning into 'Kitura-Starter'...
remote: Counting objects: 750, done.
remote: Compressing objects: 100% (38/38), done.
remote: Total 750 (delta 19), reused 0 (delta 0), pack-reused 710
Receiving objects: 100% (750/750), 137.06 KiB | 78.00 KiB/s, done.
Resolving deltas: 100% (397/397), done.
```

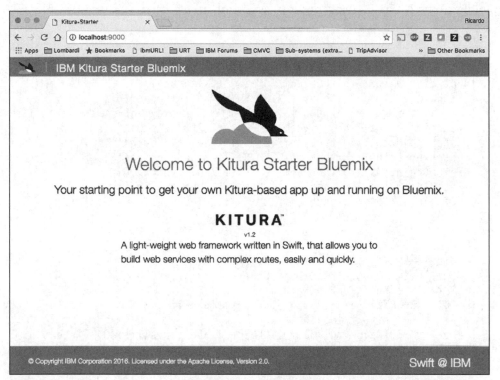

Figure 5-1: Using your browser to access the Kitura Starter application running inside a
Docker container

Change to the folder that contains the project that we just cloned and execute the following
command:

```
$ cat docker-compose.yml
app:
  image: ibmcom/swift-ubuntu:3.1
  ports:
  -"8080:8080"
```

```
volumes:
-.:/root/Kitura-Starter
command: bash -c "cd /root/Kitura-Starter && swift package clean && swift build
&& ./.build/debug/Kitura-Starter"
```

The `image` field in the `docker-compose.yml` file specifies that the `ibmcom/swift-ubuntu:3.1` Docker image should be used to instantiate the Docker container, while the `command` field states that the Kitura Starter sample application should be compiled and started in the container. Also, note that the `volumes` field states that the *current* folder on the host system should be mounted to the `/root/Kitura-Starter` folder in the container. With that in mind, let's now execute the `docker-compose up` command from the root folder of the Kitura Starter repository, as it contains a `docker-compose.yml` file:

```
$ docker-compose up
Recreating kiturastarter_app_1
Attaching to kiturastarter_app_1
app_1  | Fetching https://github.com/IBM-Swift/Kitura.git
app_1  | Fetching https://github.com/IBM-Swift/HeliumLogger.git
app_1  | Fetching https://github.com/IBM-Bluemix/cf-deployment-tracker-client-swift.git
app_1  | Fetching https://github.com/IBM-Swift/Kitura-TemplateEngine.git
app_1  | Fetching https://github.com/IBM-Swift/SwiftyJSON.git
app_1  | Fetching https://github.com/IBM-Swift/BlueSocket.git
app_1  | Fetching https://github.com/IBM-Swift/Swift-cfenv.git
app_1  | Fetching https://github.com/IBM-Swift/LoggerAPI.git
app_1  | Fetching https://github.com/IBM-Swift/CloudConfiguration.git


...


app_1  | Compile Swift Module 'Kitura' (43 sources)
app_1  | Compile Swift Module 'Kitura_Starter' (2 sources)
app_1  | Linking ./.build/debug/Kitura-Starter
app_1  | [2017-03-30T21:57:36.365Z] [INFO] [main.swift:28 Kitura_Starter] Server
will be started on 'http://localhost:8080'.
app_1  | [2017-03-30T21:57:36.373Z] [INFO] [HTTPServer.swift:104 listen(on:)]
Listening on port 8080
```

As you can see in the output, the application is compiled and started inside the Docker container! Using `docker-compose`, you can quickly determine if your Swift application compiles and runs on Linux without any errors. You can do this for your own application by making a copy of the `docker-compose.yml` file found in the Kitura Starter repository, adding it to your Swift application, and then updating the value for the `command` field so that you can build and execute your program.

Why Use Containers on Bluemix?

Using Containers on Bluemix gives you the flexibility to run an application in the Cloud without having to make changes to it. This is possible because the Containers offering on Bluemix leverages Docker and Kubernetes.

Containers for Packaging and Deployment of Swift Applications

Developers can package an application in a Docker container and have it run in any environment that supports Docker. Therefore, having an application up and running in the development, testing, and production environment zones is a matter of instantiating the corresponding Docker image in each one of those zones. Gone are the days when developers had to install and configure the application and its dependencies from scratch in each environment. Instead, they can now simply "move" the application artifact from one environment zone to another by creating a Docker container (think of the Docker container as the deployable unit that encapsulates your application). This enormously simplifies the process of deploying applications, and portability is no longer just a concept.

It is also possible to package an application and all the services (CouchDB, MongoDB, and so on) that it depends on into a single unit. Although you may want to de-compose your application from the services it leverages to separate containers, you could package all components into a single deployable unit for testing the functionality of your application or for building a quick prototype or proof of concept. Using Containers on Bluemix, you can then instantiate this deployable unit to validate the functionality of your application.

Swift packages that serve as wrappers for system-level packages (for example, libhttp-parser) require those packages to be installed before you attempt to build your application using Swift Package Manager. These system packages can be specified in a Docker image as dependencies. Creating containers using a Docker image that has the system dependencies needed for your application will provide the required runtime for executing it on the Cloud.

Also, Swift packages may have complex installation steps that go beyond just executing apt-get to install and configure those dependencies. For instance, non-Swift repositories may have to be cloned and built before a given Swift package can be used. Such complex steps can be taken care of as part of the Docker image creation phase, leaving developers to concentrate on what they enjoy doing: writing the business and application logic (and not being concerned about setting up the environment).

The Kubernetes Platform

Kubernetes is an open-source platform for orchestrating the deployment and management of the runtime operations (such as scaling) of containerized applications. Using Kubernetes on Bluemix allows you to take advantage of crucial built-in capabilities you'll need for your applications once they are running on the Cloud such as load balancing, clustering, and automated rollouts and rollbacks. These capabilities can eliminate downtime to your users and maximize for availability and capacity. The Kubernetes platform has gained a lot of traction, and we believe it provides the essential building blocks for delivering a production-grade environment for container orchestration.

A Kubernetes cluster is a collection of worker nodes found within the same network configuration, while a worker node can be a physical or virtual machine configured to run containers managed by Kubernetes. The Kubernetes orchestration platform takes into account several factors, such as hardware limitations and the amount of requested memory for figuring out which nodes should be used for executing containers. It is worth mentioning that worker nodes are not inherently created by Kubernetes. Instead, worker nodes are created externally by Bluemix. Hence, when Kubernetes creates a worker node, it is just creating an object that represents the node provisioned by Bluemix.

Along with worker nodes, a Kubernetes cluster has at least one master node, which provides a set of APIs that system administrators can interact with to configure and manage the cluster. As a failover mechanism, it is not uncommon for a cluster to have more than one master node.

Containers created from the same template and that run on a same worker node are grouped into a pod, while the object that contains the template for creating pods is known as a deployment. When you create a deployment, you specify the Docker image that should be used for the creation of containers in the cluster. Finally, the object that contains the networking rules that allow pods to be accessed from the Internet is known as a service.

Running Your Docker Image in the Bluemix Cloud

In this section, I will go over the steps for creating a Kubernetes cluster on Bluemix to host a Swift sample server application. Before you begin these steps, make sure you have installed Docker, as documented earlier in this chapter.

Install the Kubernetes Command Line

The Kubernetes command line, `kubectl`, should be installed on your development system so you can interact with the management APIs and run commands against clusters. To install this command line tool, you should follow the instructions for your platform at `https://kubernetes.io/docs/tasks/kubectl/install/`.

Install the Bluemix Command Line

The Bluemix Command Line Interface (CLI) provides the required infrastructure for executing commands against the Bluemix cloud for managing Kubernetes clusters on the IBM Cloud. Therefore, it is necessary to install the Bluemix CLI on your development system. To do so, you should follow the instructions at `https://console.ng.bluemix.net/docs/cli/reference/bluemix_cli/index.html#getting-started`. Once it is installed, you should configure it so that it communicates with your Bluemix region. At the time of writing, the following are the public regions available (you should check the documentation at `https://console.ng.bluemix.net/docs/public/index.html` since additional regions may now be available):

- **United Kingdom**—`https://api.eu-gb.bluemix.net`
- **Sydney**—`https://api.au-syd.bluemix.net`
- **U.S. South**—`https://api.ng.bluemix.net`
- **Germany**—`https://api.eu-de.bluemix.net`

You specify your Bluemix region URL using the bx api command, as shown here (I am using U.S. South as the region for this example):

```
$ bx api https://api.ng.bluemix.net
Setting api endpoint to https://api.ng.bluemix.net...
OK

API endpoint: https://api.ng.bluemix.net (API version: 2.54.0)
```

Let's now authenticate and access your Bluemix organizations and spaces using the bx login command (https://plugins.ng.bluemix.net/ui/home.html):

```
$ bx login
API endpoint: https://api.ng.bluemix.net

Email> roliv@us.ibm.com

Password>
Authenticating...
OK

Select an account (or press enter to skip):
1. Ricardo Olivieri's Account (866573739108948289 45dd81b01281e3)
2. Swift DevOps functionalid's Account (629e1d16217c8ad85ccb31f33bd6cd37)
Enter a number> 1
Targeted account Ricardo Olivieri's Account (866573739108948289 45dd81b01281e3)

Targeted org roliv@us.ibm.com

Select a space (or press enter to skip):
1. dev
2. test
Enter a number> 1
Targeted space dev



API endpoint:   https://api.ng.bluemix.net (API version: 2.54.0)
Region:         us-south
User:           roliv@us.ibm.com
Account:        Ricardo Olivieri's Account (866573739108948289 45dd81b01281e3)
Org:            roliv@us.ibm.com
Space:          dev
```

Your Bluemix account probably only has one organization and one space; if so, then those will be automatically selected for you after you authenticate. In this case, there were multiple organizations and spaces bound to the Bluemix account, and so you had to choose which ones to reference (roliv@us.ibm.com for the organization and dev for the space).

Install the IBM Container Registry Plug-In

You will be uploading Docker images to your private image registry in Bluemix. Images stored in your private registry can be used to build containers that run on the Bluemix cloud. To manage these images, you should install the IBM Container Registry plug-in on your development system:

```
$ bx plugin install container-registry -r Bluemix
Looking up 'container-registry' from repository 'Bluemix'...
Attempting to download the binary file...
10911504 bytes downloaded
Installing binary...
OK
Plug-in 'container-registry 0.1.109' was successfully installed into
/Users/olivieri/.bluemix/plugins/container-registry.
```

You can verify the installation of the plug-in using the following command:

```
$ bx plugin list
Listing installed plug-ins...

Plugin Name         Version
container-registry  0.1.109
```

It is worth mentioning that frequent updates and enhancements are added to the plug-ins that IBM develops for the Bluemix CLI. Therefore, a newer version of the IBM Container Registry plug-in more than likely will be available by the time you are reading this. At the time of writing, the latest version for the IBM Container Registry plug-in was 0.1.109.

Install the IBM Container Service Plug-In

Let's now proceed to install and initialize the IBM Bluemix Container Service plug-in also on your development system:

```
$ bx plugin install container-service -r Bluemix
Looking up 'container-service' from repository 'Bluemix'...
Attempting to download the binary file...
52278336 bytes downloaded
Installing binary...
OK
Plug-in 'container-service 0.1.219' was successfully installed into
/Users/olivieri/.bluemix/plugins/container-service.
```

You can verify the installation of the Container Service plug-in by executing the bx plugin list command one more time (at the time of writing, the latest version for the IBM Container Service plug-in was 0.1.219):

```
$ bx plugin list
Listing installed plug-ins...

Plugin Name         Version
container-registry  0.1.109
container-service   0.1.219
```

After installing the IBM Container Service plug-in, you need to initialize it by executing the `bx cs init` command:

```
$ bx cs init
Using default API endpoint: https://us-south.containers.bluemix.net
OK
```

Create a Runtime Image for Swift Applications

In this section, you will be creating a Docker image that extends the `ibmcom/swift-ubuntu-runtime` image. The `ibmcom/swift-ubuntu-runtime` image is much smaller in size (approximately 300 MB) than the `ibmcom/swift-ubuntu` image and is tailored for provisioning your Swift applications to cloud environments, such as Bluemix. The `ibmcom/swift-ubuntu-runtime` image does not include any of the build tools required for compiling, linking and testing Swift applications. Therefore, this Docker image is not suited for application development, testing, or debugging but exclusively for running Swift applications.

Let's start by downloading the `ibmcom/swift-ubuntu-runtime` image from Docker Hub using the `docker pull` command:

```
$ docker pull ibmcom/swift-ubuntu-runtime:latest
```

If you haven't already cloned the Kitura Starter application, let's take care of that now:

```
$ git clone https://github.com/IBM-Bluemix/Kitura-Starter
Cloning into 'Kitura-Starter'...
remote: Counting objects: 750, done.
remote: Compressing objects: 100% (38/38), done.
remote: Total 750 (delta 19), reused 0 (delta 0), pack-reused 710
Receiving objects: 100% (750/750), 137.06 KiB | 78.00 KiB/s, done.
Resolving deltas: 100% (397/397), done.
```

We should now compile the Kitura Starter application on a system that runs Ubuntu 14.04. To do so, we will use the `ibmcom/swift-ubuntu` development image:

```
$ docker pull ibmcom/swift-ubuntu:latest
```

We can now create a new Docker container, mount the folder that contains the Kitura Starter project, and compile this sample application in release mode instead of debug mode. Compiling a Swift application in release mode ensures that the binary generated is optimized for a production deployment. Go to the folder that contains the Kitura Starter project and execute the following command to start the container:

```
$ docker run -i -t -v $PWD/:/root/Kitura-Starter ibmcom/swift-ubuntu:latest
```

Once the container is running, execute each one of the following commands to compile the application in release mode:

```
root@c528db75744e:~# cd Kitura-Starter/
root@c528db75744e:~/Kitura-Starter# swift package clean
root@c528db75744e:~/Kitura-Starter# swift build --configuration release
Compile Swift Module 'Socket' (3 sources)
Compile Swift Module 'LoggerAPI' (1 sources)

...

Compile Swift Module 'Kitura_Starter' (2 sources)
Linking ./.build/release/Kitura-Starter
```

After compiling the Kitura Starter application, you can exit the Docker container by executing the exit command:

```
root@baa0bfcda066:~/Kitura-Starter# exit
exit
$
```

Using your favorite text editor on your host system (e.g., macOS), create a new Dockerfile named Dockerfile.run in the root folder of the Kitura Starter project and add the contents shown below:

```
# Builds a Docker image for running the Kitura-Starter sample application.

FROM ibmcom/swift-ubuntu-runtime:latest
MAINTAINER IBM Swift Engineering at IBM Cloud
LABEL Description="Docker image for running the Kitura-Starter sample application."

USER root

# Expose default port for Kitura
EXPOSE 8080

# Binaries should have been compiled against the correct platform (i.e. Ubuntu
14.04).
COPY .build/release/Kitura-Starter /root/Kitura-Starter/.build/release/Kitura-
Starter
COPY .build/release/*.so /root/Kitura-Starter/.build/release/
COPY public /root/Kitura-Starter/public
CMD [ "sh", "-c", "cd /root/Kitura-Starter && .build/release/Kitura-Starter" ]
```

This Dockerfile extends the `ibmcom/swift-ubuntu-runtime` image, exposes port 8080, adds the necessary project files and generated binaries for the Kitura Starter application, and specifies the command to execute when a container that uses this image as its specification is run. Since the `public` folder in the Kitura Starter project contains static HTML content that is served by the sample application, we include this folder along with the generated binaries in the new Docker image. Let's create a runtime image named `kitura-starter-runner` by executing the following command in the root folder of the Kitura Starter project:

```
$ docker build -f Dockerfile.run -t kitura-starter-runner:latest .
Sending build context to Docker daemon 39.22 MB
Step 1/9: FROM ibmcom/swift-ubuntu-runtime:latest
--> 345128fc1110
Step 2/9: MAINTAINER IBM Swift Engineering at IBM Cloud
--> Using cache
--> f30c6cabdf27
Step 3/9: LABEL Description "Docker image for running the Kitura-Starter sample
application."
--> Using cache
--> 2c492e91a0a1
Step 4/9: USER root
--> Using cache
--> 9d9191e51bf6
Step 5/9: EXPOSE 8080
--> Using cache
--> 507873633116
Step 6/9: COPY .build/release/Kitura-Starter /root/Kitura-Starter/.build/release/
Kitura-Starter
--> fd3919e8189d
Removing intermediate container 312da9b59c1d
Step 7/9: COPY .build/release/*.so /root/Kitura-Starter/.build/release/
--> fa6fbfb14964
Removing intermediate container 5049dbe7ea34
Step 8/9: COPY public /root/Kitura-Starter/public
--> 2568632dc83a
Removing intermediate container b8545143149e
Step 9/9: CMD sh -c /root/Kitura-Starter/.build/release/Kitura-Starter
--> Running in 9de51ff314b4
--> abe294836728
Removing intermediate container 9de51ff314b4
Successfully built abe294836728
```

We have now a new image that extends the `ibmcom/swift-ubuntu-runtime` image and contains the binaries for the Kitura Starter application. Since we already downloaded the `ibmcom/swift-ubuntu-runtime` image, creating the `kitura-starter-runner` image should only take a few seconds. Executing the following command finally creates a new container for running the kitura-starter-runner image on your local development system:

```
$ docker run -p 8080:8080 -i -t kitura-starter-runner:latest
[2017-03-31T16:56:32.599Z] [INFO] [main.swift:28 Kitura_Starter] Server will be
started on 'http://localhost:8080'.
[2017-03-31T16:56:32.685Z] [INFO] [HTTPServer.swift:104 listen(on:)] Listening on
port 8080
```

Now that the Docker container is running, you can access the Kitura Starter application by using the browser of your choice and pointing to localhost:8080. (To stop the Docker container, you can use Control-C.)

Tag a Docker Image

Before tagging the Docker image, you need to obtain the registry and namespace values assigned to your organization:

```
$ bx cr info

Container Registry:                 registry.ng.bluemix.net
Container Registry API endpoint:    https://registry.ng.bluemix.net/api
Bluemix API endpoint:               https://api.ng.bluemix.net
Bluemix organization ID:            b3b24762-96dc-4438-98b5-82dc4e5fa411

OK
$ bx cr namespaces
Listing namespaces...

Namespace
olivieri

OK
```

As you can see in the output, the bx cr info command displays relevant information about your IBM Containers environment, such as the hostname of your private registry (in this case, registry.ng.bluemix.net). The bx cr namespaces command lists the namespaces available to you (in this case, olivieri). With these two values at hand, you can now proceed to tag the kitura-starter-runner Docker image. Tagging an image with the registry information lets the Docker tool know that you intend to push that image to the Bluemix registry instead of Docker Hub. Make sure you replace <bluemix registry> with the name of the registry for your Bluemix region, and <namespace> with the namespace assigned to your organization. For instance, for the U.S. South region, the name of the registry is registry.ng.bluemix.net. Also, note that kitura-starter is the name you are assigning to the image within the Bluemix namespace:

```
docker tag kitura-starter-runner:latest <bluemix registry>/<namespace>/kitura-
starter:latest
```

Keep in mind that executing the `docker tag` command creates a reference to the original Docker image. You can verify this by executing the `docker images` command (note that the `IMAGE ID` value is the same for both images):

```
$ docker images
REPOSITORY                                          TAG       IMAGE ID        CREATED             SIZE
kitura-starter-runner                               latest    2804c8244a3f    About an hour ago   294 MB
registry.ng.bluemix.net/olivieri/kitura-starter     latest    2804c8244a3f    About an hour ago   294 MB
```

Push a Docker Image to Bluemix

Before uploading your Docker image to Bluemix, you should have logged the local Docker client in to Bluemix Container Registry. If you haven't done so, then uploading the image to your Bluemix registry will fail with an `unauthorized: authentication required` error. The `bx cr login` command will log you in as shown below:

```
$ bx cr login
Logging in to 'registry.ng.bluemix.net'...
Logged in to 'registry.ng.bluemix.net'.

OK
```

You are now ready to push the tagged image to Bluemix. Make sure you replace `<namespace>` with your namespace and `<bluemix registry>` with the name of the registry for your Bluemix region:

```
docker push <bluemix registry>/<namespace>/kitura-starter:latest
```

As reference, here's the output from uploading this image to my private registry on Bluemix:

```
$ docker push registry.ng.bluemix.net/olivieri/kitura-starter:latest
The push refers to a repository [registry.ng.bluemix.net/olivieri/kitura-starter]
d6d7d35d5ace: Pushed
51df01e31b90: Pushed
8b51567be46b: Pushed
fb6621a3f7f6: Pushed
330d55a2b35b: Pushed
bd00cdbae641: Pushed
af43131c4039: Pushed
9bd4c7af882a: Pushed
04ab82f865cf: Pushed
c29b5eadf94a: Pushed
latest: digest: sha256:60f083936fb41dd237e3afaef3828af796857b58441b54513c102778e5d
9aa21 size: 2408
```

Let's verify that the image was successfully uploaded to your private registry in Bluemix by executing the `bx cr images` command:

```
$ bx cr images
Listing images...

REPOSITORY                                        NAMESPACE  TAG     DIGEST        CREATED    SIZE    VULNERABILITY STATUS
registry.ng.bluemix.net/olivieri/kitura-starter   olivieri   latest  e7d884bbf082  1 day ago  294 MB  OK

OK
```

Create a Kubernetes Cluster on Bluemix

You can create free and paid Kubernetes clusters in Bluemix. For this sample, we will create a free cluster which consists of one worker node. For comprehensive information on free and paid clusters and their available options, please check the Bluemix documentation at `https://console.ng.bluemix.net/docs/containers/cs_cli_devtools.html`.

Let's execute the following command to create a free cluster named swift-cluster in the Bluemix cloud:

```
$ bx cs cluster-create --name swift-cluster
Creating cluster...
OK
```

Since the creation process runs asynchronously and may take several minutes before it is provisioned, you should verify the creation of the Kubernetes cluster (the State value will change to normal and a value of 1 should appear under the Workers column once the cluster is created) by executing the following command:

```
$ bx cs clusters

Listing clusters...
OK
Name           ID                                State      Created                   Workers
swift-cluster  0d04cd961bcd4674bdc4722606e0482b  deploying  2017-05-24T18:09:11+0000  0

$ bx cs clusters
Listing clusters...
OK
Name           ID                                State      Created                   Workers
swift-cluster  0d04cd961bcd4674bdc4722606e0482b  deploying  2017-05-24T18:09:11+0000  0

$ bx cs clusters
Listing clusters...
OK
Name           ID                                State    Created                   Workers
swift-cluster  0d04cd961bcd4674bdc4722606e0482b  normal   2017-05-24T18:16:32+0000  1
```

After the cluster is created, we should verify the status of the worker nodes in the cluster by executing the following command (you should update the command below with your cluster ID value, which can be obtained from the execution of the bx cs clusters command):

```
$ bx cs workers 0d04cd961bcd4674bdc4722606e0482b
Listing cluster workers...
OK

ID                                                 Public IP  Private IP  Machine
Type  State          Status
kube-dal10-pa0d04cd961bcd4674bdc4722606e0482b-w1-     -          free
provisioning   Waiting for IP addresses
$ bx cs workers 0d04cd961bcd4674bdc4722606e0482b
Listing cluster workers...
OK

ID                                                 Public IP       Private IP
Machine Type     State          Status
kube-dal10-pa0d04cd961bcd4674bdc4722606e0482b-w1 169.47.249.231  10.177.161.64
free             bootstrapping   Starting worker deployment

$ bx cs workers 0d04cd961bcd4674bdc4722606e0482b
Listing cluster workers...
OK

ID                                                 Public IP       Private IP
Machine Type     State     Status
kube-hou02-pa0d04cd961bcd4674bdc4722606e0482b-w1 50.23.5.226     10.77.223.131      free
normal    Ready
```

As shown above, you may have to execute the bx cs workers <cluster ID> command above several times since the status changes periodically. When the worker nodes are ready, the state changes to normal and the status to Ready.

Next you should set the cluster you created as the context for this session by setting the KUBECONFIG environment variable. Doing so ensures that the operations executed using the Kubernetes command line tool target the correct cluster. You should do this every time that you intend to work with a given Kubernetes cluster:

```
$ bx cs cluster-config 0d04cd961bcd4674bdc4722606e0482b
Downloading cluster config for
0d04cd961bcd4674bdc4722606e0482b
OK

The configuration for
0d04cd961bcd4674bdc4722606e0482b
```

```
    was downloaded successfully. Export environment variables to start using
    Kubernetes.

    export KUBECONFIG=/Users/olivieri/.bluemix/plugins/container-service/clusters/
    0d04cd961bcd4674bdc4722606e0482b/kube-config-prod-dal10-swift-cluster.yml

    $ export KUBECONFIG=/Users/olivieri/.bluemix/plugins/container-service/clusters/
    0d04cd961bcd4674bdc4722606e0482b/kube-config-prod-dal10-swift-cluster.yml
```

You are now ready to create a deployment in the Kubernetes cluster you just created using the Kubernetes command line. This deployment should reference the `kitura-starter` image that you just pushed to your Bluemix registry (remember to replace the `bluemix registry` and `namespace` values accordingly):

```
    kubectl run kitura-starter --image=<bluemix registry>/<namespace>/kitura-
    starter:latest --port=8080
```

As reference, here's the output after executing the command by referencing the `kitura-starter` image that I had previously uploaded to my private image registry on Bluemix:

```
    $ kubectl run kitura-starter --image=registry.ng.bluemix.net/olivieri/kitura-
    starter:latest --port=8080
    deployment "kitura-starter" created
```

After creating the deployment object, you should create a service object that exposes the deployment and makes it available for clients establishing inbound connections from the Internet:

```
    $ kubectl expose deployment kitura-starter --type=NodePort
    service "kitura-starter" exposed

    $ kubectl get services
    NAME            CLUSTER-IP      EXTERNAL-IP    PORT(S)           AGE
    kitura-starter  10.10.10.169    <nodes>        8080:31772/TCP    4s
    kubernetes      10.10.10.1      <none>         443/TCP           4d
```

With the service object in place, you should now be able to access the Kitura Starter application that is running in the Kubernetes cluster. To do so, we first need to obtain the IP address assigned to our worker node and the port number assigned to the service object:

```
    $ kubectl describe nodes | grep hostname
          kubernetes.io/hostname=169.47.249.231
    $ kubectl get services | grep kitura-starter
    kitura-starter  10.10.10.60    <nodes>           8080:30482/TCP   15h
```

Looking at the output above, we can see that 169.47.249.231 is the IP address assigned to our worker node, and that 30482 is the port number associated with the service object we just created for exposing the Swift application (when you execute the above commands, you will more than likely get different values). Using the browser of your choice, you can then access the Kitura Starter application in the cluster by pointing the address bar to the corresponding IP address and port number as shown in Figure 5-2:

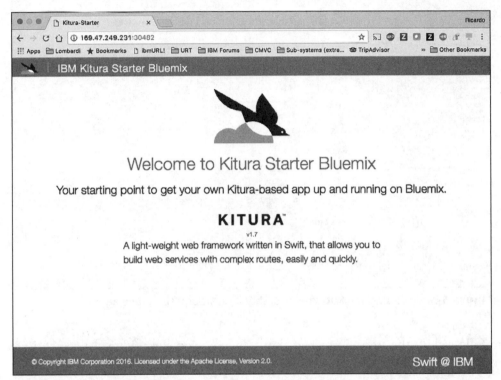

Figure 5-2: The Kitura Starter application running inside a Kubernetes cluster

You should know that you can also access a dashboard from your browser to manage your Kubernetes cluster. To do so, you need to start a proxy agent first by executing the following command:

```
$ kubectl proxy
Starting to serve on 127.0.0.1:8001
```

Once the proxy agent is up and running, you can access the Kubernetes dashboard by pointing your browser to http://localhost:8001/ui as shown in Figure 5-3.

The Kubernetes dashboard provides a web-based user interface that you can use for deploying and troubleshooting applications and for managing a cluster and its associated resources. For more information on the capabilities provided by the Kubernetes dashboard (https://kubernetes.io/docs/tasks/web-ui-dashboard/), please see the Kubernetes documentation.

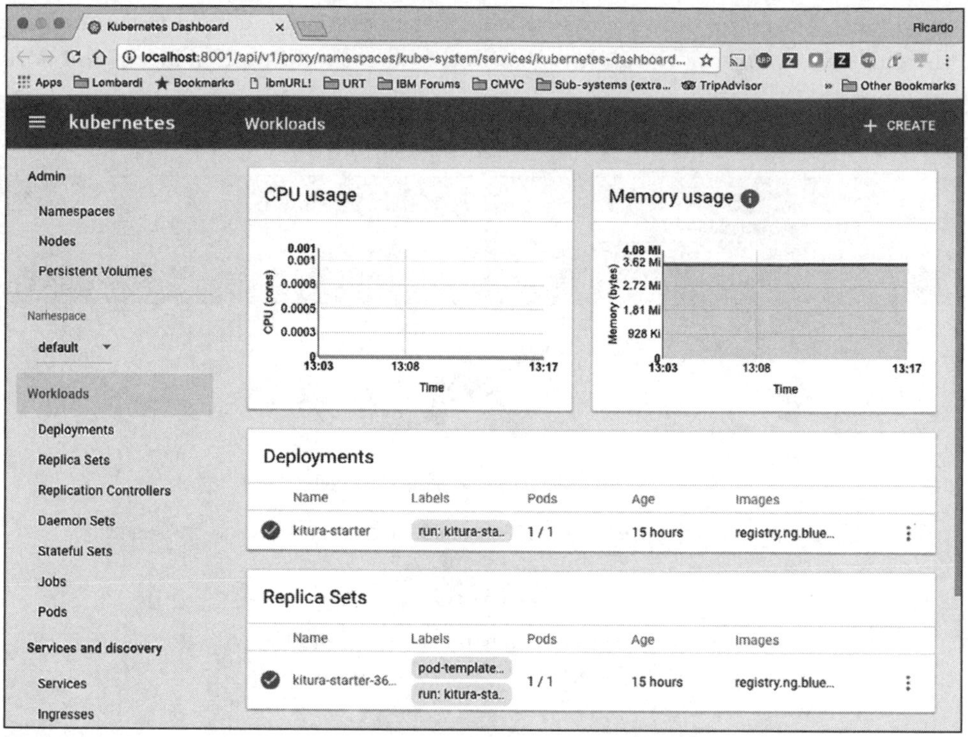

Figure 5-3: Accessing the Kubernetes dashboard through the proxy agent

If you followed all the steps described above, by now you should have successfully created a Kubernetes cluster on Bluemix and deployed the Kitura Starter application to it!

High Availability in Kubernetes Clusters

In the previous section, you deployed a Swift sample application to a Kubernetes cluster that has a single worker node, which is great for development, testing, and educational purposes. However, more than likely, when you deploy your Swift application to the Bluemix cloud, you will want to leverage all the scalability and reliability features that Kubernetes offers out of the box. These capabilities are priceless because you'll definitely want your application to handle unexpected increases in the number of users and workloads. For instance, to achieve redundancy, you should deploy the same container that hosts your Swift application to a Kubernetes cluster that contains more than one worker node. If at some point one of the hosts running your application becomes unavailable (e.g., goes down), having other hosts running your application will minimize the possibility of downtime for your users.

Kubernetes also allows you to scale your Swift applications horizontally based on CPU usage by defining a scaling policy for your application. In this policy, you can specify the target average CPU usage over all the pods for your application and the upper and lower limits for the number of pods that can be set by the Kubernetes' autoscaler.

It is beyond the scope of this book to cover the recommended architectures for achieving high availability for your Swift applications in Kubernetes. For in-depth details on planning your Kubernetes cluster for high availability, you should review the following documentation on Bluemix and the Kubernetes websites:

- Planning Kubernetes clusters and apps with IBM Bluemix (`https://console.ng.bluemix.net/docs/containers/cs_planning.html`)
- Deploying highly available (HA) apps in Kubernetes clusters with IBM Bluemix Container Service (`https://console.ng.bluemix.net/docs/containers/cs_apps.html`)
- Building High-Availability Clusters (`https://kubernetes.io/docs/admin/high-availability/`)

Binding Bluemix Services to IBM Containers

Bluemix gives you access to many services so that you can build applications that provide value to your customers. For instance, your application may need to store and retrieve binary data, consume and persist structured or non-structured data, use the power of data analytics to personalize the content for your users, or consume data collected by sensors. In the Bluemix catalog (`https://console.ng.bluemix.net/catalog/`), you will find services to address these and many other needs.

For your Swift applications running as a containerized application in a Kubernetes cluster to leverage Bluemix services, you should bind those services to the Kubernetes cluster. For example, using the `bx service create` command, let's create an instance of the Object Storage service and name it `Kitura-Object-Storage`. Once you've done this, we will then bind this service instance to the Kubernetes cluster you recently created, `swift-cluster`:

```
$ bx service create Object-Storage Free "Kitura-Object-Storage"
Invoking 'cf create-service Object-Storage Free Kitura-Object-Storage'...

Creating service instance Kitura-Object-Storage in org roliv@us.ibm.com / space dev as roliv@us.ibm.com...
OK

Create in progress. Use 'cf services' or 'cf service Kitura-Object-Storage' to check operation status.

$ bx service show Kitura-Object-Storage
Invoking 'cf service Kitura-Object-Storage'...


Service instance: Kitura-Object-Storage
Service: Object-Storage
Tags:
Plan: Free
Description: Provides a cost-effective, scalable, unstructured cloud data store to build and deliver cloud apps and services.
Documentation url: https://www.ng.bluemix.net/docs/services/ObjectStorage/index.html
Dashboard: https://objectstorage-ui.ng.bluemix.net/v2/service_instances/67bc2280-c3ad-469c-bd7d-75dec948867d

Last Operation
Status: create succeeded
Message: Provision request state
```

```
Started: 2017-04-17T19:04:10Z
Updated: 2017-04-17T19:05:14Z

$ bx service list
Invoking 'cf services'...

Getting services in org roliv@us.ibm.com / space dev as roliv@us.ibm.com...
OK


name                        service           plan          bound apps       last operation
Kitura-Object-Storage       Object-Storage    Free                           create succeeded
$ bx cs clusters
Listing clusters...
OK
Name               ID                                        State     Created                   Workers
swift-cluster      0d04cd961bcd4674bdc4722606e0482b          normal    2017-05-24T18:16:32+0000  1

$ bx cs cluster-service-bind 0d04cd961bcd4674bdc4722606e0482b default Kitura-Object-Storage
Binding service instance to namespace...
OK
Namespace:         default
Secret name:       binding-kitura-object-storage
```

As you can see above, the `bx cs cluster-service-bind <cluster ID> <namespace> <service instance name>` was used to bind the Kitura-Object-Storage instance to the Kubernetes cluster we created earlier (note the name of the namespace where the swift-cluster was created is default). Binding the Kitura-Object-Storage service to the Kubernetes cluster creates a secret named binding-kitura-object-storage. To verify that the service instance is bound to the cluster and that the corresponding secret was created, you can execute the following command:

```
$ kubectl get secrets
NAME                              TYPE                                   DATA     AGE
binding-kitura-object-storage     Opaque                                 1        16m
bluemix-default-secret            kubernetes.io/dockercfg                1        10d
default-token-r9ftt               kubernetes.io/service-account-token    3        10d
```

You can also use the Kubernetes dashboard to verify that a secret named `binding-kitura-object-storage` was created as shown in Figure 5-4 and Figure 5-5.

Looking at Figure 5-5, you can see that the `binding-kitura-object-storage` secret has a key named binding with its data being a JSON string that contains the necessary credentials to connect to the object storage instance we created just a few minutes ago. The next step is to map the `binding-kitura-object-storage` secret into the container as an environment variable. The name of this environment variable can be anything you'd like, though it is recommended to use a meaningful and descriptive name. For this sample, let's use `KITURA_OBJECT_STORAGE` as the name for this variable. To define this environment variable and map it to the `binding-kitura-object-storage` secret, we need to update the Kubernetes pod configuration using the following command:

```
$ kubectl edit deployment
```

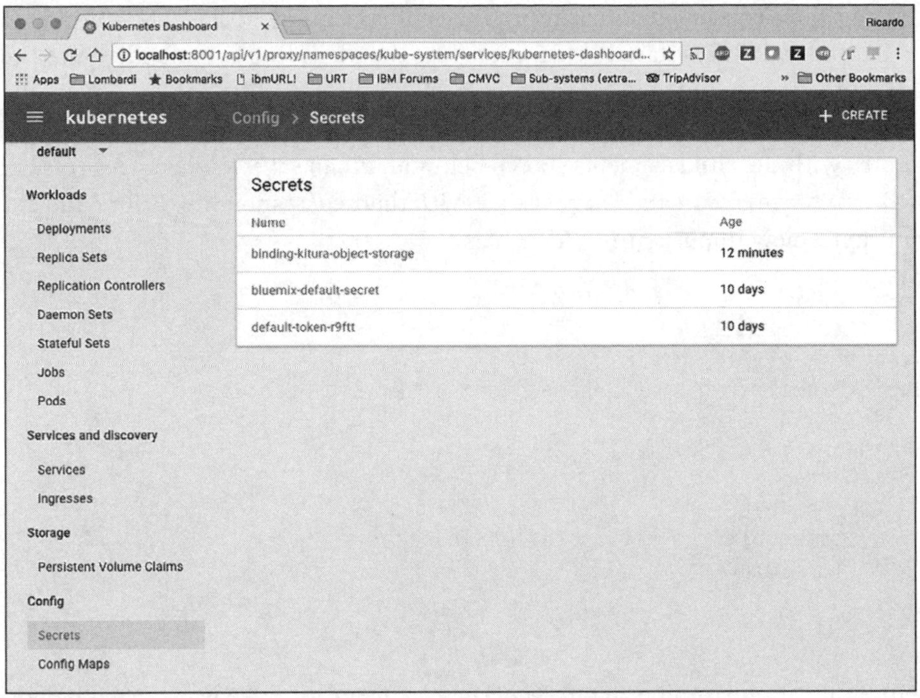

Figure 5-4: List of secrets for the Kubernetes cluster, swift-cluster

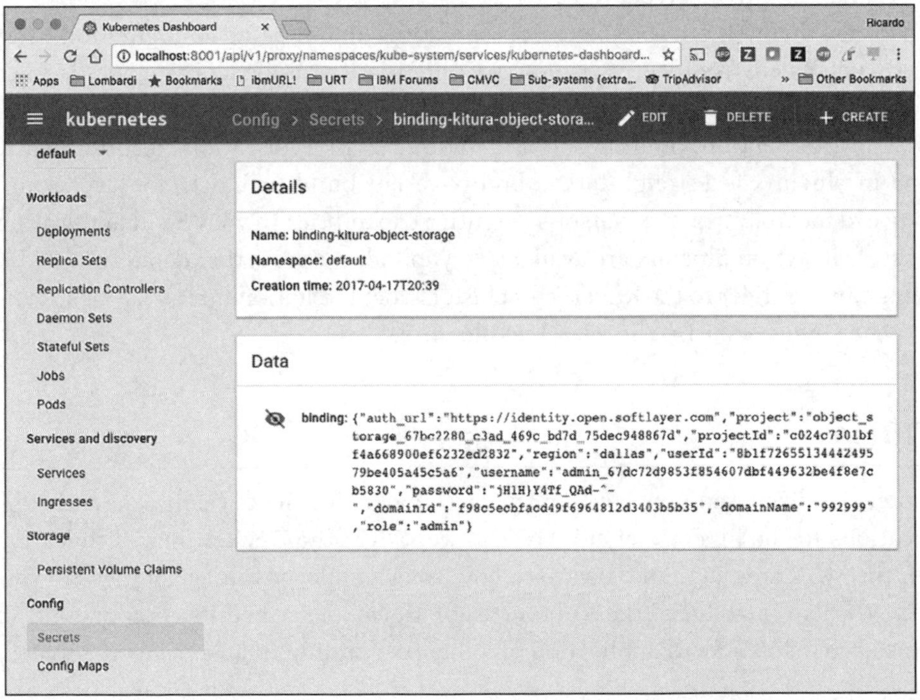

Figure 5-5: Secret details for the binding-kitura-object-storage secret

Executing the above command will bring up the deployment metadata YAML file and allow you to edit it (note that the vi editor is started when executing the preceding command). Once the YAML file is opened for edits, you should look for the `containers` element under the `spec` element. Under the `containers` element, you should see an `image` entry. Right underneath the `image` entry, you should add an `env` entry with the child elements shown below and then save your changes (please remember to replace `<bluemix registry>` and `<namespace>` with their corresponding values and also note that indentation is extremely important in YAML files):

```
...
spec:
  containers:
  - image: <bluemix registry>/<namespace>/kitura-starter:latest
    env:
      - name: KITURA_OBJECT_STORAGE
        valueFrom:
          secretKeyRef:
            name: binding-kitura-object-storage
            key: binding

...
```

For a Swift application running in our Kubernetes cluster to make use of the credentials for the `Kitura-Object-Storage` instance, it is a matter of accessing the `KITURA_OBJECT_STORAGE` environment variable and parsing its credentials.

A Swift package that will prove to be useful for loading and merging configuration data from multiple sources, such as environment variables, is Configuration. We encourage you to check out this library especially if you find yourself writing code for parsing data stored in environment variables.

As we saw in this section, binding services to your Swift application running in a Kubernetes environment in Bluemix is a straightforward process. The building blocks for leveraging the power of, for instance, data analytics and Watson's cognitive capabilities in your Swift applications running in a Kubernetes cluster on Bluemix are available to you today. For further details on binding services to Kubernetes clusters, refer to the Kubernetes clusters documentation (`https://console.ng.bluemix.net/docs/containers/cs_cluster.html`) on Bluemix.

Summary

In this chapter, we discussed how you can leverage Docker for the development and deployment of Swift applications to the Bluemix cloud. We also went over the Docker images that IBM has made available for the Swift language and discussed how you can take advantage of these in your development efforts. We also introduced the Kubernetes platform, described its components, and demonstrated how to provision a Swift application on Bluemix running in a Kubernetes cluster.

Docker allows developers to package an application and its dependencies in a deployable unit. Using the Kubernetes offering on Bluemix, you can then instantiate that deployable unit to execute your Swift application in a scalable environment. This makes deploying applications to the Bluemix cloud a simple task and puts portability in the front seat.

These are very exciting times for Swift developers. Initially, the Swift language was used only for the development of iOS applications. Now, you can also use it to develop the back-end components that mobile platforms and other clients (such as web clients) can leverage to deliver unique experiences and functionality to your users.

CHAPTER 6

Swift Package Management

Every large software project has unique requirements and challenges. As a developer, you want to focus your attention on the problems that haven't been solved before. Common, repeatable aspects of your solution can be addressed by third-party components and libraries. You may also find that your project is well suited to contribute its own components to be reused by others.

Swift has all the pieces in place to make modularization possible. In this chapter, you'll explore each aspect of the Swift package management ecosystem, including Swift Package Manager and the Swift Package Catalog. I'll also walk you through some usage and code examples, so that you're ready to use Swift packages right away.

Swift Package Manager

The concept of package management has been around for a while. The number of files on a computer system can be so numerous that it can be difficult to manage files individually. A package encapsulates multiple files into a more manageable chunk. A user can then perform operations at the package level, such as viewing its contents, installing it, uninstalling it, and so on.

Packages can be especially useful for managing source code. Not only can a package contain source code files for its own functionality, but a package can also specify dependencies on other packages. With dependency management, modular code is made possible by enabling package authors to break up the structure of their own code and to reuse code from other sources.

Another key feature of package management systems is versioning. Source code can seem like it has a life of its own over time—adding capabilities, refactoring, supporting different platforms, and so on. Each package contains metadata that includes the version number of the package. That version number ensures that other packages that depend on the package will get what they expect. Also, the version number can convey how significant a change is using a scheme called semantic versioning.

In modern software development, there is a virtually limitless number of scenarios for using packages. For example, some common types of packages include networking utilities, web frameworks, and database connectors. There is no minimum or maximum size for a package or number of packages that can be depended on. Of course, there are best practices and practical considerations that you must consider when you are including packages.

Using Swift Package Manager

Swift Package Manager is the Swift solution for package management. It supports the key capabilities we've discussed so far, such as dependency management and versioning. Swift Package Manager also has some useful features for systems programming, including specifying system modules and integration with C modules.

Swift Package Manager is included with any of the Swift development snapshots that can be downloaded from Swift.org. Just like the Swift language, Swift Package Manager is open source and available on GitHub.

Now that you're familiar with what Swift Package Manager is, let's look at the package specification that it supports. The `Package.swift` file is the manifest file in the root of a package, and drives the behavior of Swift Package Manager for that package. It is actually compilable Swift code, which provides more flexibility than a declarative file format. In its simplest form, the manifest file should import the `PackageDescription` module and declare the package's name. Let's say that you want to define a package called MyPackage. Inside a directory called `MyPackage`, you'd create a `Package.Swift` file like this:

```
import PackageDescription

let package = Package(
    name: "MyPackage"
)
```

The source code for the package goes into the `Sources/` subdirectory. Tests belong in the `Tests/` subdirectory. By the way, the package directory structure and files can automatically be created by Swift Package Manager when you run the `swift package init` command. By default, this command creates a library structure. You will later see how to create an executable.

You've now seen how simple it is to create a package. Next, you'll see how to add dependencies to the package. Inside the package declaration, you can also define a dependencies array with an entry for each package you'd like to include. For example, to include Kitura, a Swift framework we will discuss further in a later chapter, you can add a comma at the end of the line with the `name`, and then add the following line:

```
dependencies: [
.Package(url: "https://github.com/IBM-Swift/Kitura.git", majorVersion: 1)
]
```

To compile your package, run `swift build`. This command downloads and compiles the source of the dependency you've specified. It also recursively downloads and compiles dependencies of the dependencies. The output includes a list of all the dependencies, to look something like this:

```
karls-mbp-2:test2 kweinmeister$ swift build
Cloning https://github.com/IBM-Swift/Kitura.git
HEAD is now at 43d9c17 IBM-Swift/Kitura#788 Avoid converting JSON serialized Data to
String and back to Data again. (#807)
Resolved version: 1.0.1
Cloning https://github.com/IBM-Swift/Kitura-net.git
HEAD is now at b61145f Merge pull request #126 from IBM-Swift/issue_784
Resolved version: 1.0.2
Cloning https://github.com/IBM-Swift/LoggerAPI.git
HEAD is now at d4c1682 Regenerated API Documentation (#15)
Resolved version: 1.0.0
...
```

Let's now change the package into an executable. In the `sources/` subdirectory, note that a Swift file has been created already with a data structure that contains "Hello World" text. Let's use that variable in a new file called `main.swift`. In that file, add a couple of lines:

```
let pkg = MyPackage()
print(pkg.txt)
```

You can now run `swift build` again, and it creates a `MyPackage` executable in the `.build/debug` directory, where build artifacts in debug mode are created. Launching the package results in the expected output, `Hello World!`. If your package contains tests, it's also helpful to try running them in your environment after building with `swift test`.

Commands

So far, I've discussed how the `init` command can create a new package directory structure. There are a few other useful actions that Swift Package Manager can help with. Developers who would like to use Xcode to develop their package can use the `swift package generate-xcodeproj` command. It creates an `.xcodeproj` file configured to include dependencies and build settings to get started quickly. Figure 6-1 displays the generated Xcode project for the project. You can see that it includes the source code for the project, as well as for dependent packages like Kitura.

The `update` command fetches any updated packages that still meet the version constraints specified in the dependency. The versions can be declared in a variety of ways. One way is as a range, such as `versions: Version(0,1,0)..<Version(2,0,0)`. Another way, shown in the initial example that pulls in Kitura, is to specify a major version, and optionally a minor version. It is also possible to fetch the dependencies without building, by using the `fetch` command.

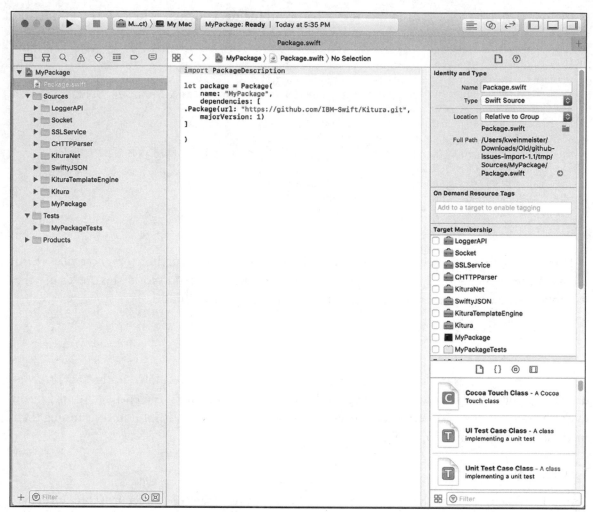

Figure 6-1: The Xcode developer tool with a generated Swift project open for editing

Swift Package Manager can also export package metadata. The `dump-package` command parses the `Package.swift` file and exports the contents as JSON. The `show-dependencies` command exports the dependency relationships in a variety of formats. By default, the output looks something like this:

```
└─ Kitura<https://github.com/IBM-Swift/Kitura.git@1.0.1>
   ├─ Kitura-net<https://github.com/IBM-Swift/Kitura-net.git@1.0.2>
   │  ├─ LoggerAPI<https://github.com/IBM-Swift/LoggerAPI.git@1.0.0>
   │  ├─ Socket<https://github.com/IBM-Swift/BlueSocket.git@0.11.33>
   │  ├─ CCurl<https://github.com/IBM-Swift/CCurl.git@0.2.3>
   │  ├─ CHTTPParser<https://github.com/IBM-Swift/CHTTPParser.git@0.3.0>
   │  └─ SSLService<https://github.com/IBM-Swift/BlueSSLService.git@0.11.46>
   │     └─ Socket<https://github.com/IBM-Swift/BlueSocket.git@0.11.33>
   ├─ SwiftyJSON<https://github.com/IBM-Swift/SwiftyJSON.git@14.2.1>
   └─ Kitura-TemplateEngine<https://github.com/IBM-Swift/Kitura-
TemplateEngine.git@1.0.0>
```

Package.Swift Details

So far, you've seen what a basic `Package.swift` file looks like. The `name` property is the bare minimum required to instantiate a `Package` object. On top of that, the `dependencies` array defines the dependencies on external packages. Let's now look at additional properties that are available to you in a Swift package.

If you have defined more than one module in your package, you can declare them individually using the `targets` array property. For each target, you can define the name, and then the dependencies, which drive the order in which the modules are built. Here is an example:

```
targets: [
        Target(name: "MyFirstModule")
        Target(name: "MySecondModule", dependencies: ["MyFirstModule"]),
    ]
```

System Module Attributes

Swift system modules wrap system libraries for easy integration. If you are writing your own system module that needs to rely on other system modules, you can specify them with the `providers` property. Swift Package Manager doesn't automatically install these modules on your system, but documenting them can enable build scripts, makefiles, and other utilities to potentially prepare the user's system with these packages. Here is an example:

```
providers: [
        .Apt("libssl-dev"),
        .Brew("openssl")
]
```

You can also use the `pkgConfig` property to find a matching `.pc` metadata with flags to build the module. With this property defined, Swift Package Manager can query the pkg-config tool for flag and path arguments.

Swift Package Catalog

How do you find the right package to do the job? As a package author, how can you publicize the great work you've done? That's where the Swift Package Catalog comes in. The catalog is a website for Swift packages, enabling users to search, browse, inspect, and bookmark their favorite packages. Whether users are just window-shopping for a package, or know exactly what they want, the Swift Package Catalog can help.

Browsing

On the home page of the Swift Package Catalog, there is a section for Popular Packages. This helps users quickly see what's hot in the community. As shown in Figure 6-2, there are three different views: Most Starred, Most Recent, and Most Essential. *Most Starred* contains the packages that have the most stars on GitHub. *Most Recent* shows packages that have been updated most recently. *Most Essential* is a useful feature that ranks each package by the number of other packages that depend on it.

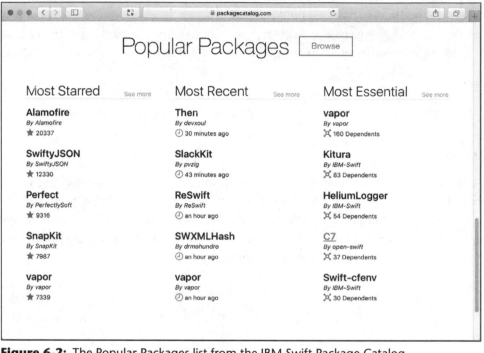

Figure 6-2: The Popular Packages list from the IBM Swift Package Catalog

Another helpful way to discover new packages is to browse the catalog. By clicking the Browse button next to the Popular Packages heading, users are guided to a menu of available categories. By clicking a category, such as JSON (shown in Figure 6-3), users can see a list of packages within that category, sorted by GitHub stars. Package authors can log in and update their package categories.

Searching

Users often know what they're looking for: either a specific package or a problem they're trying to solve. The Swift Package Catalog has a robust search engine that indexes the package name, author organization, URL, and more, to return relevant search results. The search results (shown in Figure 6-4) offer detailed information in each row, such as the package name, author, description, Swift version, rating, and last update.

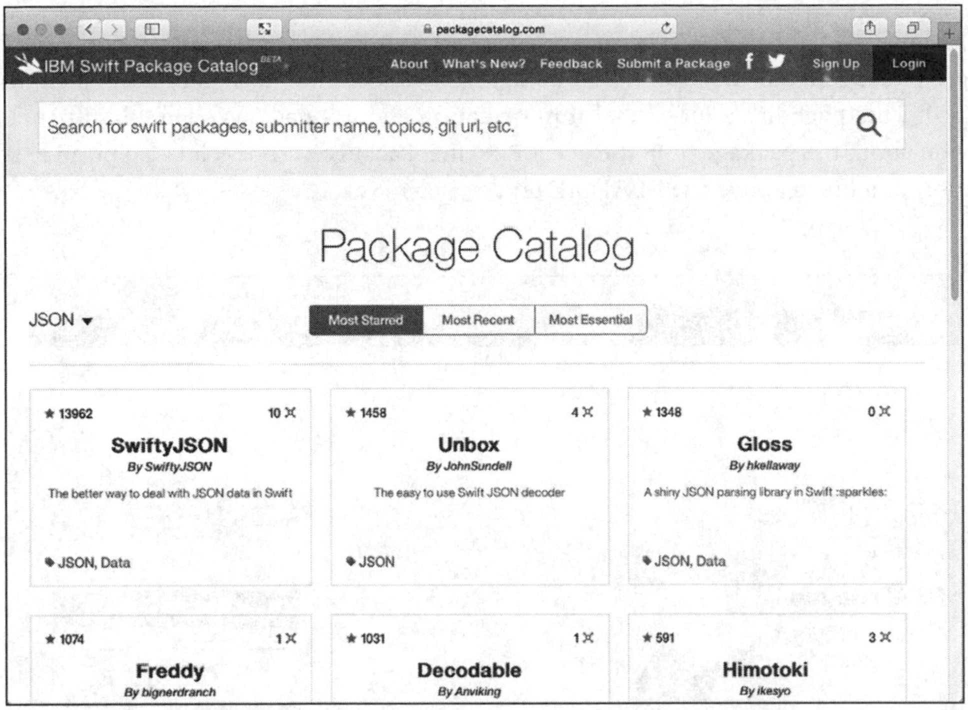

Figure 6-3: A view of the JSON category on the IBM Swift Package Catalog

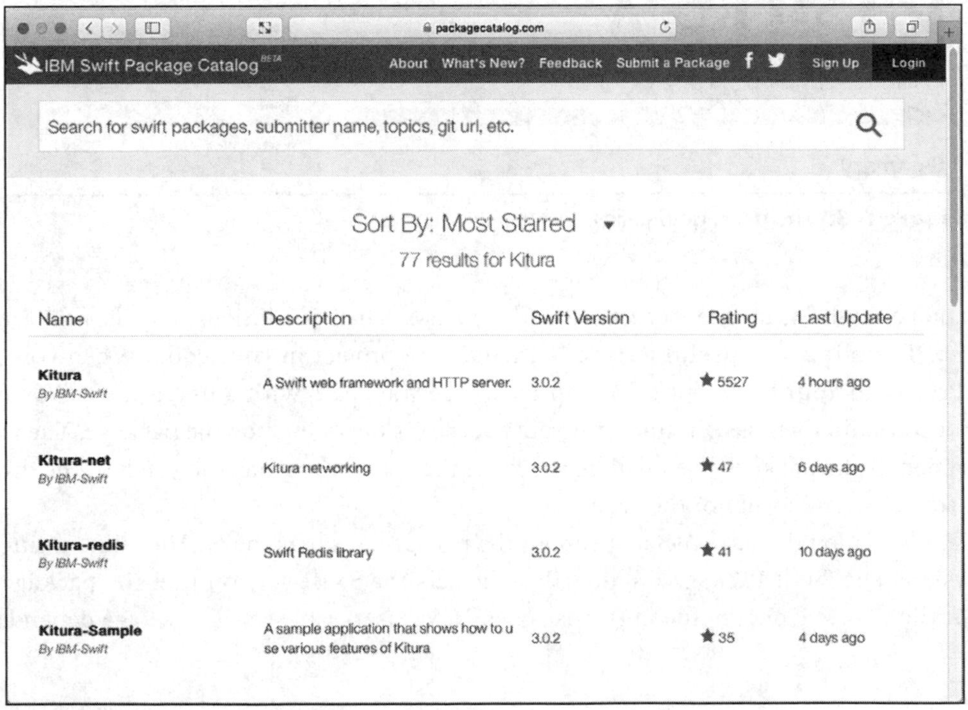

Figure 6-4: Search Results for Kitura in the IBM Swift Package Catalog

Package Details

Clicking a package from the search results brings users to the package details page (shown in Figure 6-5). This page has a lot of useful information about a package. The main panel displays information about the package from the README.md file. Package authors can also provide additional information in a blurb above the README text.

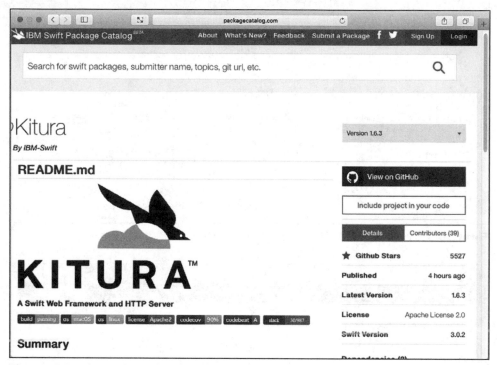

Figure 6-5: The package details page

The right panel shows a variety of actions and metadata. There is a link to view the package directly on GitHub. There is also a useful feature to include the project in your code. When you click the Include Project in Your Code button, a pop-up window appears with a line of code. You can copy this line of code and then paste it into your Package.swift file to include the package. The major and minor version of the package used will be based on the version you have selected in the drop-down menu in the top-right corner of the page.

The *Details* section displays metadata about the package, such as the GitHub stars rating and the latest version. The Swift Package Catalog also extracts the Swift version that the package uses by looking at the .swift-version file in the package. Next, users can see the package dependencies as well as *dependents* (other packages that depend on this package). Finally, users can see keywords that package authors have added to the package. The *Contributors* panel displays the contributors to the project, sorted by the number of commits.

If you have logged into the Swift Package Catalog, you can bookmark your favorite packages. By clicking the heart icon next to a package name, you can favorite or unfavorite the package. You can also view your favorites in the User Profile menu, and subscribe to notifications of changes to your favorite packages.

Dependency Visualization

The dependencies graph is a very helpful way to see the relationship between a package and its dependencies. The graph is displayed as a circle, with the package displayed at the top (see Figure 6-6). Any dependency that does not have any dependencies of its own is unfilled. A dependency that has further dependencies has a filled node. Clicking the node shows its dependencies, using a line color that matches the color of the node. You can also click the node again to hide its dependencies. Below the graph, you also see some dependency information for the selected package, and you can navigate to its entry in the catalog.

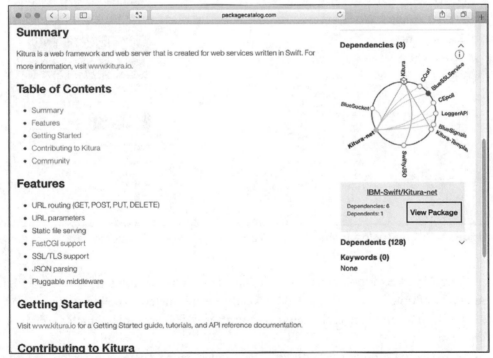

Figure 6-6: The Dependency Visualization view of the IBM Swift Package Catalog

Trying Out a Package in the Sandbox

When you're choosing between several packages that all do the same thing, it can be helpful to actually try out a package to see if you like it. You may also want to quickly learn how a package works. Fortunately, there is a capability within the Swift Package Catalog to try out a package's APIs from within the IBM Swift Sandbox.

For this feature to be enabled, package authors need to add a .swift-sample to their package, which points the Swift Package Catalog to a sample package. A sample package depends on the original package, and includes typical use cases and comments in the main.swift file. When a package has a sample, it includes a Try in Sandbox button, as shown in Figure 6-7.

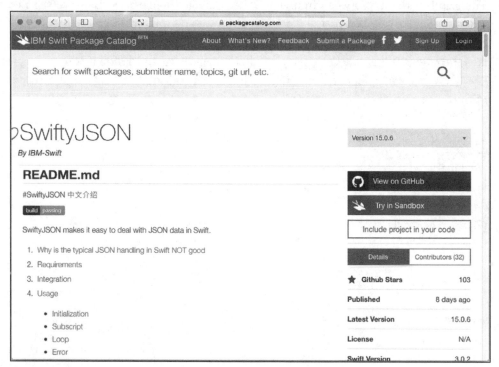

Figure 6-7: The Try in Sandbox button enables users to try out a package.

After clicking Try in Sandbox, users see a menu of available samples, as shown in Figure 6-8. Projects can have multiple samples defined. Based on the sample metadata defined in the .swift-sample file, users see information such as the name and purpose of the sample, which version of Swift it runs on, and more.

After the user selects a sample, the Swift Package Catalog opens a new browser tab with the sample loaded into the sandbox, as shown in Figure 6-9. On the left panel, the user can view the sample code and then execute it by pressing the play button. The right panel shows the output from the sample. The use of the sandbox is covered in more depth in Chapter 3.

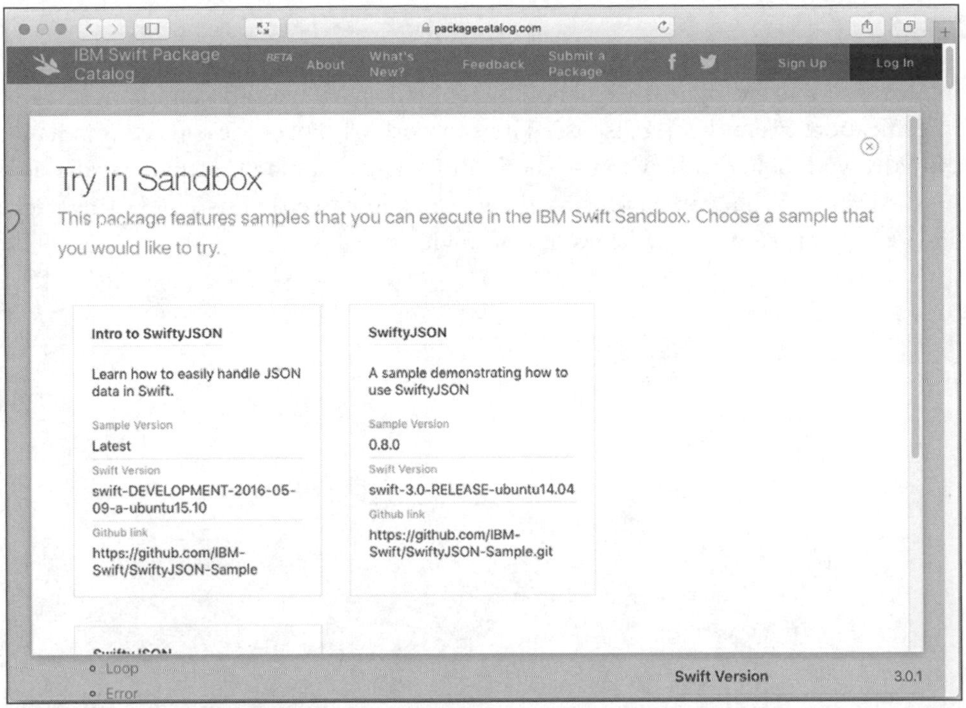

Figure 6-8: Users can select from a variety of samples available.

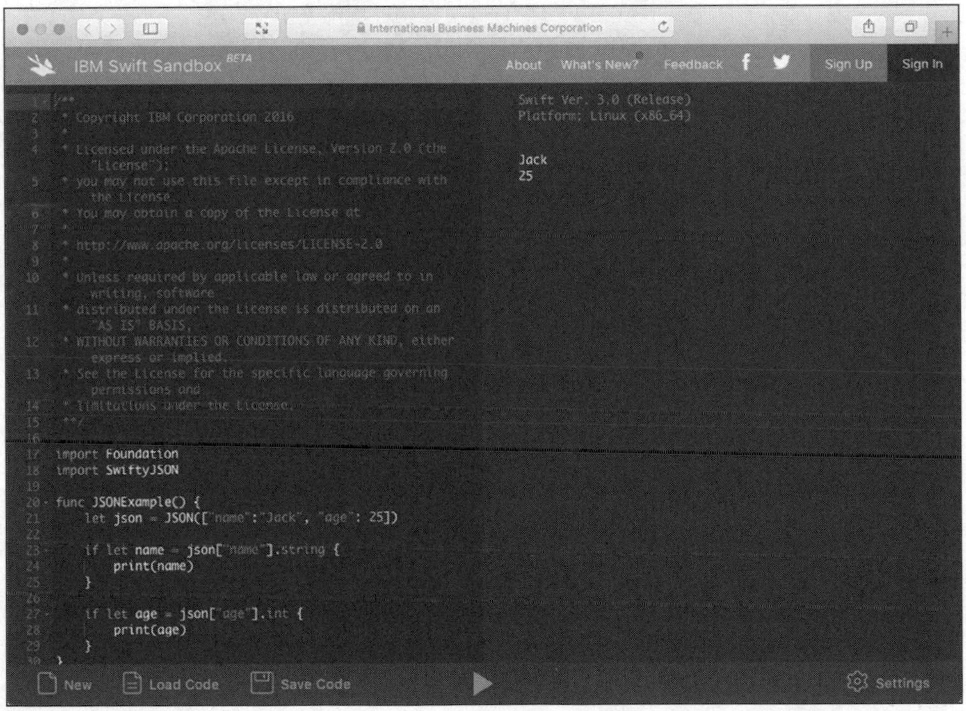

Figure 6-9: After selecting a sample, the user can run the code in the IBM Swift Sandbox.

Summary

In this chapter, you started by learning about what Swift packages are, and about Swift Package Manager specification. From there, I discussed how to work with packages on the command line and in Xcode. Finally, you looked at how to use the Swift Package Catalog to explore available packages in the Swift ecosystem. What you have learned here can apply to either using existing packages in a new application, or contributing packages of your own.

CHAPTER 7

Swift and Kitura for Web Applications

Modern user-facing applications are typically built as two separate parts, a front end and a back end. This is especially true in the enterprise application space. This separation of the front end and back end enables user-facing applications to offer great user experiences and user interfaces, while enforcing enterprise and legal requirements in the server. This also enables multiple front ends, such as mobile apps and web applications with the same back end.

Enterprise applications are typically built with a large set of technologies, often using very different technologies on both the front end and the back end. In larger projects this may not be a problem, as different teams may be writing different parts of the application. In smaller projects where the same people are writing both the client side and the server code, this use of different technologies causes loss of productivity due to mental model switches when people switch "sides" of the application.

Web applications are sometimes written using JavaScript on the client, in the browser, and on the server, using Node.js.

Mobile applications, especially those that use iOS-based clients, have until now also suffered from this problem, with the client side more recently being written in Swift, and the server side being written in Java or JavaScript.

With the open sourcing and porting to Linux of the Swift language, its compiler, debugger, standard library, and the Foundation framework, the base was set to write the server side of applications in Swift. Developers now had one language, compiler, debugger, and so on, on both the client side, for iOS mobile clients, and on the server side.

An architecture that is often used when building back ends, is the so-called microservice architecture. In a microservice architecture, a monolithic server is broken up into many smaller services. One of these services acts as the main interface to the overall back end, exposing the public APIs. This main service communicates with other services (which in turn may communicate with other services) to handle requests it receives. The main advantage here is the decoupling of the entire back end. This way, each microservice can be developed and deployed with its own schedule, dev ops flow, and scale as needed, making it much easier to manage the back end.

In some cases the application back end is built using a microservice in front of an existing legacy application. This is often done with an enterprise's legacy applications in which they have invested heavily over the years, but are not always able to move quickly enough to meet the needs of fast-moving and changing client apps. This micro-service fills in that gap and provides application programming interfaces (APIs) over the network that are more consumable and tailored to the various client apps. Such micro-services often manipulate, aggregate, and filter data, deal with authenticating users, and act as proxies for the client apps.

In addition, a new paradigm has emerged in which there is a separate main interface micro-service for each front end (i.e., web application, iOS app, Android app, etc.). This paradigm is called back end for front end (BFF). BFFs come to make the back end even more consumable for the front ends, as they often want data in different groupings or amounts to deal with form factors and network connectivity. BFFs are typically written by the team developing the front end. They are typically written to be as thin as possible and try to reuse as much as possible the existing set of micro-services. This often also makes it easier for the front-end team to deal with changes in the back end as it can often take several weeks to distribute a new mobile app, while the BFF can be changed and deployed immediately.

For BFFs that are application and front-end specific and for larger systems built using a microservice architecture, you want a lightweight runtime because you want to be able to run a lot of them with as few resources as possible. The Swift language and its runtime are well suited for this.

The over-the-wire protocol of choice between the client app and the BFF—as well as between the various microservices that make up an application back end—is often Representational State Transfer (REST). REST is a stateless protocol that is almost always transmitted using HTTP as the underlying transfer protocol. Data is exchanged between the client and server as a combination of parts of the URL path, HTTP query parameters, and contents of the body of the HTTP message. The body is most often sent using JavaScript Object Notation (JSON).

Because you want to maximize the business value of your efforts in building a BFF, you want to use reusable components wherever possible. These reusable components should do the following:

- Accept incoming HTTP requests and parse them.
- Hand off incoming requests to appropriate pieces of code that will process them.
- Enable these pieces of code to do the following:
  - Access information in the request, such as
    - Pieces of the URL
    - HTTP query parameters
    - HTTP headers
    - The body of the HTTP request
  - Send a response, including
    - The HTTP response code
    - HTTP headers
    - The body of the HTTP response
- Enable the application to be secure both by allowing only authorized users access and by using secure communications.

This chapter will describe how you can build application back ends for web applications and RESTful end points using Kitura, an open source Swift-based web server framework.

Kitura

Kitura is a set of open source projects whose goal is to provide a web server framework written in Swift. Kitura aims to be lightweight and performant. Kitura exploits the Apple Foundation library for common low-level functions, and Grand Central Dispatch (GCD) for multi-programming. GCD simplifies multi-programming by managing the threading for you. You simply have the system run a block of code on one of many queues. These queues can run the blocks added to the queue either sequentially or in parallel, depending on how the queue was configured. Kitura runs on both Linux and macOS, using the Linux ports of Foundation and GCD.

The Kitura framework, or simply Kitura, is compiled and linked with your application for execution. There is no application server into which you deploy your code; the application simply becomes the server. The executable for your application can be deployed locally or in the Cloud—in particular, on the IBM Bluemix using IBM Bluemix Runtime for Swift.

Kitura is packaged as a set of GitHub repositories for inclusion in your application back end using Swift Package Manager (SPM), which is shipped with the Swift toolchain.

The simplest "Hello World" Kitura-based server can be built as follows:[1]

1. Create a directory called `example1`.
2. In the `example1` directory, edit the file `Package.swift`. It should have the following contents:

```
import PackageDescription

let package = Package(
    name: "HelloWorld",
    dependencies: [
        .Package(url: "https://github.com/IBM-Swift/Kitura.git",
                majorVersion: 1, minor: 7),
        .Package(url: "https://github.com/IBM-Swift/HeliumLogger.git",
                majorVersion: 1, minor: 7)
    ]
)
```

3. Create a `Sources` directory, and in it a `HelloWorld` directory.

---

[1] This assumes that the Swift 3.x toolchain has been installed on your computer. Installing the Swift 3.x toolchain is not described in this chapter.

4. In the `Sources/HelloWorld` directory, edit the file `main.swift`.[2] It should have the following contents:

```
import Kitura
import HeliumLogger

HeliumLogger.use()

let router = Router()

Kitura.addHTTPServer(onPort: 8080, with: router)
Kitura.run()
```

From the top HelloWorld directory, run the command `swift build`.

Swift Package Manager is invoked and starts compiling the code. It fetches the dependencies, compiles the code, and finally links the executable.

You can run the server by simply typing the following from the command line:

```
.build/debug/HelloWorld
```

Once the server is running, you can point your favorite browser at `http://localhost:8080`. You see the page shown in Figure 7-1.

The displayed page is the default root page for Kitura, and is shown whenever anyone sends an empty request (/) to a Kitura-based server.

"How do you do that?" you ask. Here are the steps:

1. In the `Package.swift` file, input the following code:

```
import PackageDescription

let package = Package(
    name: "HelloWorld",        // Named our executable HelloWorld
    dependencies: [            // Listed our dependencies
        .Package(url: "https://github.com/IBM-Swift/Kitura.git",
                majorVersion: 1, minor: 7),
        .Package(url: "https://github.com/IBM-Swift/HeliumLogger.git",
                majorVersion: 1, minor: 7)

    ]
)
```

---

[2] You could have simply created the `main.swift` file in the parent directory. However, as the application grows, it is better to have it in a directory under `Sources`.

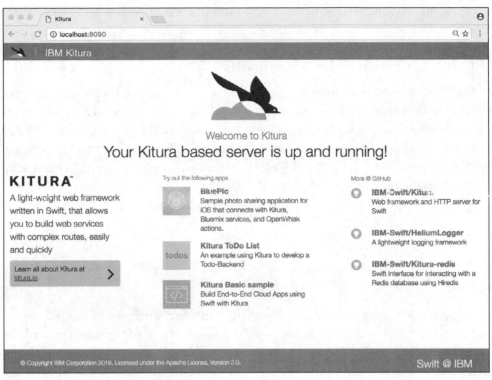

Figure 7-1: The Kitura default root page

2. There is a main.swift file in the Sources/HelloWorld directory. In this file, input the following code:

```
import Kitura
import HeliumLogger

HeliumLogger.use()          // Setup the HeliumLogger as our logging package

let router = Router()       // Created a router to route requests

                            // Created a HTTP server that will listen
Kitura.addHTTPServer(onPort: 8080, with: router)     // on port 8080
Kitura.run()                // Started all created servers
```

In the Package.swift file, there is the dependency HeliumLogger. HeliumLogger is a lightweight implementation of the LoggerAPI package. The LoggerAPI package is a protocol for a logger that is used throughout Kitura. It is designed to enable the use of any compatible implementation, whether simple or advanced. The HeliumLogger is a simple implementation that prints the logged messages to the console. The messages can be colorized and tailored.

Keep in mind that the call to Kitura.run() doesn't return until all of the started servers are stopped. As such, it should be the last statement in the main.swift file.

Sending Simple Responses to Requests

While it's nice to have a server up and running that can show the default root page, it can't do any real work. Let's change that and add some code that will handle a request and send a response to the client.

The Router class has functions for designating code that should be invoked when HTTP requests come to the server. These functions can cause the designated code to be invoked when a specific HTTP method (that is, GET, POST, PUT, DELETE, and so on) is used in the HTTP request, or if the path of the URL in the request matches a specific pattern.

After the let router = Router() statement, add the following code:

```
router.get("/hello") { request, response, next in
    response.send("Hello world")
    next()
}
```

The added code causes the code in the closure to be invoked when an HTTP GET request comes to the server with a URL with a path of /hello—in other words, if the request from a browser was http://localhost:8090/hello. This closure is known as a *RouterHandler*. RouterHandlers are passed three parameters:

- request, an instance of the class RouterRequest, which enables the code in the closure to get information from the request
- response, an instance of the class RouterResponse, which enables the code in the closure to build the response sent back to the client who issued the request
- next, a callback to be invoked to let more code process the request. While you don't have to invoke next, doing so allows code that processes the request to be much more decoupled.

In the previous code snippet, the code in the RouterHandler sends a simple string, "Hello world", as the response. The last line in the RouterHandler, the call to next(), has Kitura check to see if there is other code to invoke for this request.

Typically, in RESTful applications, you set the Content-Type HTTP header to convey the type of data being sent back to the client. In the previous example, in which the response was plain text, you would like the Content-Type header to have the value of text/plain. To do so, you simply add response.headers.setType("text") to the previous example, after the line response .send("Hello world"). The Kitura API setType makes it easier on the developer by accepting well-known file extensions (for example, .txt, .html, .css, .js, .jpeg, and so on) and setting the header to the correct standard mime type (for example, text/plain, text/html, text/css, application/javascript, image/jpeg, and so on).

You also usually set the Content-Length header to indicate the number of bytes being sent in the body of the response. Kitura sets that header for you automatically by counting the bytes that will be sent before sending them.

You can use the same `RouterResponse.send(:String)` API that sends any type of text to send XML by simply writing code as follows:

```
response.send("<data><name>Judah</name><age>57</age></data>")
response.headers.setType("xml")
```

When writing RESTful end-points, you most often want to send JSON-formatted responses. JSON is a text-based method for sending data between a client and a server. It enables the sending of structured but freeform data in a very simple way. The previous XML example code could have been sent as JSON, as follows:

```
{
    "name": 'Judah',
    "age": 57
}
```

Kitura uses the `SwiftyJSON` package, included as a dependency of Kitura, to make it easier to work with JSON. The JSON could have been sent as follows:

```
let json = JSON(["name": "Judah", "age": 57])
response.send(json: json)
```

The Kitura `RouterResponse.send(json:JSON)` API automatically sets the Content-Type for you. You also need to add an `import SwiftyJSON` to the beginning of your Swift file when working with `SwiftyJSON`.

Binary data can be sent using the `RouterResponse.send(data:Data)` API to send the bytes stored in a `Data` struct. Again, you should use the `RouterResponse.headers.setType(:String)` API to set the Content-Type.

A Real-World Library Example

To make the examples in this chapter more concrete and understandable, throughout the chapter you are going to see how to build a simple back end for a library. This chapter purposely does not cover the front end for the library "application," which might be an entire family of applications and mobile apps, as it only focuses on building servers with Kitura.

The back-end server for a library needs to support many functions, including the following:

1. Letting people search for books, both by title and by ISBN
2. Checking the availability of a book

3. Reserving a book for later checkout
4. Checking out and returning books
5. Adding and removing books from the collection

The security and authentication requirements vary from function to function. For example, anyone can search for books and check on their availability. Any registered and authenticated person can reserve and check out books. Only authorized staff members can return books and manage the collection.

You will now see how you can implement those functions with the required authentication and authorization using Kitura.

Accessing Information Sent in Requests

Real-world RESTful applications often model a collection of items. To this collection, you add, retrieve, update, and delete items. The HTTP method, usually POST, GET, PUT, or DELETE, is used to differentiate between the various operations that you want to do. In addition, at least part of the path in the request is used to identify the collection being worked with.

In the library example, the main collection is the collection of books, where you might have code that looks like this:

```
let router = Router()

router.post("/books") {request, response, next in
...
}
router.get("/books") {request, response, next in
...
}
router.put("/books") {request, response, next in
...
}
router.delete("/books") {request, response, next in
...
}
```

Accessing Parts of the URL Path

If you were to use code like this, you could add a book via a POST to /books, and get all the books via a GET to /books. However, to update or delete a book, you need more information, specifically the identity of the book being updated or deleted. Fortunately, not much code is needed to access a book identifier in the URL path. The following will do it for an update request:

```
router.put("/books/:id") {request, response, next in
    let id = request.parameters["id"] ?? ""
...
}
```

This code snippet enhances the previous `router.put` code snippet by requiring a second element in the path or the request. This second element is identified in the path pattern by the text `:id`. This string provides an identifier, id, for accessing a section of a URL path. The section of the URL path can be accessed via the `RouterRequest.parameters` API as shown in the example. In particular, if in the example the incoming request had a path of `/books/123`, then the variable id would have the value 123.

Accessing the Query Parameters of the URL

In many requests, you want to add various parameters that affect the results of the HTTP request. This is often done by using what is called the query string of the URL. The query string of a URL is the part after the question mark (?). The query string is made up of a set of parameter/value pairs. In line with the library example, if you wanted to fetch all the books written by a certain author, you might perform a GET against the following URL: `http:/books?author=Twain`. In a RouterHandler, you can access the author query parameter via `request.queryParameters["Author"]`.

Accessing the Body of the Request

In the skeletal code for the books collection, many of the route handlers need the data with which to create or update a book collection. Typically, this data is sent to the server via the body of the HTTP request. Such data is often sent in JSON format.

Because the contents and format of the body of a request are tied to a specific request or set of requests, Kitura doesn't automatically try to parse the body of requests. Instead, Kitura provides reusable code that parses a variety of common body formats. This reusable code is in the form of a `RouterMiddleware`, commonly known as middleware.

Middleware are simply RouterHandlers packaged as a class or struct that implement the `RouterMiddleware` protocol. Because they are classes or structs, they can have state and configuration information.

The BodyParser middleware can be used to parse request bodies that are in JSON format, URL-encoded format, multi-part form format, or plain text.

If in the library book collection code, you want the BodyParser to parse the bodies of the requests, you can change the code to the following:

```
let router = Router()

router.all("/books", middleware: BodyParser())

router.post("/books") {request, response, next in
...
}
...
```

Note the use of the `Router.all()` function to add the middleware to the list of code to process the request. Code added with the `Kitura.all()` function will process a request regardless of the HTTP method of the request.

The order here is important. The Kitura router maintains a list of handlers and middleware to be invoked when requests arrive. The order of the code to be invoked is simply the order in which the pieces of code, RouterHandlers, or middleware were added to the list.

In this snippet, the code in RouterHandler processing the POST request could include the following to get the body as a SwiftyJSON object:

```
if let book = request.body?.asJSON
```

Starting the Library Application

Using these basic Kitura concepts, let's start building a library back end by doing the following:

1. Create a directory library.
2. In the library directory, edit the file `Package.swift`. It should have the following contents:

```
import PackageDescription

let package = Package(
    name: "Library",
    dependencies: [
        .Package(url: "https://github.com/IBM-Swift/Kitura.git",
                majorVersion: 1, minor: 7),
        .Package(url: "https://github.com/IBM-Swift/HeliumLogger.git",
                majorVersion: 1, minor: 7)
    ]
)
```

3. Create a `Sources` directory, and in that directory, create a `Library` directory.
4. In the `Sources/Library` directory, edit the file `main.swift`. It should have the following contents:

```
import Kitura
import HeliumLogger

HeliumLogger.use(.info)

var books = Books()

let router = setupRoutes()

Kitura.addHTTPServer(onPort: 8090, with: router)
Kitura.run()
```

This code is not yet complete because it depends on files that will be described shortly. In the meantime, let's learn about a couple of the differences between these files and those in the HelloWorld example shown earlier.

In the `main.swift` file, HeliumLogger was imported and then set up as the logger to be used via the `HeliumLogger.use(.info)` statement, which also filters the log by limiting the printed log message to informational, warning, and error messages.

If you are following along with this example and developing the library server on a Mac with Xcode 8 installed, you now probably want to issue the `swift package generate-xcodeproj` command, in your root library directory. This command generates an Xcode project, named `Library.xcodeproj`, that can be opened in Xcode to edit, debug, and run the library server. If you do this and open the project in Xcode right now, it will look like Figure 7-2.

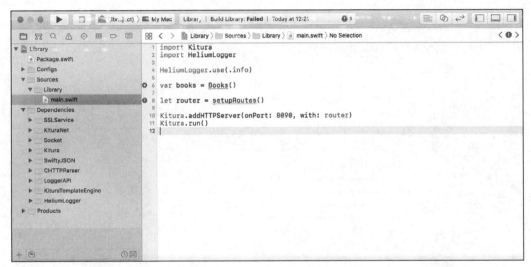

Figure 7-2: Library's main.swift shown in XCode

If you use Xcode to build your Kitura-based application, not only do you get auto-completion (using Ctrl-space) on the Kitura APIs, but you also get to view the documentation directly in Xcode (using the Alt key), as shown in Figure 7-3.

Next, in the `Sources/Library` directory, edit the `Book.swift` file, which will be the basic structure for an item in the collection of books. The file should have the following contents:

```
struct Book {
    var id = 0
    var isbn: String
    var title: String
    var author: String
    var checkedOut = false

    init(json: JSON) {
        id = json["id"].intValue
        isbn = json["isbn"].stringValue
        title = json["title"].stringValue
```

```
        author = json["author"].stringValue
        checkedOut = json["checkedOut"].boolValue
    }

    func toDictionary() -> [String: Any] {
        return ["id": id,
                "isbn": isbn,
                "title": title,
                "author": author,
                "checkedOut": checkedOut
                ]
    }

    func toJSON() -> JSON {
        return JSON(toDictionary())
    }

}
```

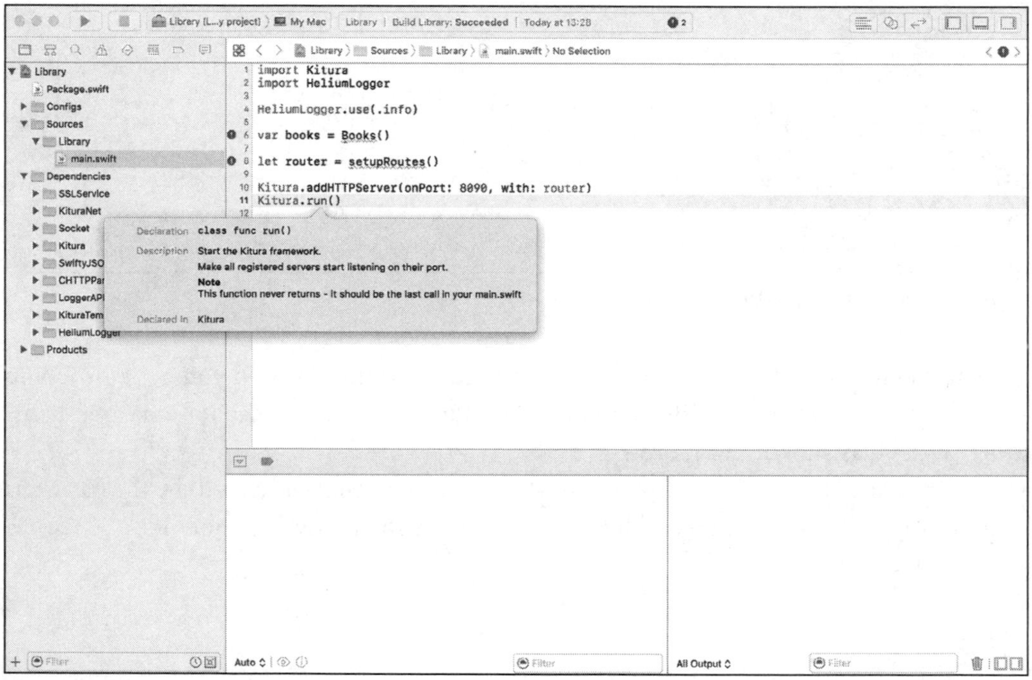

Figure 7-3: API documentation for Kitura shown in XCode

One nice feature of the Book struct is a constructor that builds an instance from a SwiftyJSON JSON object. SwiftyJSON is a very popular package that wraps the Apple Foundation JSONSerialization class, providing all sorts of helper functions and computed variables. Kitura uses the SwiftyJSON class when processing JSON data.

Next, in the `Sources/Library` directory, edit the `Books.swift` file, which will contain the data access code, or in Model View Controller (MVC) terms, the model. For now, it is a simple in-memory database. The file should have the following contents:

```
struct Books {
    var lastId = 0
    var theCollection = [Int: Book]()

    mutating func nextId() -> Int {
        lastId += 1
        return lastId
    }

    mutating func add(book: Book) -> Book {
        let id = nextId()
        theCollection[id] = book
        theCollection[id]?.id = id
        return book
    }

    mutating func delete(id: Int) {
        theCollection.removeValue(forKey: id)
    }
}
```

In the `Sources/Library` directory there will be another file, `Controller.swift`, that contains the RouterHandlers, or in MVC terms, the controller of the application. Because this file is probably the most interesting one from a Kitura perspective, you'll build it slowly. Let's start with the following code:

```
import Foundation

import Kitura

import SwiftyJSON

func setupRoutes() -> Router {
    let router = Router()

    router.all("/books", middleware: BodyParser())

    return router
}
```

The main contents of the `Controller.swift` file include the function `setupRoutes`, which as its name implies, sets up the routes using the Kitura `Router` class. So far, you have created an instance of the `Router` class and had Kitura invoke the BodyParser middleware on any request whose path begins with `/books`. The BodyParser will parse the body of any requests that have one.

Now let's continue by adding code that will add books to the book collection. Before the `return router` statement in the `Controller.swift` file, add the following:

```
router.post("/books") { request, response, next in
    if let bookJSON = request.body?.asJSON {
        let book = Book(json: bookJSON)
        let addedBook = books.add(book: book)
        response.status(.OK).send(json: addedBook.toJSON())
    }
    else {
        response.status(.badRequest)
    }
    next()
}
```

A RouterHandler is defined that will be invoked on POST requests to the path `/books`.

The statement `if let bookJSON = request.body?.asJSON` tries to get the payload as a SwiftyJSON JSON. If it fails, either because there is no body at all or because it isn't in JSON format (that is, with a mime type of application/json), the status code of the response is set to 400 (bad request). Note that the code uses an enum available with Kitura.

On the other hand, if a JSON-formatted payload is received and accessed, the RouterHandler proceeds by creating a book instance from the JSON and adding that book to the books collection. Finally, the response's status code is set to 200, and the added book is sent back in JSON form as the payload. Keep in mind that many of the response functions return the response itself as the result, enabling function calls to be chained.

There is now enough code to run the server. To do so, run the swift build command, in your root library directory, which builds the server executable. If there are no errors, you can start the server by simply running the command `.build/debug/Library` in the same directory. You can test your server by sending a request using your favorite browser HTTP request tool, or you can use the following curl command:

```
curl --header "Content-Type: application/json"
    --data-binary "{\"isbn\": \"1234-5678\",
                    \"title\": \"A test book\",
                    \"author\": \"Tester 1\"}"
    http://localhost:8090/books
```

as shown in Figure 7-4.

Note that neither an id nor a `checkedOut` value is sent in the request. The id value is set by the `Books.add` function to the next sequential id value, and `checkedOut` received a default value of false.

Figure 7-4: Adding a book to the library using curl

Now that books can be added to your collection, it would be nice to be able to retrieve them as well. Items can be retrieved from a collection like this one in three different ways:

1. All of them
2. All of them filtered by some value
3. A specific item in the collection, identified by its id

Let's start by fetching all the books in the collection. Before the `return router` statement in the `Controller.swift` file, add the following:

```
router.get("/books") { request, response, next in
    var result = [[String: Any]]()
    let allBooks = books.getAll()

    for book in allBooks {
        result.append(book.toDictionary())
    }

    response.status(.OK).send(json: JSON(result))
    next()
}
```

The added code handles a GET request to the path /books. It builds up a result that is an array of dictionaries whose keys are strings and whose values are Any Swift type. It gets all the books from the collection, loops through them, and adds them in dictionary form to the result array. Finally, the response is sent with a status of 200 (OK) with a body of the result array in JSON format.

If you were to rebuild the server, start it, and add a few books to the collection, issuing a request against /books, it might return results similar to those in Figure 7-5.

While being able to fetch all the books in the collection is nice, it doesn't necessarily work well when the collection is large, as it should be in a normal library. This is especially true if the clients are mobile devices on mobile networks with poor bandwidth and latency. You also won't be presenting the entire book collection to the user for them to scroll through. Instead, you will probably be enabling the user to search the book collection, and presenting the results of the search, which in most cases is a much shorter list.

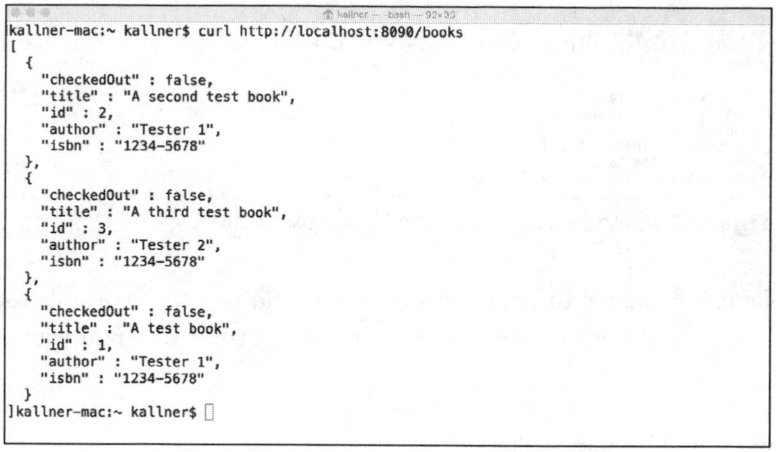

Figure 7-5: Fetching all of the books in the library using curl

Let's add some simple searching by author. To do so, you change the code you just added to read as follows:

```
router.get("/books") { request, response, next in
    var result = [[String: Any]]()
    let allBooks = books.getAll()

    for book in allBooks {
        let temp = request.queryParameters["author"]
        if let author =  temp?.removingPercentEncoding {
            if book.author == author {
                result.append(book.toDictionary())
            }
        }
        else {
            result.append(book.toDictionary())
        }
    }

    response.status(.OK).send(json: JSON(result))
    next()
}
```

This code differs from the code you added before in the for loop that was scanning the collection. Instead of simply adding all the book structures to the result, the new code checks to see if there is an author query parameter, and compares the value with the author field in the Book struct. If they match or there is no author query parameter in the request, the book is added to the result. Keep in mind that before using the value of the author query parameter, the function String.removePercentEncoding is invoked. The path in an HTTP request is a UTF-8 string. However, certain characters aren't allowed as part of the string, but can still be sent in an *escaped* form. This escaped form is simply a percent sign (%) followed by two hexadecimal digits of the code point (00–7f) of the character you want to send. The function String.removePercentEncoding simply converts any such escaped characters back to their unescaped form.

If you were to rebuild and restart the server, and load the same three books that loaded in Figure 7-5, you could search for books by the author "Tester 2", as shown in Figure 7-6.

```
kallner-mac:~ kallner$ curl http://localhost:8090/books?author=Tester%202
[
  {
    "checkedOut" : false,
    "title" : "A third test book",
    "id" : 3,
    "author" : "Tester 2",
    "isbn" : "1234-5678"
  }
]kallner-mac:~ kallner$ []
```

Figure 7-6: Searching for books authored by Tester 2

You saw earlier that there are three ways to fetch an item from a collection, with the last one being to fetch by id. To implement this in your server, you simply add the following code before the return router statement in the Controller.swift file:

```
router.get("/books/:id") { request, response, next in
    if let id = request.parameters["id"],
            let book = books.get(byId: Int(id)!) {
        response.status(.OK).send(json: book.toJSON())
    }
    else {
        response.status(.notFound)
    }
    next()
}
```

Notice that the code adds a second RouterHandler to be invoked on HTTP GET requests. The new RouterHandler and the previous one are differentiated by the specified path. The new RouterHandler has added /:id to the path, which indicates that unlike the previous RouterHandler, where GET requests to the path /books were processed, this RouterHandler only gets requests if the path is /books/*something*, where *something* is the identifier of the book to fetch from the book collection.

Basically, the RouterHandler accesses the second element of the path via the request parameter *id*, using the request.parameters API, and looks up the book by converting the String received from request.parameters. If the book is found, it is returned in JSON format. If it isn't found, a result is sent with a status of 404 (not found).

An invocation of this RouterHandler is shown in Figure 7-7, both where there was a book of the specified id and where there wasn't one.

```
|kallner-mac:~ kallner$ curl http://localhost:8090/books/2
{
  "checkedOut" : false,
  "title" : "A second test book",
  "id" : 2,
  "author" : "Tester 1",
  "isbn" : "1234-5678"
|}kallner-mac:~ kallner$
|kallner-mac:~ kallner$
|kallner-mac:~ kallner$
|kallner-mac:~ kallner$ curl http://localhost:8090/books/5
 kallner-mac:~ kallner$ []
```

Figure 7-7: Retrieving books by id

This code is simplistic in that it "trusts" that the user sends an identifier that is an integer. This probably isn't a good thing because a non-integer value could cause a crash, as shown in Figures 7-8 and 7-9.

```
|kallner-mac:~ kallner$ curl http://localhost:8090/books/test
curl: (52) Empty reply from server
kallner-mac:~ kallner$ []
```

Figure 7-8: Retrieving a book with a non-integer id

```
kallner-mac:Library kallner$ .build/debug/Library
 INFO: listen(socket:port:) HTTPServer.swift line 128 – Listening on port 8090
 INFO: listen(socket:port:) HTTPServer.swift line 133 – Accepted connection from: 127.0.0.1:
61268
fatal error: unexpectedly found nil while unwrapping an Optional value
Current stack trace:
0     libswiftCore.dylib                    0x00000001103c9580 swift_reportError + 132
1     libswiftCore.dylib                    0x00000001103e6850 _swift_stdlib_reportFatalError +
61
```

Figure 7-9: The library server crashing when an invalid id was sent in a request

To fix this, you can add code to check that the second path element was an integer and to send back perhaps a status code of 400 (bad request). Another simpler way to prevent such problems is to add a regular expression to the path to check that the second element is of the correct format. You can do this by changing the following line from

```
router.get("/books/:id") { request, response, next in
```

to

```
router.get("/books/:id(\\d+)") { request, response, next in
```

The text in the path in the parenthesis is a Perl-compatible regular expression that is checking for one or more decimal digits. In general, any Perl-compatible regular expression can be used.

To finish up the database operations on the book collection, you will now add the ability to update and delete books. To do so, add the following code before the return router statement in the Controller.swift file:

```
router.put("/books/:id(\\d+)") { request, response, next in
    if let id = request.parameters["id"],
            let bookJSON = request.body?.asJSON {
        var book = books.get(byId: Int(id)!)
        if book != nil {
```

```
            book?.isbn = bookJSON["isbn"].stringValue
            book?.title = bookJSON["title"].stringValue
            book?.author = bookJSON["author"].stringValue
            books.update(book: book!)

            response.status(.OK).send(json: book!.toJSON())
        }
    }
    else {
        response.status(.badRequest)
    }
    next()
}

router.delete("/books/:id(\\d+)") {
                        request, response, next in
    if let id = request.parameters["id"] {
        books.delete(id: Int(id)!)
        response.status(.noContent)
    }
    else {
        response.status(.notFound)
    }
    next()
}
```

This code adds a pair of handlers: one for HTTP PUT requests and the other for HTTP DELETE requests. These handlers are adding the ability to update and delete books, respectively. By now, you should understand the RouterHandlers. Note that in the update code, the id and checkedOut fields aren't being updated. This is not by accident, as the ids of books are assigned by the server and never change. Checking out and returning books is not something you want to do by handling update requests to a book. Instead, you want to use special HTTP requests for that to minimize what external components need to know about the inner workings of the library server. You'll get back to checking out and returning books later in this chapter.

Working with Various HTTP Features Using Kitura

So far you've learned how to work with the basic features of HTTP used in client-server communication. Kitura supports more than just that. Here is an overview of how to work with some of these HTTP features. Keep in mind that Kitura doesn't support all of these features by itself; some of them require add-on middleware in order to work.

HTTPS

HTTPS, or secure HTTP, uses the Transport Layer Security (TLS) protocol, sometimes still called SSL, to provide secure end-to-end HTTP requests and responses. It is used to provide privacy and integrity of requests and responses because they cannot be read or modified by any entities in the network. Additionally, when certificates signed by trusted certificate authorities are used, the client can verify the identity of the server and thus trust it with sensitive information.

In the background, Kitura uses OpenSSL on Linux and Apple Secure Transport on macOS. As a result, there are some subtle differences in setting up Kitura for HTTPS on Linux versus on macOS.

To set up a Kitura server to receive HTTPS requests, you need a certificate and key pair. For development and testing purposes, this pair can be self-certified—in other words, generated by yourself. For real production use, you should get a certificate and key pair from a trusted certificate authority.

The certificate and key pair will be a pair of files in PEM format. On Linux these files are used as is, while on macOS they need to be converted into a single file in PKCS#12 format.

If you are working with HTTPS just for testing and will be using a self- certified certificate, you can use the following commands to generate the necessary files:

```
openssl genrsa -out key.pem 2048

openssl req -new -sha256 -key key.pem -out csr.csr

openssl req -x509 -sha256 -days 365 -key key.pem -in csr.csr
               -out certificate.pem
```

If you are running your server on macOS, you also need to run the following command:

```
openssl pkcs12 -export -out certificate.pfx -inkey key.pem
               -in certificate.pem
```

These commands generate four files: csr.csr, key.pem, certificate.pem, and certificate.pfx. The csr.csr file can be deleted. The key.pem and certificate.pem files are the only ones that are needed on Linux, and certificate.pfx is the only file needed on macOS.

When you have the appropriate key and certificate files, assuming you use these names and that they are in the root directory of your project, you can add HTTPS support to the library server. You do this by adding to the code in Sources/Library/main.swift [just before the Kitura.run()] either the following code on macOS:

```
let ssllsConfig =
    SSLConfig(withChainFilePath: "./certificate.pfx",
              withPassword: "the password",
              usingSelfSignedCerts: true)
Kitura.addHTTPServer(onPort:8443, with: router,
                     withSSL: sslConfig)
```

or the following code on Linux:

```
let sslConfig =
    SSLConfig(usingCertificateFile: "./certificate.pem",
              withKeyFile: "./key.pem",
              withPassword: "the password",
              usingSelfSignedCerts: true)
```

```
Kitura.addHTTPServer(onPort:8443, with: router,
                     withSSL: sslConfig)
```

In both code snippets, an SSL configuration is being set up in the first statement. In both of them, if a password is entered when creating the certificate, the entered password needs to be used in the withPassword parameter. You probably want to read the password from a file or an environment variable and not have it in the source code in plain text as a string. The usingSelfSignedCerts parameter is set to true because, in this example, you're using a self-signed certificate.

The second statement of both code snippets is starting an HTTP server listening on port 8443 for HTTPS requests. This server will use the same routes that were set up for the server listening for regular HTTP requests.

You can easily set the server to only listen for HTTPS requests, removing the statement Kitura .addHTTPServer(onPort: 8090, with: router) from the main.swift file. If, on the other hand, you want some requests to be handled via HTTP and others to be handled via HTTPS, you can simply set up two different router objects, one for the HTTP server and the other for the HTTPS server.

HTTP Headers

HTTP headers allow HTTP clients and servers to exchange extra information in their requests and responses. This extra information is often related to security, for example, sending API tokens, which contain information about the payload such as its length, type, or format. Headers can also be used to request that responses be sent in certain formats.

The Kitura RouterRequest and RouterResponse classes have a headers field that can be used to access and set headers using a simple subscript syntax. For example, to get the value of the "Cache-Control" header sent by the client, you simply write the following in a RouterHandler or RouterMiddleware:

```
let cacheControl = request.headers["cache-control"]
```

To set a header in a response, you simply write something like this:

```
Response.headers["Cache-Control"] = "max-age=3600"
```

When retrieving header values, the header name is case-insensitive. When setting headers, it is preferable to use the mixed-case name of the header, although it isn't required.

Kitura provides a set of helper functions for setting a variety of HTTP headers. These functions include the following:

- RouterResponse.headers.addAttachment—Sets the Content-Disposition header to *attachment*, optionally adding the specified filename.
- RouterResponse.headers.addLink—Adds an HTTP Link header
- RouterResponse.headers.setLocation—Sets the Location header
- RouterResponse.headers.setType—Sets the Content-Type header to the mime type associated with the specified *file extension*. In many cases Kitura sets the Content-Type header for you automatically.

Cookies

Cookies are used in HTTP responses to store a piece of information that will be sent back with subsequent requests. This technique is typically used in web applications. Historically this was often used to maintain state, specifically session state, that is sent from the browser back to the server on subsequent requests.; however, it is not a good idea because the amount of cookie storage in a browser is not that large. A better solution is to send one cookie that contains a session key, which is used to retrieve the user's session data stored on the server.

If you need to work with cookies, Kitura provides a pair of APIs for extracting cookies sent to the server and setting cookies to be sent to the client. To extract a cookie from a request, you can simply write something like this:

```
let cookie = request.cookies["app-cookie"]
```

The retrieved cookie is an Apple Foundation `HTTPCookie` object.
To send a cookie in a response, you can simply write something like this:

```
response.cookies["app-cookie"] = cookie
```

Again, this is where `cookie` is an instance of the Apple Foundation `HTTPCookie` class.

Sending Results in the Format Requested by the Client

Many RESTful APIs provide results in several formats. This is often useful in supporting a variety of clients from the same RESTful end-point. The standard way for an HTTP client to tell the server what format of response body the client is willing to accept is to use the Accept HTTP Header in the request. In the Accept Header you specify the mime type of the response body you want.

The Kitura `RouterResponse` class has a function format, which makes it easier to write simpler code to deal with such situations.

In the following example, the `Book` struct used in the library example has been extended with a function called `toHTML`. The `toHTML` function returns the book in question in the form of an HTML snippet, suitable for embedding in a large HTML document. Using that extension, you could change the `RouterHandler` that retrieves a book by id to read as follows:

```
router.get("/books/:id") { request, response, next in
    if let id = request.parameters["id"],
           let book = books.get(byId: Int(id)!) {
        response.format(callbacks: [
            "application/json": { request, response in
                response.status(.OK)
                response.send(json: book.toJSON())
            },
            "text/html": { request, response in
                response.status(.OK)
                response.send(json: book.toHTML())
```

```
            }
        ])
    }
    else {
        response.status(.notFound)
    }
    next()
}
```

The `RouterResponse.format` function automatically sets the status of the response to 406 (not acceptable) if the Accept header in the request has a value other than either `"application/json"` or `"text/html"`.

Compressing Data Sent Back to the Client

Many RESTful requests can send large responses to the client. Very often the response is text that is readily compressed to enable a smaller payload to be sent to the client. This is particularly helpful with devices on mobile networks where bandwidth can often be limited. The HTTP standard lists a few compression methods including the deflate and gzip methods. A client can use the HTTP Accept-Encoding header to indicate what, if any, compression methods it understands.

Kitura-Compression middleware, when added to your server, automatically compresses responses using either the deflate or gzip method. A threshold can be specified such that if the response body's length is less than the threshold, the response body is not compressed. In any event, the response body is only compressed if the client sent an appropriate Accept-Encoding header.

If you want to use Kitura-Compression in the library server, you can change the `Package.swift` file to read as follows:

```
import PackageDescription

let package = Package(
  name: "Library",
  dependencies: [
    .Package(url: "https://github.com/IBM-Swift/Kitura.git",
            majorVersion: 1, minor: 7),
    .Package(url: "https://github.com/IBM-Swift/HeliumLogger.git",
            majorVersion: 1, minor: 7),
    .Package(url: "https://github.com/IBM-Swift/Kitura-Compression.git",
            majorVersion: 1, minor: 7)
  ]
)
```

In addition, you can modify the beginning of the `Controller.swift` file to read as follows:

```
import Kitura
import KituraCompression
import SwiftyJSON

func setupRoutes() -> Router {
```

```
let router = Router()

router.get(middleware: Compression(theshold: 50*1024))
router.all("/books", middleware: BodyParser())


...
```

In this example, any GET request whose response is over 50KB and has an appropriate Accept-Encoding header is compressed.

Cross-Origin Resource Sharing

JavaScript applications running in browsers have typically been limited to making HTTP requests back to the server from which the application was loaded. This sandboxing was done for security purposes to prevent JavaScript applications from reaching out maliciously to other servers.

Cross-Origin Resource Sharing (CORS) is a set of HTTP extensions that enable a JavaScript application that is running in a browser and that was loaded from site A, to make a request to site B, typically a GET request, and have site B allow the request. If site B doesn't allow the request, the browser running the JavaScript application does not allow the request to be made.

Kitura-CORS middleware can be configured to automatically send the needed responses to preflight-requests issued by browsers.

If you want to use Kitura-CORS in the library server, you can change the Package.swift file to read as follows:

```
import PackageDescription

let package = Package(
    name: "Library",
    dependencies: [
        .Package(url: "https://github.com/IBM-Swift/Kitura.git",
                majorVersion: 1, minor: 7),
        .Package(url: "https://github.com/IBM-Swift/HeliumLogger.git",
                majorVersion: 1, minor: 7),
        .Package(url: "https://github.com/IBM-Swift/Kitura-CORS.git",
                majorVersion: 1, minor: 7)
    ]
)
```

In addition, you can modify the beginning of the Controller.swift file to read as follows:

```
import Kitura
import KituraCORS
import SwiftyJSON

func setupRoutes() -> Router {
```

```
let router = Router()

router.all(middleware:
              CORS(options: Options(
                  allowedOrigin: .origin("www.acme.com"),
                  methods: ["GET"]
              ))
)
router.all("/books", middleware: BodyParser())

...
```

Other Ways of Serving Content Using Kitura

Kitura is a framework for web server applications. But what would a web server be without the ability to serve content? You might ask, "Isn't that what was described earlier in the chapter, when handling HTTP requests was described?" Well, sort of. Those requests were about handling data that would be used by mobile apps or Web 2.0 applications in AJAX requests. Content is more about serving files for mobile and web applications.

Content can be either static or dynamic in nature. Dynamic content is generated on the server before being sent to the client. To help with this type of content, Kitura has two features: static file serving and templating.

StaticFileServer

Static file serving in Kitura is accomplished via the `StaticFileServer` middleware. The `StaticFileServer` middleware maps HTTP requests to specific files on the file system, which are then sent to the client. The Content-Type header is set based on a popular convention of file extensions to mime type (for example, `.html` to `text/html`).

Each instance of the `StaticFileServer` middleware serves a set of files from the server's file system for a specific URL path prefix from a specific root directory in the file system. The prefix is specified when the `StaticFileServer` middleware is added to the list of routes. The root directory is specified by a parameter to the `StaticFileServer` instance's constructor, which defaults to `"./public"`.

The name of the file served under the root directory is the path in the HTTP request, with the route used for the `StaticFileServer` removed.

In the following example,

```
router.all("/static", middleware: StaticFileServer())
```

if the client in a browser makes the HTTP request for `http://server:port/static/application.css`, the file `public/application.css` is served.

If the root directory is specified in a relative fashion, StaticFileServer looks for it—first, under the current directory, and if that fails, under the root of the SPM project that was compiled to build the running server. In other words, if the Kitura-based server is executing from `/servers/myapp` and is built from `/applications/myapp`, in this example StaticFileServer first looks for `/servers/myapp/public/application.css` and then `/applications/myapp/public/application.css`.

Templates

Often the content you want to send to the client varies only by a few values. Other times you want to convert content from one easier-to-create format to another easier-to-consume format and you don't want to do the conversion up front. Kitura templates can do both. The idea is to pass a template and set of values to an appropriate template engine. The template engine processes the template with the specified values and produces content in some format.

Template engines for Kitura implement the Kitura Template Engine protocol, found in the `https://github.com/IBM-Swift/Kitura-TemplateEngine.git` repository.

At the time of this writing, three template engines have implemented the Kitura Template Engine protocol:

1. `https://github.com/IBM-Swift/Kitura-Markdown.git` generates HTML pages from Markdown files.
2. `https://github.com/IBM-Swift/Kitura-MustacheTemplateEngine.git` uses the GRMustache template engine.
3. `https://github.com/IBM-Swift/Kitura-StencilTemplateEngine.git` uses the Stencil template engine.

Template engines are used by invoking the `RouteResponse.render()` function within a RouterHandler or middleware. The "extension" of the name of the template passed in is used to select the template engine to be used. In the following example, Markdown files are served from the `views` directory. The `Package.swift` file would contain the following:

```
import PackageDescription

let package = Package(
  name: "DocServer",
  dependencies: [
    .Package(url: "https://github.com/IBM-Swift/Kitura.git",
             majorVersion: 1, minor: 7),
    .Package(url: "https://github.com/IBM-Swift/Kitura-Markdown.git",
             majorVersion: 0, minor: 9)
  ]
)
```

The `main.swift` file would contain the following:

```
import Kitura
import KituraMarkdown
```

```
let router = Router()

router.add(templateEngine: KituraMarkdown())

router.get("/docs/*") { request, response, next in
    if let path = request.parsedURL.path {
        try response.render(path, context: [String:Any]())
        response.status(.OK)
    }
    next()
}

Kitura.addHTTPServer(onPort: 8090, with: router)
Kitura.run()
```

Other Useful Kitura Middleware

There are other Kitura middleware available that add various useful capabilities to your server. Here are some of them:

Kitura-Session

Often a web application has a collection of interactions with the server that have some collective meaning, such as a visit to a web commerce site or a visit to a private site requiring authentication. This collection of interactions with a server is often called a session. The session is often used to track session-related information about the client, such as the contents of a shopping cart, or whether or not the client has authenticated.

Kitura-Session provides session support within a Kitura-based server, extending the RouterRequest with an API to access and store session-related data. The stored data must be JSON-serializable data, that is, a dictionary or an array. The session data is automatically saved to a data store when the request ends. The data store itself is pluggable. The Kitura team has provided two data store implementations:

1. An in-memory data store, suitable for development
2. A data store that stores the data in Redis, a high-performance Key-Value data store. This data store is available in the repository https://github.com/IBM-Swift/Kitura-Session-Redis.git.

Kitura-Session takes a "secret" provided by the application and uses it to digitally sign and encrypt the HTTP cookie used to transfer the session identifier between the client and the server.

To use Kitura-Session, you add https://github.com/IBM-Swift/Kitura-Session.git to the application's dependencies in the Package.swift file, and you add code like this to the definition of the application's routes:

```
import Kitura
import KituraSession
import SwiftyJSON

...
```

```
let router = Router()

...

let session =
        Session(secret: "a secret value",
                cookie: [.maxAge(TimeInterval(48*60*60))])
router.all(middleware: session)
```

In this example the cookie sent to the client with the session identifier will "live" for forty-eight hours and is signed and encrypted with the string, `"a secret value"`.

Because a store is not provided, the default in-memory store is used. There are other options that can be specified for the cookie, to control its name, its path, and whether it should be treated as a secure cookie. Keep in mind that specifying that the cookie should be a secure cookie requires the application to be using HTTPS to receive requests.

The following code snippet shows the easy-to-use API added by `Kitura-Session` to store and retrieve session state:

```
router.post("/addtocart") { request, response, next in
    var cart = request.session["cart"]
    let items = cart["items"]
...
    cart["items"] = updatedItems
    next()
}
```

In this example the item cart is retrieved from the overall session state. From the cart, the existing list of items is retrieved. At the end, the items in the cart are replaced with the new list of items.

Kitura-CSRF

One of the known Internet attacks is the Cross-Site Request Forgery (CSRF) attack, in which an unknowing user can be coerced into performing various actions for a particular web application. This is often done by placing into web pages, hidden requests that the browser will perform, without the user knowing, within the session they have with the application they are using.

One way to prevent these attacks is to add a secure token in requests sent by the client to the server. These tokens can be stored in several places, depending in part on the way requests are sent to the server. For example, if requests are sent by posting an HTML form, a hidden field in the form can be used to hold the token. This hidden field can be set when the empty form is sent to the user. Other ways include adding a URL query parameter or an extra header.

`Kitura-CSRF` is middleware that can be used to generate and check for such tokens in a variety of ways. `Kitura-CSRF` uses `Kitura-Session` to track the session-related token of the client.

To use `Kitura-CSRF`, you first add `https://github.com/IBM-Swift/Kitura-CSRF.git` to the dependencies of your application. Then, in the code where the routes are defined, you add code like the following:

```
import Kitura
import KituraCSRF
import KituraSession

...

let router = Router()

...

let csrf = CSRF()

let session = Session(secret: "a very big secret",
                      cookie: [.maxAge(TimeInterval(60*60))])
router.all(middleware: session)

router.all("/transfer", middleware: csrf)

router.get("/transfer") { request, response, next in
    let token = csrf.createToken(request: request)
    try response.render("transfer-page.stencil",
                        context: ["csrfToken": token])
    response.status(.OK)
    next()
}

router.post("/transfer") { request, response, next in
...
    next()
}
```

In this example both the Kitura-Session and Kitura-CSRF middleware are set up. It is important that the Kitura-Session middleware be added first to the router. This ensures that Kitura-Session has set up the session and fetched any prior session data before Kitura-CSRF is invoked.

In the GET request to `/transfer`, an HTML page is generated using the Stencil template `transfer-page.stencil`. The template is passed in the context, a "variable" `csrfToken`, which contains the CSRF token to be inserted into the HTML form in the field _csrf. The _csrf field is the default field in an URL-encoded body where Kitura-CSRF looks for a token.

In the POST request, there is no need to check for the token, because if it isn't present, that `RouterHandler` executing won't execute.

Authentication Using the Kitura-Credentials Framework

In many applications, users are required to authenticate themselves before being able to use various sensitive parts of the application. Sometimes this authentication is then used to authorize a specific user to perform various actions within the application. Other times it is just important to know who the user is, to track various actions that are performed.

Authentication is often done in many ways using one or more trusted identity providers. Which ones are used in a specific application depends on the application. In enterprise applications, you often want to use an enterprise directory of some kind. In customer-facing applications, you often use well-known social identity providers such as Facebook and Google.

`Kitura-Credentials` is a pluggable authentication framework, providing a single API to the application developer to authenticate users via a variety of identity providers. When a client has successfully authenticated, the userProfile field of the Kitura `RouterRequest` will contain information about the user from the identify provider. The information provided includes the user's id and name as they are known to the identity provider.

At the time of this writing, there are `Kitura-Credentials` plug-ins for the following identity providers:

1. Facebook, both web login and OAuth2 tokens. These are available in the repository `https://github.com/IBM-Swift/Kitura-CredentialsFacebook.git`.
2. GitHub, which is available in the repository `https://github.com/IBM-Swift/Kitura-CredentialsGitHub.git`.
3. Google, both web login and OAuth2 tokens. These are available in the repository `https://github.com/IBM-Swift/Kitura-CredentialsGoogle.git`.

Although it recommended that use an OAuth provider for authentication, you can, instead, use HTTP Authentication, if needed. Both Digest and Basic authentication are supported by the repository `https://github.com/IBM-Swift/Kitura-CredentialsHTTP.git`. When using the HTTP authentication plug-ins, the developer is responsible for providing code that will validate the user id/password combination sent in the HTTP request.

The Library Sample with Authentication

To show the `Kitura-Credentials` APIs, extend the library example to add a shell for checking out books. The code will show how to set up authentication and a very simplistic use of the information retrieved about the client.

When someone checks out a book, you would like to know who it is. For this example, assume that to check out a book, you must identify yourself using your Facebook login. A real example should include other social identity providers, such as a Google login.

To add this to my example, there is some setup that must be done in the apps part of the Facebook for Developers website (`https://developers.facebook.com/apps/`). This setup includes the following steps:

1. Create an app.
2. Add a Facebook login to your new app.
3. In the "Valid OAuth redirect URIs" section, add `http://yourhost:8090/login/facebook/callback`

After performing the setup, you need to add `https://github.com/IBM-Swift/ Kitura-CredentialsFacebook.git` to the dependencies in the `Package.swift` file. Then, you modify the `Controllers.swift` file as follows:

1. At the top of the file among the other `import` statements, add the following:

```
import KituraSession
import Credentials
import CredentialsFacebook
```

2. Right after the `let router = Router()` statement, add the following:

```
let session = Session(secret: "<some secret value>")
router.all(middleware: session)

let credentials = Credentials()

credentials.options["failureRedirect"] = "/login"

let fbClientId = "<your Facebook app id>"
let fbClientSecret = "<your Facebook app secret>"
let fbCallbackURL = "<your Facebook Oauth redirect URI>"

let fbCredentials =
        CredentialsFacebook(clientId: fbClientId,
                            clientSecret: fbClientSecret,
                            callbackUrl: fbCallbackURL)
credentials.register(plugin: fbCredentials)

router.all("/books/:id/checkout", middleware: credentials)
```

This code does the following:

a. Adds session support to the Library application, which is required by the Kitura-CredentialsFacebook plug-in.

b. Creates an instance of Credentials and configures it so that when requests come in where the user is not authenticated, or if there is a failure in authentication, the user is redirected to `/login` on this same server.

c. The CredentialsFacebook plug-in is configured and instantiated. You should replace the bracketed text with the appropriate values from the Facebook for Developers website information for your app.

d. Registers the CredentialsFacebook plug-in with Credentials

e. Adds Credentials as a middleware that will be invoked on any path that matches `/books/<something>/checkout`.

3. After the code in Step 2, add the following code:

```
router.get("/login") { request, response, next in
    response.headers["Content-Type"] =
                            "text/html; charset=utf-8"
    response.status(.OK).send(
        "<!DOCTYPE html><html><body>" +
            "<p>To checkout a book you must login<br>" +
            "<a href=/login/facebook>" +
                    "Log In with Facebook" +
            "</a><br>" +
        "</body></html>\n\n")
    next()
}
```

This code displays a simple HTML page that tells the user they need to log in using Facebook to check out a book. Keep in mind that in a real-world server, the page could be statically served or generated from a template for a much better user experience.

4. After the code in Step 3, add the following code:

```
router.get("/login/facebook",
            handler: credentials.authenticate(
                    credentialsType: fbCredentials.name))

router.get("/login/facebook/callback",
            handler: credentials.authenticate(
                    credentialsType: fbCredentials.name,
                    failureRedirect: "/login"))

router.get("/books/:id/checkout") {
                        request, response, next in
    let checkedOutBy =
        request.userProfile?.displayName ?? "unknown")"
    response.send("<!DOCTYPE html><html><body>" +
                "The book is checked out by " +
                    checkedOutBy +
                " (\(request.userProfile?.id ?? ""))" +
                "</body></html>\n\n")
    response.status(.OK)
    next()
}
```

When a user clicks the hyperlink, a request is made to the library server that causes the user's browser to be redirected to the Facebook login page.

Kitura and Data Access

Without a set of data access APIs, it would be very hard to write real-world application back ends. Kitura, in an attempt to be open and enable you to do what you want the way you want, does not come with a set of data access APIs. There are many data access APIs available from the open source community. Two such data access APIs have been started by the Kitura team, one for working with data stored in relational databases via SQL and another for working with data stored in Redis servers. The following sections will discuss those APIs.

Swift-Kuery

Many teams try to keep their SQL-based applications as pure as possible from an SQL standards perspective in order to avoid locking in to a specific database engine. They do this because often the engine that is convenient to develop with may not be the one they deploy on in production. This may be due to reasons of scalability, engines supported by the production support teams, and so on.

However, each relational database engine comes with its own SDK or driver, which you need to use to write SQL applications. This makes it more difficult to keep your code database engine-independent. Some projects attempt to overcome this problem by placing all the database access code in as few files as possible. This, however, makes application development and maintenance more difficult because many developers are trying to update the same small set of files. Additionally, this almost always requires some sort of mapping code to be written to copy data from various proprietary database SDK formats to a common one.

Swift-Kuery provides an easily consumable and very Swift like, or Swifty, set of relational database APIs while solving this problem with database engine lock-in. It does this by providing an SQL-like abstraction layer above various database engine SDKs. This abstraction layer has been designed so that, as much as possible, code written using the API reads as if you wrote it in SQL. Swift-Kuery connects to specific database engines via plug-ins. Each plug-in provides the connection to the actual database SDK involved along with any changes needed when generating the SQL query being sent to the database engine.

As of this writing, two Swift-Kuery plug-ins are available:

- **For PostgreSQL**—https://github.com/IBM-Swift/Swift-Kuery-PostgreSQL.git
- **For SQLite**—https://github.com/IBM-Swift/Swift-Kuery-SQLite.git
- **For MySQL**—https://github.com/IBM-Swift/SwiftKueryMySQL.git

Library Using Swift-Kuery

The best way to describe how to work with Swift-Kuery is by using example code. To do so, you'll see how you can improve the library example used in this chapter by using a relational database to store the book collection.

To simplify this example, it will be a "pure" Swift-Kuery example, without the use of a specific database plug-in. To run it, you should create a real connection to a database using one of the available plug-ins.

For this example there is an existing table named *Books* in the database with the columns shown in Table 7-1.

Table 7-1: SQL schema for the Books table

Column name	Column type
id	integer
isbn	varchar(20)
title	varchar(100)
author	varchar(30)
checkedOut	boolean

To work with this table, you need to create a metadata class that describes the table *Books*, which inherits from the Swift-Kuery class Table. To do so, you add the file `Sources/Library/BooksTable.swift` to your project, with the following contents:

```
import SwiftKuery

class BooksTable: Table {
    let name = "Books"

    let id = Column("id")
    let isbn = Column("isbn")
    let title = Column("title")
    let author = Column("author")
    let checkedOut = Column("checkedOut")
}
```

The class `BooksTable` identifies the table it represents via the name field, and the columns of that table via a set of fields that are instances of the `Column` class. Any other fields and functions in this class are ignored by Swift-Kuery.

You also need to add an Error type for use in your application. This type will be in the `Sources/Library/LibraryError.swift` file, which should have the following contents:

```
enum LibraryError: Error {
  case failedToConnect(error: Error)
  case failedToExecuteQuery(error: Error)
}

extension LibraryError: CustomStringConvertible {
  var description: String {
```

```
    switch self {
      case .failedToConnect(let error):
        return "Failed to connect to the database: \(error)"
      case .failedToExecuteQuery(let error):
        return "Failed to execute query \(error)"
    }
  }
}
```

Next, you need to make changes to the `Books` struct.

Until now the functions `get(byId id: Int)`, `getAll()`, `add(book: Book)`, `delete(id: Int)`, and `update(book: Book)` were all synchronous in nature, in that it was assumed that anything they did was complete when they returned, and if they returned results, it was via the return value of the function. They will all be changed to require an extra parameter, a callback. This parameter will signify that the function is complete, along with conveying any results of the function including an optional Error field, indicating any error that might have occurred.

Now for the details of those changes. First you add the necessary imports to the top of the `Books.swift` file:

```
import SwiftKuery
import (Swift-Kuery plugin)
```

You need to replace `(Swift-Kuery plugin)` with the appropriate module to import for your Swift-Kuery plug-in.

In the `Books` struct, replace the declaration of the field `theCollection` with the following code:

```
private var databaseConnection =
                    (the init of your connection)
private let booksTable = BooksTable()
private var connected = false
```

You need to replace `(the init of your connection)` with the appropriate constructor for the database plug-in you have chosen.

At the end of the `Books` struct, you need to add a helper function for connecting to the database as needed:

```
private mutating
        func connect(callback: @escaping (Error?)->()) {
    if connected {
        callback(nil)
        return
    }
    databaseConnection.connect() { error in
        if let error = error {
            let connectError =
                LibraryError.failedToConnect(error: error)
```

```
                    callback(connectError)
                }
                else {
                    connected = true
                    callback(nil)
                }
            }
        }
    }
```

The `func connect` function will connect to the database if you haven't connected yet. If an error occurs while trying to connect, the callback is called with a LibraryError wrapping the error received from the Swift-Kuery plug-in.

Let's start with adding a book, that is, a SQL INSERT query. For example, you might want to execute a query like the following one:

```
INSERT INTO Books
    VALUES (2, '1234-5678', 'A second test book',
            'Tester 1', false)
```

Executing such a query from code by inserting text directly into the query is a very bad practice because it opens you up to SQL injection attacks. These attacks cause applications to issue SQL queries that weren't intended by inserting text that ends clauses in the query and starts other ones.

The correct query to issue from a programming perspective is one that uses *parameters*. Parameters are values that are inserted when the query is executed, and they can't change the clauses of the query. Parameters are inserted into queries in a database engine–specific way; some support SQL statements that look like this:

```
INSERT INTO Books VALUES (?, ?, ?, ?, ?)
```

You can change the `add` function of the `Books` struct to issue such an SQL INSERT statement as follows:

```
mutating func add(book: Book,
                  callback: @escaping (Book, Error?)->()) {
    connect() { error in
        if let error = error {
            callback(book, error)
            return
        }

        let id = nextId()
        var newBook = book
        newBook.id = id
```

```
        let query = Insert(into: booksTable,
                           values: Parameter(), Parameter(),
                                   Parameter(), Parameter(),
                                   Parameter())
        let parameters: [Any] =
                [newbook.id, newbook.isbn, book.title,
                    book.author, newbook.checkedOut]
        databaseConnection.execute(query: query,
                               parameters: parameters)
                                         { queryResult in
            if let queryError = queryResult.asError {
                let error =
                    LibraryError
                        .failedToExecuteQuery(error: queryError)
                callback(newBook, error)
            }
            else {
                callback(newbook, nil)
            }
        }
    }
}
```

In this code, the database is connected, if necessary, and an id for the book is generated. The query is then described and executed.

The Insert statement is described with code in a way that reads similarly to a standard SQL Insert statement using an instance of the Insert struct. It should be noted that the instances of the Parameter struct are used to mark parameters to be inserted at execution in the query.

The execute function of the Swift-Kuery plug-in's connection for an Insert query is asynchronous, because database operations may take a while, and it calls a callback when it completes. The callback is of the type QueryResult. The QueryResult callback enumerates the possible outcomes of query execution. In this case you only need to check whether or not there was an error, as was done with the following code from a previous example:

```
if let queryError = queryResult.asError {
    let error =
        LibraryError.failedToExecuteQuery(error: queryError)
    callback(newBook, error)
}
else {
    callback(newbook, nil)
}
```

The updated add function indicates that its work is complete by calling the callback function with a tuple of the added book and an optional LibraryError. If the LibraryError is nil, then the book was added.

The changes to the `Books.add` function need to be reflected in the RouterHandler in `Controllers.swift` that calls it, as shown in the following code:

```
router.post("/books") { request, response, next in
    if let bookJSON = request.body?.asJSON {
        let book = Book(json: bookJSON)
        books.add(book: book) { addedBook, error in
            if let error = error {
                response.error = error
            }
            else {
                response.status(.OK)
                response.send(json: addedBook.toJSON())
            }
            next()
        }
    }
    else {
        response.status(.badRequest)
        next()
    }
}
```

Continuing this process of updating functions in `Books.swift` and `Controllers.swift`, you can update the `Books.getAll` function to use a Select query. It can be as simple as:

```
SELECT * FROM Books
```

or, if you are filtering by author, you can use the following Select query:

```
SELECT * FROM Books WHERE author = 'some text'
```

Considering SQL injection attacks, you probably want something like this:

```
SELECT * FROM Books WHERE author = ?
```

The code then looks like this:

```
mutating func getAll(author: String?,
            callback: @escaping ([Book]?, Error?)->()) {
    connect() { error in
        if let error = error {
            callback(nil, error)
            return
        }

        let completion: ((QueryResult) -> ()) =
                                    { queryResult in
```

```
            if let (_, rows) = queryResult.asRows {
                var result = [Book]()
                for row in rows {
                    let book = Book(row: row)
                    result.append(book)
                }
                callback(result, nil)
            }
            else if let queryError = queryResult.asError {
                callback(nil,
                         LibraryError
                             .failedToExecuteQuery(
                                 error: queryError))
            }
        }

        var query = Select(from: booksTable)
        if let author = author {
            query =
                query.where(
                    booksTable.author == Parameter())
            databaseConnection.execute(query: query,
                             parameters: [author],
                             onCompletion: completion)
        }
        else {
            databaseConnection.execute(query: query,
                             onCompletion: completion)
        }
    }
}
```

In this code, you connect to the database, returning right away if there is a failure in connect-ing. Next, a callback closure is set up for running the queries. You run one of two slightly different queries depending on whether the getAll function received an author value to filter by. The same callback closure is used for both. This closure, if no error occurred with the query, takes the rows of the result set, an array of arrays of Any, and creates an array of Book structs, one per row in the result set.

The code then creates the Select query. It first creates a simple Select query from the table Books, without a where clause. The code then checks whether an author-filtering value was passed in. If one was, a where clause is added to the query using a parameter for the value to insert, and the query is executed using the value passed in for author filtering for the parameter value and callback closure defined in the code. If there was no author filter, the simple Select query is executed with the call-back closure defined in this example.

You can update the other functions in Books.swift and Controllers.swift in a similar fashion.

More Complicated Queries Using Swift-Kuery

Swift-Kuery can be used to create SQL queries that are more complex than those shown in the updates to the Library in the previous example. Let's say you want to get a list of the authors with at least two books that are not checked out. You want to see the number of such books per author as well, calling this column in the result *books*, and sorting the results by the authors' names in an ascending order. Here is the corresponding SQL query:

```
SELECT author, COUNT(title) AS books
FROM Books
WHERE checkedout = false
GROUP BY author
HAVING COUNT(title) >= 2
ORDER BY author ASC
```

Here is how you build this query in Swift-Kuery:

```
let query =
    Select(booksTable.author,
           count(booksTable.title).as("books"),
           from: booksTable)
    .where(booksTable.checkedOut == false)
    .group(by: booksTable.author)
    .having(count(booksTable.title) >= 2)
    .order(by: .ASC(booksTable.author))
```

Kitura-redis

Redis is an open source high-performance Key-Value store. It is often used for persistent state storage, caching, and statistics of high-volume systems. It can also be used as a simple pub/sub hub. Commands can be sent to Redis for execution individually or within the scope of a transaction in which either all or none of the commands succeed, with appropriate rollbacks.

Kitura-redis (`https://github.com/IBM-Swift/Kitura-redis.git`) provides APIs for most Redis commands in a completely type-safe way. These APIs can be invoked within the scope of a Redis transaction or by themselves. To make Kitura-redis easier to use by someone familiar with Redis, the function names for the various Redis commands match, in almost all cases, the Redis command names. There is also a set of lower-level APIs to enable the issuing of any Redis command whatsoever.

Adding Statistics to the Library Server

Say that you'd like to add some statistics to your library server. Specifically you'd like to track the number of books being checked out daily over a rolling period of three months. I should also point out that while gathering the statistical information is important, it's generally not important enough to fail the request when there are failures in gathering or storing the data. As such, in your case you will simply log errors using the LoggerAPI protocol. This is the same protocol that Kitura uses internally for its own logging.

To store the statistical data, you use a Redis hash—a collection of fields, each with its own value stored under a single key. The fields are named by the date of the day when statistics are being stored. The set of fields in the hash are pruned on every request.

To get started, you need to update the `Package.swift` file of the library server by adding `https://github.com/IBM-Swift/Kitura-redis.git` to the dependencies.

Next you add a few things to `Controllers.swift`. First you add some imports:

```
import SwiftRedis
import LoggerAPI
```

Then you add some global variables that you will use in multiple places:

```
let redis = Redis()
let statisticsKey = "checkout-statistics"
```

The `redis` variable is the Kitura-redis handle that you will use to work the Redis server, and `statisticsKey` is the key you will use for the Redis hash that you will use to store the statistical data.

Next you need to add a helper function to the end of `Controllers.swift` to connect to the Redis server when needed:

```
func connectToRedis(callback: (Bool) -> Void) {
    if !redis.connected {
        redis.connect(host: "the-host", port: 6379) { error in
          guard error == nil else {
            Log.error("Failed to connect to the Redis server.")
            callback(false)
            return
          }

          redis.auth("the-password") { error in
            guard error == nil else {
                Log.error("Redis authentication failed.")
                callback(false)
                return
            }
            callback(true)
          }
        }
    }
    else {
        callback(true)
    }
}
```

This code checks if the Kitura-redis handle is already connected to the server; if not, it calls the `connect()` function to connect to the server. The Kitura-redis connect takes a callback as a parameter, as do all the Kitura-redis APIs that communicate with the server. In this case the callback receives an optional error, which is not-nil if an error occurred while connecting to the Redis server. Having connected to the server, the code authenticates to the Redis server, using the `auth()` function, passing in the server's password. If either the `connect()` or the `auth()` function fails, a message is logged using the `Log.error()` function.

For this example, assume that a book is checked out via an HTTP POST request to `/books/:id/checkout`. If you leave out the code that does the actual checkout of a book, then code like the following will be the shell of the RouterHandler:

```
router.post("/books/:id/checkout")
                        { request, response, next in

...

    response.status(.OK)

    connectToRedis() { connected in
        guard connected else {
            next()
            return
        }

        let formatter = DateFormatter()
        formatter.dateFormat = "YYYY-MM-dd"

        let field = formatter.string(from: Date())

        redis.hincr(statisticsKey, field: field,
                                    by: 1) { _, error in
            guard error == nil else {
                Log.error("Failed to increment " +
                        "\(statisticsKey).\(field). " +
                        "Error=\(error)")
                next()
                return
            }

            let dateToRemove =
                Date().addingTimeInterval(-3600 * 24 * 93)
            let fieldToRemove =
                formatter.string(from: dateToRemove)
            redis.hdel(statisticsKey,
                    fields: fieldToRemove) { _, error in
                if error != nil {
                    Log.error("Failed to remove " +
                            "\(fieldToRemove). " +
                                "Error=\(error)")
                }
```

```
                next()
              }
          }
      }
  }
```

The code invokes the `connectToRedis` function to ensure that the library server is connected to the Redis server. If the connect fails, this code simply calls `next()` because the error was already logged. Note that it does not change the status of the response nor does it set the `response.error` field to indicate that an error occurred. The code uses a date formatter to get the current date in the form of year-month-day, to be used as the name of the field in the hash. The Kitura-redis `hincr()` function is invoked to increment the field by one. The `hincr()` function's callback returns two values: the new value of the incremented field and an optional error. In your case, you don't need the new value of the field and so you have passed in the special underscore placeholder for that value. If no error occurs, the code computes the name of the hash field for the data that was stored about three months ago (ninety-three days ago to be precise) and deletes that field from the hash.

Summary

Kitura is a web server framework written in Swift with an un-opinionated set of APIs that help you build real-world application back-end servers. The APIs are type-safe and Swifty in nature to provide a truly consumable framework with which to write your application back-end servers.

It is designed in many areas to be pluggable and therefore extendable by the community.

There will be more contributions from the community, which will make Kitura even greater.

CHAPTER 8

Serverless Programming with Swift

In previous chapters of this book, you've read about Swift being used to implement cloud-hosted services that fit typical traditional server-side functions, such as web applications and data sources. However, there are some newer programming models that have arisen in cloud computing environments that offer distinct benefits for certain workloads. Swift also supports these models, and this chapter covers how the Swift language is used in one of these cloud environments—namely event-driven, or serverless, environments.

Microservices and Serverless Computing

An approach to cloud-native application architecture that has gained popularity and support in recent years involves multiple small, focused microservices being stitched together to form a full application. There are many advantages to structuring an application this way. Although a microservice-based architecture isn't appropriate for every application, when it can be used, there are both economic and technical benefits to be exploited.

Because each microservice component of the overall application is independently deployable, it is easier to tune the application for maximum efficiency at scale than is the case for more monolithic application architectures. If one microservice is more resource intensive and requires more instances under heavy load than the others, then more instances of that one microservice can be deployed while the other microservices run fewer instances. In Figure 8-1 you can compare a microservice approach to a monolithic application where the number of instances of the entire workload must match the instances required to scale the most resource-intensive component. With a microservice architecture, each functional component of the application can be configured to run exactly the number of instances necessary for just that one component.

For some of the same reasons, it is simpler and faster to deliver a focused modification to one of the microservices than to an entire monolithic architecture. In a monolithic application, the entire application, including all components, must be redeployed in order to deliver an update to any single part of the application. The microservices that form an application are loosely coupled with each other via calls to each other's programmatic interfaces (APIs). As long as the update to one microservice does not have an impact on its API, it should be possible to redeploy that microservice without having to change any of the other microservices that make up the application.

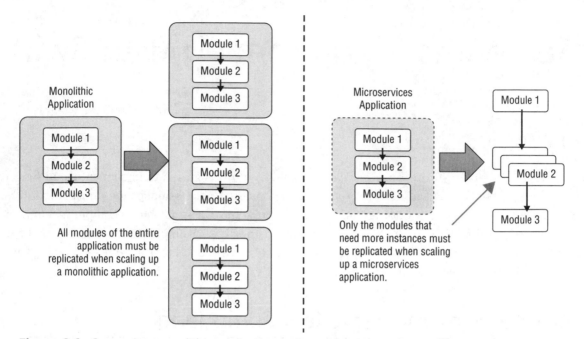

Figure 8-1: Comparing monolithic application scaling with microservices scaling

Of course, a poorly designed and implemented microservices application can negate this advantage. However, it is equally feasible to design a microservices application where the individual microservice components are sufficiently encapsulated from each other to support this targeted and lightweight update strategy. Redeployment of an individual microservice is also typically much faster than for monolithic applications, because the amount of code in a microservice implementation is smaller, and restarting the runtime hosting of the microservice is typically quicker.

The economic advantage of using microservices in a cloud application is that you pay for the minimum cloud resources needed for the aggregate function delivered by the sum of the microservices. If a particular microservice is rarely used, then you can reduce the resources assigned to it and only pay for what's needed to "keep the lights on" in case that microservice gets a call. For the same reasons that a microservice application can be more efficiently tuned for scale, there is more flexibility in how its individual component microservices are hosted to minimize costs. The microservices that form one application do not all have to be running in the same cloud environment!

There are many other advantages to using microservices. Because the ideally designed microservice is small and focused in function, it is easier for developers to understand and troubleshoot. Also, an individual microservice can be implemented using whatever programming language best fits the function delivered by that microservice, allowing for a polyglot style employing multiple languages within the entire application.

Despite the many advantages offered by microservices, there are also drawbacks to consider. These applications can become complex as the number of different individual microservices incorporated into the overall application grows. Although the work of the application developers can become easier using microservices, the work of the operations team for the application can become more complex. Automation of the deployment is more crucial for microservices applications because of the larger number of modules that need to be deployed and the differences in deployment activity in a polyglot environment.

Inter-module communication can be more challenging, or at least require more careful consideration, in a microservices application. Monolithic applications can rely on fast in-process method invocations between modules, and they frequently evolve into rather "chatty" implementations. Because each microservice runs in a separate process, more care is required when designing the communication between them, and the results of poor communication can obliterate any other benefits of choosing microservices. Synchronous inter-process communication between microservices may be easier to develop and troubleshoot, but it can also negatively impact overall application performance. Non-blocking cross-microservice communication is more complicated to design, develop, and troubleshoot.

Serverless Computing Concepts

The philosophy of microservice architecture, along with cloud computing, has given rise to another concept: *serverless* computing (sometimes called event-driven computing). If you extend the cloud computing ideal of elastic resource usage in the direction of scaling *down*, not just scaling up, it is perfectly reasonable to ask why you should have to pay for *any* resources when your application isn't being used at all. With traditional architecture applications, you end up paying for some cloud resources even when no one is using your application, because you must have some application logic running that listens for the requests from your users whenever they do engage with your application.

But suppose that something else, something that was part of the cloud environment supporting your application, did that listening for user requests on your behalf. If some other element of the environment took care of listening for user requests and routing those requests to your application when the requests occurred, then your application code would not need to be running until you actually had real users (and you would also not have to pay for your application resources unless there were real users).

This is the fundamental concept behind event-driven or serverless programming, and it lends itself to microservices application architecture beautifully. If you use event-driven programming with a monolithic cloud application, you have to pay for all of the resources for all of your application logic each time a user request triggers your application to run. But if you can factor your application into multiple small, independent, event-driven microservices, then you only pay for the resources used by the subset of those microservices that the specific user request needs. In other words, the logic to respond to the request has a specific path through the microservices that it traverses, and you only have to pay for the microservices that are in that path. The rest of the microservices available to be used for the application remain "stopped" because no event has occurred that triggers the need for them.

A serverless computing environment offers many advantages for application developers, and it is no wonder that it has become so popular with them:

- As the name implies, there is no server runtime to provision and configure. The system takes care of that detail for you.
- You do not have to worry about maintaining the operating system for the application—patching and updating it.
- Middleware installation and maintenance concerns are eliminated.
- The serverless approach is inherently scalable because each incoming event triggers a separate process to handle that event. This allows the environment to scale the resources up and down for a given application based on demand.
- There is no need to worry about over-provisioning of resources (or under-provisioning either) because you always get exactly the resources devoted to your application that it needs, based on usage driven by the requests of your users.

The key thing about serverless computing that makes it attractive to developers is that they can concentrate solely on application business logic development and avoid spending any time whatsoever dealing with infrastructure or application environment provisioning or deployment. It's an extremely simple and economical way to run an application in the cloud.

The unit of execution for serverless computing must be small, typically the size of a single function. It must also be able to execute in the pre-defined size and the constraints imposed by the serverless cloud environment. The function implemented for the unit of execution of a serverless environment cannot require large amounts of memory, and it should not require a long time to complete its work. The supporting environment in which a serverless task executes only exists for the lifetime of that one task and then disappears. The logic must be stateless and efficient. Many serverless environments have time constraints on the tasks that run within them and will terminate a task if it remains running for too long.

Because of the constraints of serverless computing, it is ideally suited to implement a microservices architecture application. Each microservice can be implemented by a single serverless task, and there are a variety of mechanisms that can be employed to invoke a serverless function. In addition to direct invocation from the end user, a timer can be configured to wake up at regular intervals and invoke the serverless logic. Many data sources can be configured to issue notifications when data is added, modified, or removed, and these notifications can be the source that drives invocation of a serverless action each time the data source is updated. In fact, there is an almost endless list of sources that could be used as the trigger to run a serverless task.

Another advantage of serverless computing is its inherent parallelism. A large processing job can be divided into multiple smaller chunks, and all of those chunks can be submitted to the serverless environment where they will be simultaneously executed for much faster job completion. A good practice when implementing serverless tasks is to create them assuming that they will be run in parallel.

Of course, no approach is perfect for all situations. In addition to living within the memory and compute restraints imposed by the serverless environment, individual serverless tasks should not be long running. If the task takes more than a handful of seconds to complete, it will run afoul of the timeout constraints imposed by its supporting environment. The length of execution time for a serverless task includes time required to start up and initialize its supporting runtime environment (language runtime, JVM, or container) before any application logic is able to run. This environment initialization time is dependent on the language used to implement the serverless task and also the amount of code written.

Serverless functions also need to be stateless, which eliminates some types of applications. Although you can certainly store the state of a serverless request in some form of persistent file or object storage, the time required for your serverless task to read and write that state data further reduces the time available to perform the intended business logic.

A common technique of employing a fast in-memory cache or a cache held in the client request header is of little use in a serverless computing environment because the cache only lives as long as a single serverless task and is destroyed as soon as that one task finishes. Use of an external cache may address this drawback but it adds overhead and, much like the mitigation for persistent state data, may not be feasible within the time constraints of a serverless task execution cycle.

There are several cloud providers that deliver an event-driven or serverless code environment. Amazon offers Lambda and Google offers Cloud Functions. Microsoft Azure Functions is a serverless cloud environment and IBM offers an open source serverless environment as part of the IBM Bluemix cloud platform: OpenWhisk.

OpenWhisk

OpenWhisk is an open source project that provides a distributed compute service to execute application logic in response to events. It delivers an event-driven platform within which you can execute code (typically a microservice) in response to the occurrence of some event.

Like other serverless environments, OpenWhisk hides the infrastructural complexity and allows you, the developer, to simply provide the code that you want to be executed. It provides you with exactly the resources (not more, not less) that you need, and only charges you for code that is truly executing.

OpenWhisk offers a flexible programming model that includes support for several languages such as Node.js and Swift. You can even execute any kind of custom logic, implemented in any manner, as long as it can be configured in a Docker container. This allows small, agile teams to reuse existing skills and to develop in a polyglot fashion. It also provides you with tools to chain together the building blocks you've developed. One of the most unique aspects of the OpenWhisk serverless environment is that it is open source and can run anywhere to avoid vendor lock-in that is common for other serverless solutions.

There are several key OpenWhisk architectural concepts:

- **Triggers**—A class of events emitted by a wide variety of event sources.
- **Actions**—Individual units of execution that encapsulate the actual code to be run whenever a given event triggers it. The implementation of an action can invoke other services accessible within the same surrounding cloud environment or any number of external services.
- **Rules**—An association between a trigger and an action.
- **Packages**—Describe external services in a uniform manner.

Figure 8-2 illustrates the basic architecture for OpenWhisk.

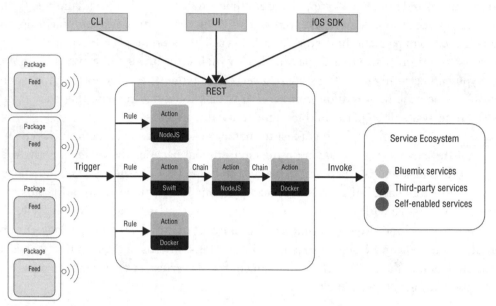

Figure 8-2: The basic OpenWhisk architecture

Setting Up OpenWhisk

You can access the open source project for OpenWhisk at `https://github.com/openwhisk/openwhisk`. You can set up an OpenWhisk environment on your local development computer or on any remote server or cloud system where you have access to login as a user. The open source project documentation includes instructions for setting up environments on macOS and Linux (Ubuntu) systems. While there are a variety of ways to create your own environment to experiment with OpenWhisk, why not just use the free cloud-hosted OpenWhisk service in the IBM Bluemix cloud platform? The service is free for low-traffic applications and easy to get up and running within just a few minutes.

Several interesting and educational OpenWhisk GitHub repositories are located under the parent repository, `https://github.com/openwhisk`. These repositories represent projects implemented in multiple different languages besides Swift. An especially valuable group of sample applications is included in the Awesome OpenWhisk project at `https://github.com/openwhisk/awesome-openwhisk`.

The Bluemix OpenWhisk Sandbox

Let's quickly do something concrete using Swift and OpenWhisk. The easiest way to do this is to use the version of OpenWhisk hosted as a service in the IBM Bluemix cloud platform. (Note: the following steps assume that you have a Bluemix account.)

In your browser, log in to your Bluemix account and click the Catalog link at the top of the page. In the IBM Bluemix catalog, locate the OpenWhisk service, as shown in Figure 8-3. Click the OpenWhisk icon and create an instance of the service.

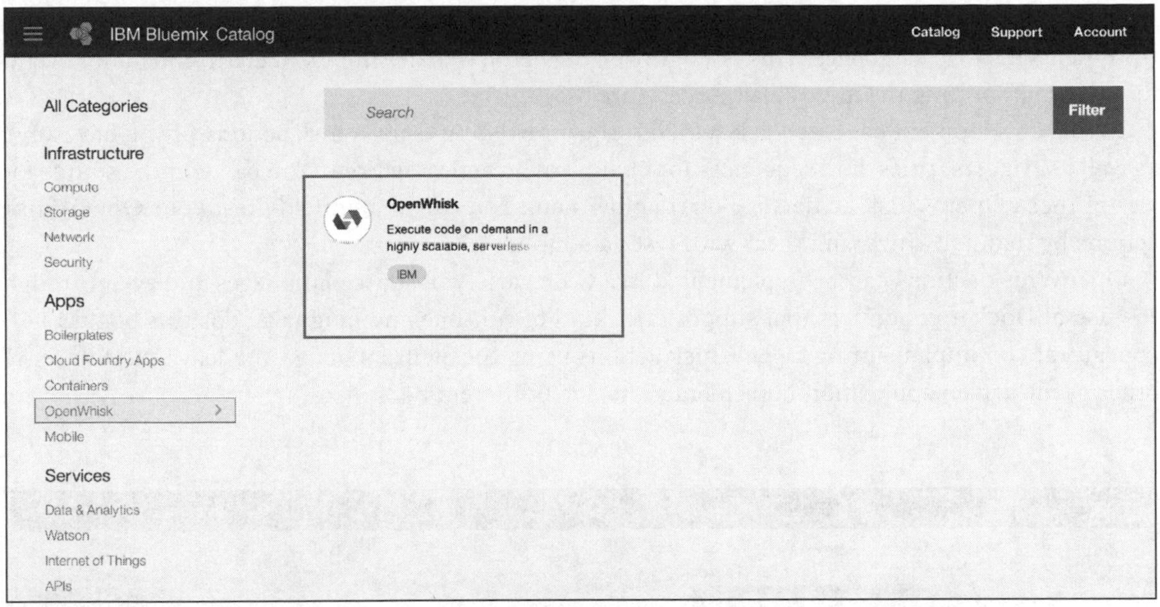

Figure 8-3: The OpenWhisk service icon in the IBM Bluemix Catalog page

Once you have created the OpenWhisk service instance, you can click the icon again to switch to the OpenWhisk home page, as shown in Figure 8-4.

Figure 8-4: The home page for the OpenWhisk service in IBM Bluemix

Click the Develop in your Browser button on the left side of the OpenWhisk home page to display the OpenWhisk Develop page. This is a lightweight, web-based development environment for event-driven programming in OpenWhisk (see Figure 8-5).

In this development page, you can see a list of your existing OpenWhisk actions (if you have any), as well as triggers, rules, and sequences (or chains) of serverless actions. You can edit the source for any of these OpenWhisk artifacts and redeploy them. You can also quickly test your OpenWhisk actions by manually invoking them with test data input.

OpenWhisk actions can be implemented in a wide variety of source languages and even through the use of Docker containers that support any kind of runtime and language. For this book, I will concentrate on implementing OpenWhisk actions using the Swift language and leave the subject of other event-driven application implementations for a different book.

Figure 8-5: The Develop page for OpenWhisk event-driven programming

Swift and OpenWhisk

You can implement event-driven microservices in OpenWhisk using the Swift programming language. In order to accomplish this, you write the logic for your OpenWhisk action using Swift instead of one of the other supported languages.

A different approach for deploying a serverless microservice implemented in Swift is to package the Swift code in a Docker container (see Chapter 5) and deploy that container as the OpenWhisk action. In this chapter, I will focus on writing snippets of Swift code and deploying those small functions as OpenWhisk actions, rather than using the container approach.

Using the Web-Based OpenWhisk Tools

To begin with, you can quickly create an OpenWhisk action in Swift by exploiting the built-in OpenWhisk Develop web page tools for the service in Bluemix. Simply click the Create an Action button in the upper-left corner of the Develop page, as shown in Figure 8-6.

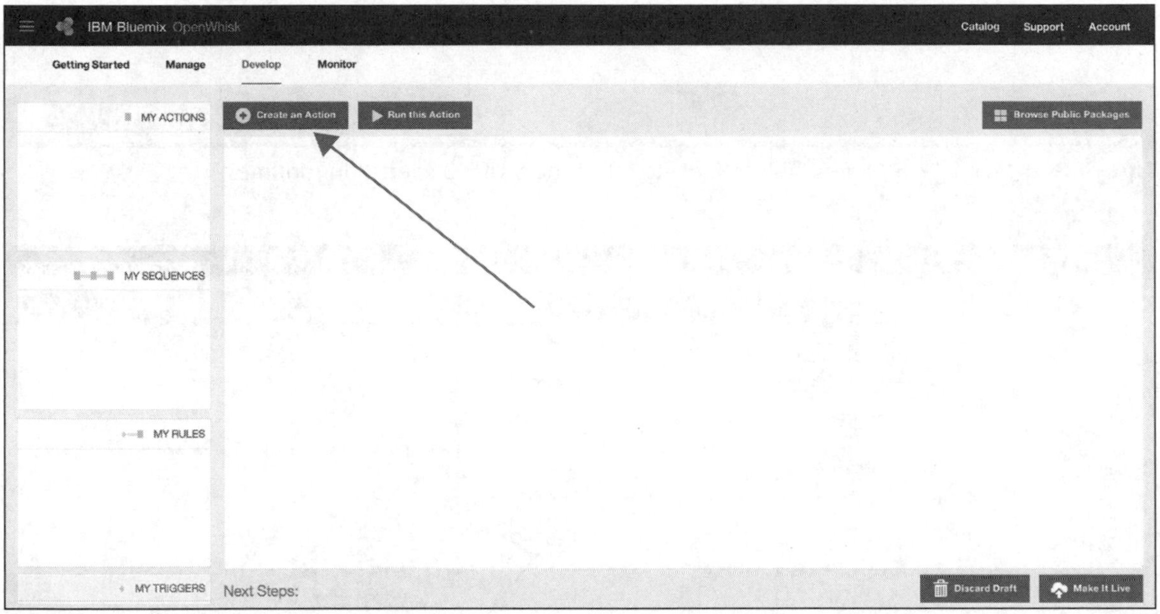

Figure 8-6: Click the Create an Action button to begin the process.

When you click the Create an Action button, you see the Create An Action web page where you can name your action and specify its runtime. For this exercise, name your action "my1st-swift-action" and select the Swift v3 runtime to use for this action, as shown in Figure 8-7.

After naming your action and selecting the Swift v3 runtime, use the drop-down menu on this page to select the "Hello World in Swift" sample starting template, as shown in Figure 8-8. Then click the Create Action button in the lower-right corner of the page.

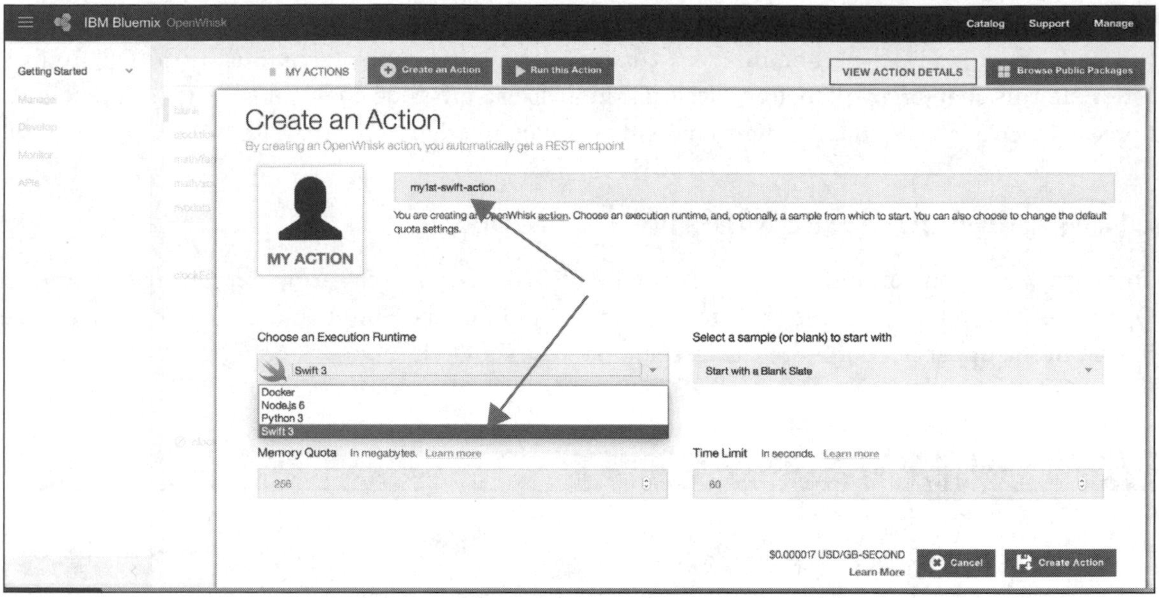

Figure 8-7: Name your OpenWhisk action and select the Swift v3 execution runtime.

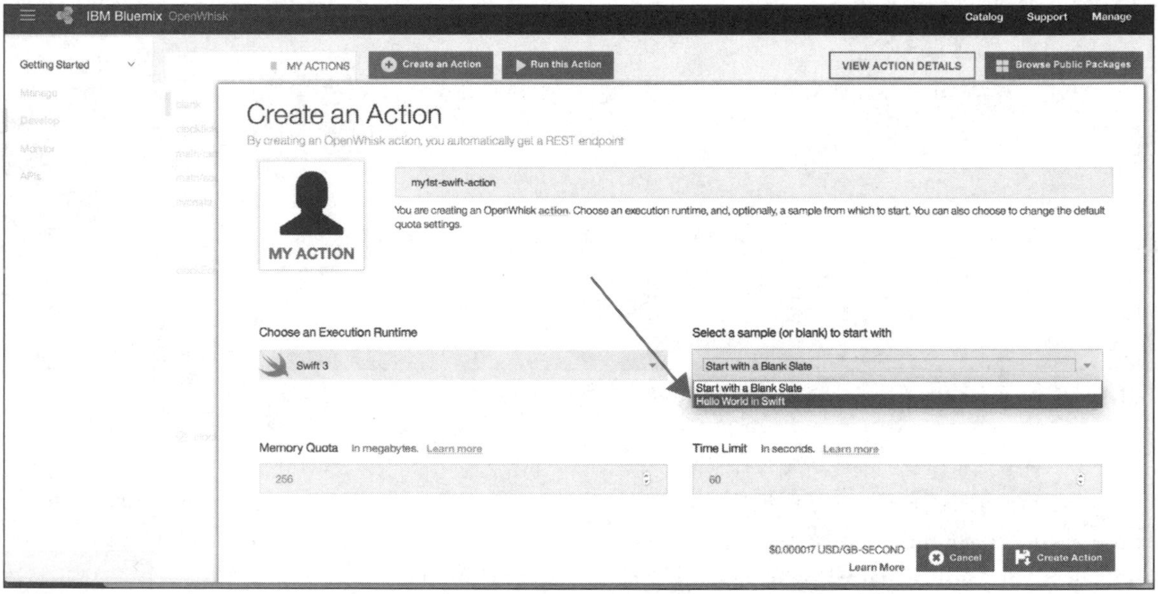

Figure 8-8: Select the sample action template for your Swift OpenWhisk action.

After you click the Create Action button, the OpenWhisk editor page opens, displaying the source code for your OpenWhisk action, as shown in Figure 8-9. Note the indicator in the upper-right corner of the editor window that tells you that this is a Swift v3 action, and the other indicator in the lower-right corner that tells you that this code is now live in the OpenWhisk environment and can be invoked.

```
≡  ◆ IBM Bluemix OpenWhisk                                    Catalog   Support   Manage

Getting Started  ˅              ▥ MY ACTIONS      ⊕ Create an Action    VIEW ACTION DETAILS    ▦ Browse Public Packages
Manage
                      math/random              my1st-swift-action                          SWIFT 3 ACTION
Develop
                      math/square              1 ▾ /**
Monitor                                        2   *
                      my1st-swift-action       3   * main() will be invoked when you Run This Action.
APIs                                           4   *
                                               5   * @param Whisk actions accept a single parameter,
                                               6   *         which must be a JSON object.
                      ▥-▥-▥ MY SEQUENCES       7   *
                                               8   * In this case, the params variable will look like:
                      clockEcho                9   *      { "message": "xxxx" }
                                               10  *
                                               11  * @return which must be a JSON object.
                                               12  *      It will be the output of this action.
                                               13  *
                                               14  */
                         ⊷▥ MY RULES          15 ▾ func main(args: [String:Any]) -> [String:Any] {
                                               16 ▾     if let message = args["message"] as? String {
                      ⊘ clockRule              17           print("parameter passed in is: \(message)")
                                               18           return [ "greeting" : "Hello \(message)!" ]

                                                                       This Code Is Live! View REST Endpoint
                         ⊹ MY TRIGGERS   Next Steps:        Link into a Sequence    Automate this Action
        ‹
```

Figure 8-9: The OpenWhisk action editor window with Swift v3 source code

Take a look at the source code for this Swift OpenWhisk action, visible in the editor. This is standard Swift 3.0 code and you can make changes to this starting template using the web browser–based action editor. Before you make any source code changes to this Swift action, let's run it once as-is. Click the Run this Action button above the editor window. You're taken to the Invoking an Action page in the browser, as shown in Figure 8-10.

Figure 8-10: The Invoking an Action web page for your Swift v3 OpenWhisk action

On this page, you identify which OpenWhisk action to run and provide the input values for the action, if any are needed. The input values are specified in JSON format near the bottom of the page. In this case, the default input value is "choose a value" For now, don't alter that input value. Click the Run with this Value button in the lower-right corner of the page.

Clicking the Run with this Value button opens the Invocation Console for OpenWhisk (shown in Figure 8-11), where the output from running the action is visible.

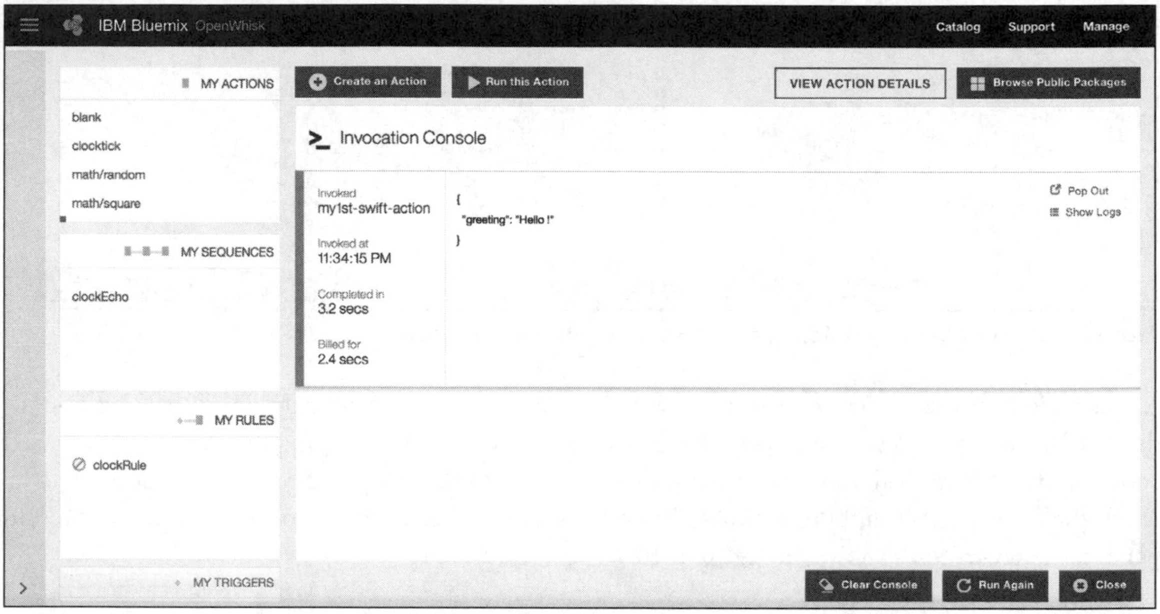

Figure 8-11: The Invocation Console for your example Swift OpenWhisk action

The Invocation Console shows you which action was executed, the time it was invoked, how long it took to execute, and the resulting JSON output from the action. Congratulations! You've just executed your first Swift serverless microservice.

Let's invoke the action with a different input value than the default. Click the Run this Action button at the top of the page. Your web browser shows the Invoking an Action page. Change the text in the JSON Input area from "choose a value" to "from planet Swift". Then click the Run with this Value button in the lower-right corner of the page, as shown in Figure 8-12.

Your web browser switches back to the Invocation Console and the output from the action now reflects the new input value, as shown in Figure 8-13.

Now let's put some debug print statements in the action source code so that some logging output is produced when the action is invoked. Click the my1st-swift-action link in the MY ACTIONS list

Figure 8-12: Change the input value to be sent to the action.

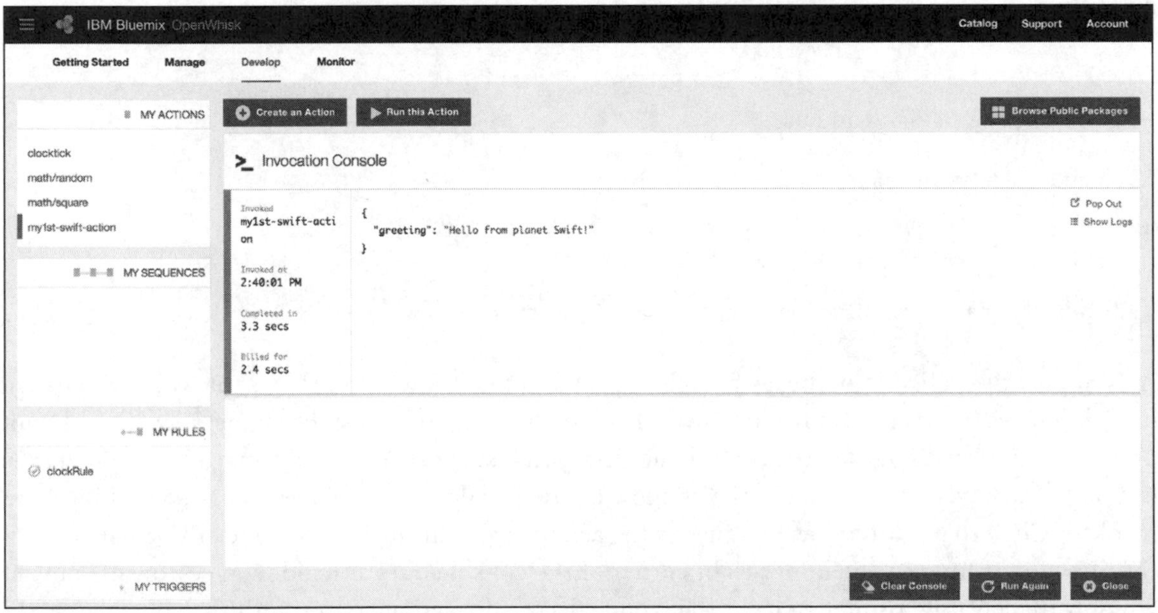

Figure 8-13: Output displayed for another invocation of the Swift action

in the top-left corner of the page. This returns your web browser to the action source code editor. Add two Swift print statements to the source code, as shown in Figure 8-14.

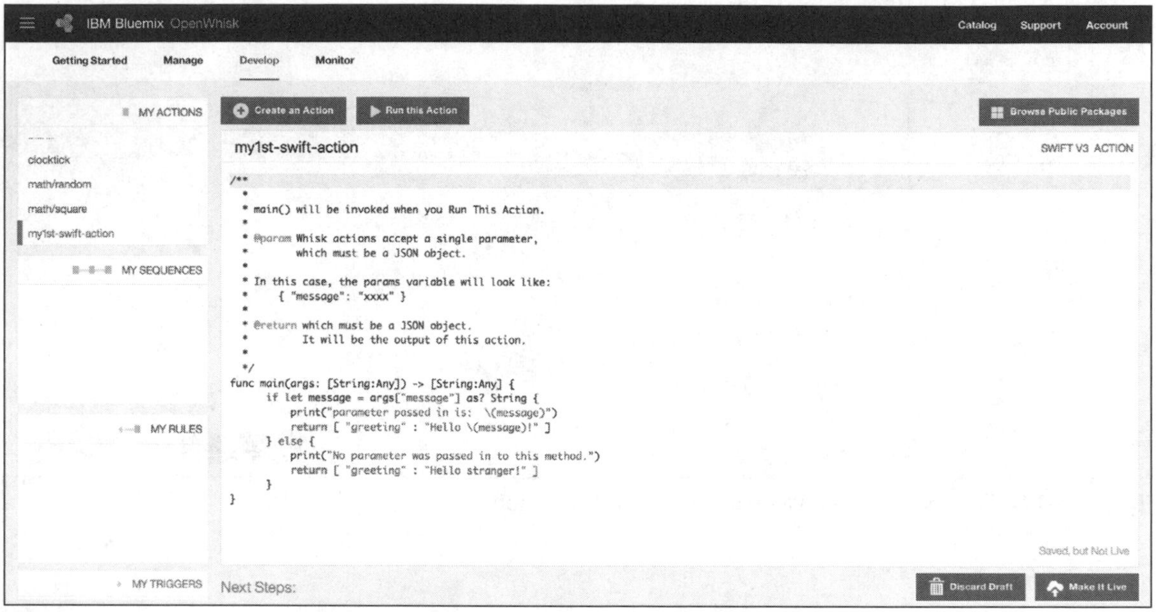

Figure 8-14: Add print statements to the action source code.

The two statements to add are

```
print("parameter passed in is:  \(message)")
```

and

```
print("No parameter was passed in to this method.")
```

Note that the indicator in the lower-right corner of the editor window shows that the code change has been saved, but is not yet live in OpenWhisk. If you were to invoke the action now, it would not produce output that reflected the code change that you just made. You need to click the Make It Live button in the lower-right corner of the window in order to deploy this code change so that it can be invoked. Click that button now and invoke the action again. In the Invocation Console panel, click the Show Logs link, in the upper-right corner of the console output window. The console output window displays the print statement that you added to the action source with the value passed in for this specific action invocation, as shown in Figure 8-15.

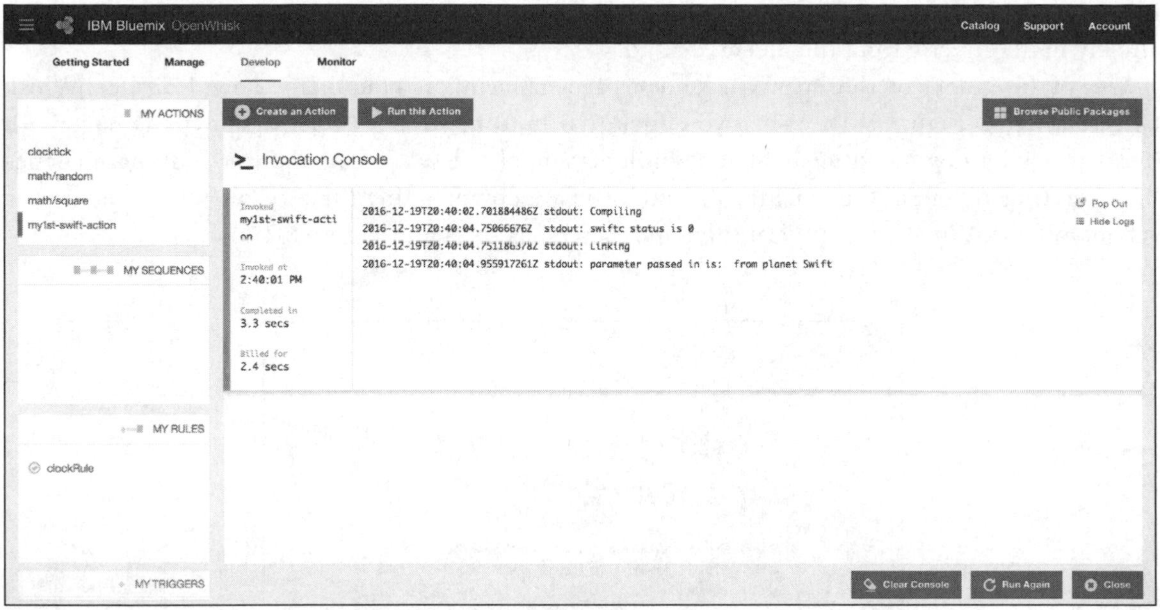

Figure 8-15: The Console output window showing debug print log data

Using the web-based OpenWhisk development tools is a great way to get started quickly. You can experiment with simple actions implemented in Swift and rapidly iterate on the action implementation, redeploying and testing the action quickly as you modify it. These web-based OpenWhisk tools can also be handy for quick patches to actions that are currently live and need immediate modification.

However, for more robust Swift code development that is integrated with a source code control system and where a team of developers is involved, it is more effective to use either a separate command line editor or one of the modern Integrated Development Environment tools such as Apple Xcode.

Command Line OpenWhisk

The command line tool for OpenWhisk, called wsk, is important to learn and understand because many of the more sophisticated development tools that support OpenWhisk build their support on top of wsk. The version of the OpenWhisk CLI tool that you use must be compatible with the version of OpenWhisk that you are running in the cloud (or on your own private computer). The best way to ensure this is to download and build the matching CLI version on your local development machine yourself. The CLI code is available in the same GitHub repository as the rest of the open-source OpenWhisk source code, in a subdirectory: `https://github.com/openwhisk/openwhisk/tree/master/tools/cli`.

You can download the CLI tool source code and build the tool yourself by following the instructions in the `README.md` file in the repository. However, if you are running your OpenWhisk actions in the IBM Bluemix cloud platform, an easier way to get the command line tool is to download it, already built, directly from the Bluemix cloud.

One of the options on the OpenWhisk home page in Bluemix is a button to "Download OpenWhisk CLI," shown in Figure 8-16. When you click that button, your browser displays the page with instructions for downloading an already-built version of the `wsk` command line tool that matches the operating system of the machine to which you are downloading the tool, and also matches the version of OpenWhisk currently running in Bluemix, as shown in Figure 8-17.

Figure 8-16: The button on the OpenWhisk home page for downloading the CLI

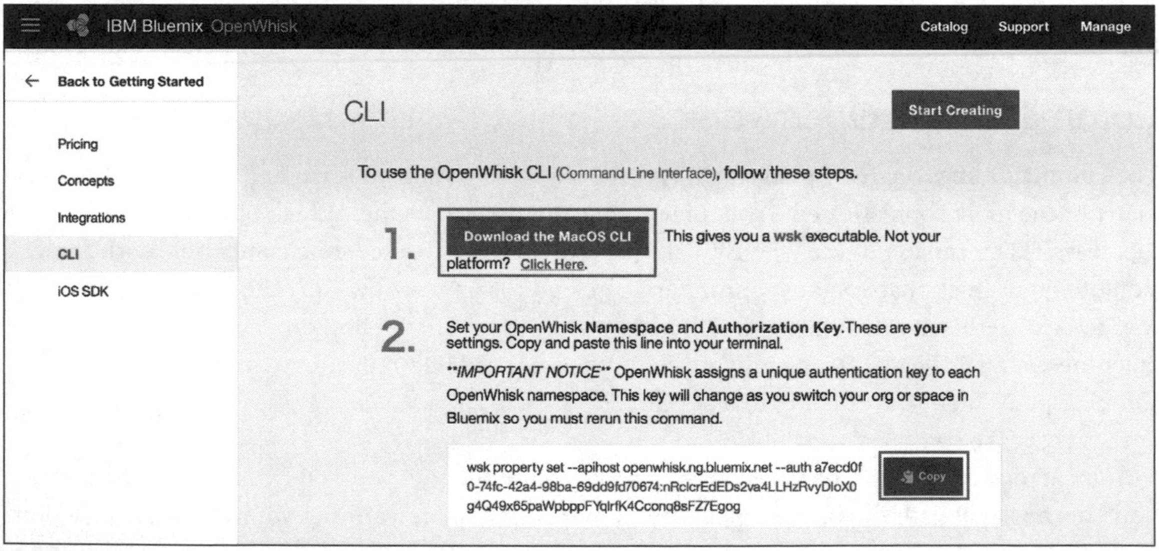

Figure 8-17: The Bluemix web page to access the OpenWhisk CLI

When you click the Download button in Step 1 of the instructions on this page, your browser downloads a compressed archive file containing the tool. For instance, for the macOS development workstation, this file is named `OpenWhisk_CLI-mac.zip`. When you uncompress (or unzip) this file after you download it, the wsk binary is extracted.

Make sure that the extracted wsk program is in a directory on your command line PATH environment variable, so that it will be found when you try to run it. Test to make sure that the command is found and executes by typing **wsk -h** on the command line.

```
$ wsk -h

     ___            ___ ___                     _     _     _
    /\  \          /   \  \__         ___      | |   (_)   | |
   /\  \_\  \     |     \   \'--.    \    \     | |    _   _| |  _
  /  \___\  \  /  |__|  |   |__/ .---' |   \    | |   | | / / | / /
  \  / /\   \/   \___  /  .---\  |__|  |   |    | |___| | \ \  _\ \
   \/_/  \___\/ tm    |_|                             |_|
```

```
Usage:
  wsk [command]

Available Commands:
  action           work with actions
  activation       work with activations
  package          work with packages
  rule             work with rules
  trigger          work with triggers
  sdk              work with the sdk
  property         work with whisk properties
  namespace        work with namespaces
  list             list entities in the current namespace
  api-experimental work with APIs

Flags:
     —apihost HOST        whisk API HOST
     —apiversion VERSION  whisk API VERSION
  -u,—auth KEY            authorization KEY
  -d,—debug               debug level output
  -i,—insecure            bypass certificate checking
  -v,—verbose             verbose output

Use "wsk [command]—help" for more information about a command.
$
```

Before you can effectively use the `wsk` command line tool, you need to set your authentication key for the target OpenWhisk service in the command line environment properties. This allows each invocation of the tool to authenticate with the cloud service before the command is executed. You can do this on the command line using the `wsk property set` command. Bluemix makes it easy for you to obtain the correct command syntax by preparing the exact command in the web page where you downloaded the binary. Just click the Copy button on that page and paste the copied command into your command line window.

```
$ wsk property set-apihost openwhisk.ng.bluemix.net-auth <big-long-auth-key-string>
ok: whisk auth set to <big-long-auth-key-string>
ok: whisk API host set to openwhisk.ng.bluemix.net
$
```

Now each invocation of the wsk command will interact with your instance of the OpenWhisk service in IBM Bluemix. Each Bluemix namespace has a unique authentication key associated with it. This key will change as you switch namespaces in Bluemix, so you must rerun this command if you switch your Bluemix organization or space. If you had previously set a namespace in your command environment, you must unset it to avoid misdirection of the command. If you had not previously set a namespace, then you do not need to set or unset it, because the namespace will be identified from the authentication key.

```
$ wsk property unset-namespace
ok: whisk namespace unset; the default value of _ will be used.
$
```

If you followed the exercise earlier in this chapter to create a few Swift language OpenWhisk actions using the web developer tools, you can see a listing of those actions by executing the wsk list command.

```
$ wsk list
Entities in namespace: default
packages
actions
/leighw@us.ibm.com_dev/my1st-swift-action                              private
/leighw@us.ibm.com_dev/swifthello                                      private
triggers
rules
$
```

If the wsk list command succeeds, try executing a synchronous echo action test. This echo action is part of the default OpenWhisk system and should always be available and succeed. Use the wsk action invoke command as shown here.

```
$ wsk action invoke /whisk.system/utils/echo -p message hello-blocking-result
{
    "message": "hello"
}
$
```

The `wsk action invoke` command does just what you would expect: It triggers the execution of the named action. Several other pre-defined actions are available in the whisk.system packages. You can get a list of the pre-defined system packages via the command line.

```
$ wsk package list /whisk.system
packages
/whisk.system/pushnotifications                          shared
/whisk.system/github                                     shared
/whisk.system/weather                                    shared
/whisk.system/utils                                      shared
/whisk.system/system                                     shared
/whisk.system/watson-speechToText                        shared
/whisk.system/slack                                      shared
/whisk.system/watson-textToSpeech                        shared
/whisk.system/samples                                    shared
/whisk.system/websocket                                  shared
/whisk.system/watson-translator                          shared
/whisk.system/watson                                     shared
/whisk.system/alarms                                     shared
/whisk.system/messaging                                  shared
/whisk.system/cloudant                                   shared
/whisk.system/util                                       shared
$
```

Let's take a closer look at what is in the whisk.system/utils package.

```
$ wsk package get-summary /whisk.system/utils
package /whisk.system/utils: Building blocks that format and assemble data
 action /whisk.system/utils/head: Extract prefix of an array
    (parameters: lines, num)
 action /whisk.system/utils/cat: Concatenates input into a string
    (parameters: lines)
 action /whisk.system/utils/date: Current date and time
 action /whisk.system/utils/split: Split a string into an array
    (parameters: payload, separator)
 action /whisk.system/utils/sort: Sorts an array
    (parameters: lines)
 action /whisk.system/utils/echo: Returns the input
    (parameters: payload)
$
```

You can see all the actions in that package, along with the parameters that each action accepts. OpenWhisk packages are a mechanism for organizing groups of actions that are all related to one particular topic or solution. You can think of packages in a similar way to the concept of how folders are used in file systems to organize and logically arrange files.

Now try to execute one of the Swift actions that you created using the web developer tools.

```
$ wsk action invoke my1st-swift-action—blocking—result
{
    "greeting": "Hello !"
}
$
$ wsk action invoke my1st-swift-action -p message "Dear Reader" —blocking—result
{
    "greeting": "Hello Dear Reader!"
}
$
```

Notice that the -p flag on the command line is how you pass arguments (parameters) into the action. After the -p you put the name of the argument (message in this example) and after that, you put the value that you want assigned to that argument (Dear Reader in this example).

The—blocking flag is important because it tells the wsk command to wait (block) until a response has been returned by the OpenWhisk task. Without that flag on the command line, the wsk command will immediately return with an output telling you that it invoked the action in a "fire and forget" mode. The only command line output that you see is the id string for the OpenWhisk action instance that is executing as a result of the command.

```
$ wsk action invoke swifthello -p message "Where are you" —result
ok: invoked /_/swifthello with id 3da0cc7f5fd24474a90d412d85bdc6cd
$
```

Non-blocking or asynchronous invocation of an OpenWhisk action is useful and common. But when using the command line tool, you will most often use the synchronous or blocking mode of execution because most of the time you will want to see the result of the action once it has completed.

The—result flag on the wsk command is also important for managing the output returned by the OpenWhisk action as the result of its execution. The full response returned by the execution of any OpenWhisk action contains many components, but you usually don't want to see all of them printed as the result of invoking the action.

```
$ wsk action invoke my1st-swift-action —blocking
ok: invoked /_/my1st-swift-action with id ce3379d0a2a1493ca4f96255a4d61b0b
{
    "namespace": "leighw@us.ibm.com_dev",
    "name": "my1st-swift-action",
    "version": "0.0.2",
    "subject": "leighw@us.ibm.com",
    "activationId": "ce3379d0a2a1493ca4f96255a4d61b0b",
    "start": 1482111701143,
    "end": 1482111703746,
    "duration": 2603,
    "response": {
        "status": "success",
```

```
            "statusCode": 0,
            "success": true,
            "result": {
                "greeting": "Hello stranger!"
            }
        },
        "logs": [],
        "annotations": [
            {
                "key": "limits",
                "value": {
                    "logs": 10,
                    "memory": 256,
                    "timeout": 60000
                }
            },
            {
                "key": "path",
                "value": "leighw@us.ibm.com_dev/my1st-swift-action"
            }
        ],
        "publish": false
    }
$
```

Thus far, I have used simple actions to illustrate how to navigate the OpenWhisk environment. Now, let's try a more involved example that begins to show the real power of a serverless system.

A More Involved Example

In this exercise, you'll write a small Swift module that will be your OpenWhisk action logic. You'll deploy that action and set it up to run automatically every 10 seconds. Then you'll add that action to a longer chain of actions (an OpenWhisk sequence), where one action takes its input from the output of the previous action.

First, use your favorite code editor to create a file named ClockAction.swift, and add the following code into the file:

```swift
func main(args:[String:Any]) -> [String:Any] {
    var result:[String:Any] = ["payload": ""]

    let currentDateTime = Date()
    let formatter = DateFormatter()
    formatter.timeStyle = .medium
    var str = formatter.string(from: currentDateTime)
    str = "[\(str)]"
    result = ["payload": "\(str)"]

    return result
}
```

This code just returns a result that is the current time from the system on which it executes. Save the file and use it as the source for a new OpenWhisk action that you create.

```
$ wsk action create clocktick ClockAction.swift
ok: created action clocktick
$
```

You can test that the action performs the intended task:

```
$ wsk action invoke clocktick-blocking-result
{
    "payload": "[10:54:55 PM]"
}
$
```

Next, use the `wsk trigger create` command to define a trigger that will fire every 10 seconds. This is similar to configuring a cron job on a Linux system. In fact, the syntax for the time interval that you use in the trigger creation command is the same as that used for a cron job setup. You'll use the alarm action that is a default part of the OpenWhisk environment, part of the /whisk.system package. You can examine the action and its parameters from the command line.

```
$ wsk package get-summary /whisk.system/alarms
package /whisk.system/alarms: Alarms and periodic utility
   (parameters: cron, trigger_payload)
 feed   /whisk.system/alarms/alarm: Fire trigger when alarm occurs
$
```

Use the alarm action as the feed for the new trigger that you create, named every10.

```
$ wsk trigger create every10-feed /whisk.system/alarms/alarm -p cron "*/10 * * * *"
-p trigger_payload ""
ok: invoked /whisk.system/alarms/alarm with id 205c30c631454ac5b8b4466ecc0a423f
{
    "namespace": "leighw@us.ibm.com_dev",
    "name": "alarm",
    "version": "0.0.99",
    "subject": "leighw@us.ibm.com",
    "activationId": "205c30c631454ac5b8b4466ecc0a423f",
    "start": 1482173474930,
    "end": 1482173474984,
    "duration": 54,
    "response": {
        "status": "success",
        "statusCode": 0,
        "success": true,
        "result": {}
```

```
        },
        "logs": [],
        "annotations": [
            {
                "key": "limits",
                "value": {
                    "logs": 10,
                    "memory": 256,
                    "timeout": 60000
                }
            },
            {
                "key": "path",
                "value": "whisk.system/alarms/alarm"
            }
        ],
        "publish": false
}
ok: created trigger every10
$
```

Now that you've created the trigger that will fire every 10 seconds, you need to tie that event to an action to execute. This is done by creating a new rule that tells OpenWhisk to invoke a specific action whenever a named trigger fires.

```
$ wsk rule create clockRule every10 clocktick
ok: created rule clockRule
$
```

The automated sequence is now set up and running. You can visually inspect the configuration of the flow in the web page for OpenWhisk development. In the Develop web page, click the clockRule link, under the MY RULES heading; you should see a similar layout to that shown in Figure 8-18.

You can switch to the Monitor web page to see the ongoing activity that is generated every 10 seconds, as shown in Figure 8-19.

Click the expansion arrows in the upper-right corner of the Activity Log frame to display the log in the entire browser window, as shown in Figure 8-20.

You can see the sequence of trigger firing, rule activation, and action invocation occur every 10 seconds in the activity log, along with the amount of time the action took to execute.

You can add more actions to this automated chain of execution. You'll now create a new action that is a sequence of the clocktick action followed by the echo action that is part of the OpenWhisk system. Use the—sequence flag on the wsk action create command.

```
$ wsk action create clockEcho—sequence clocktick,/whisk.system/utils/echo
ok: created action clockEcho
$
```

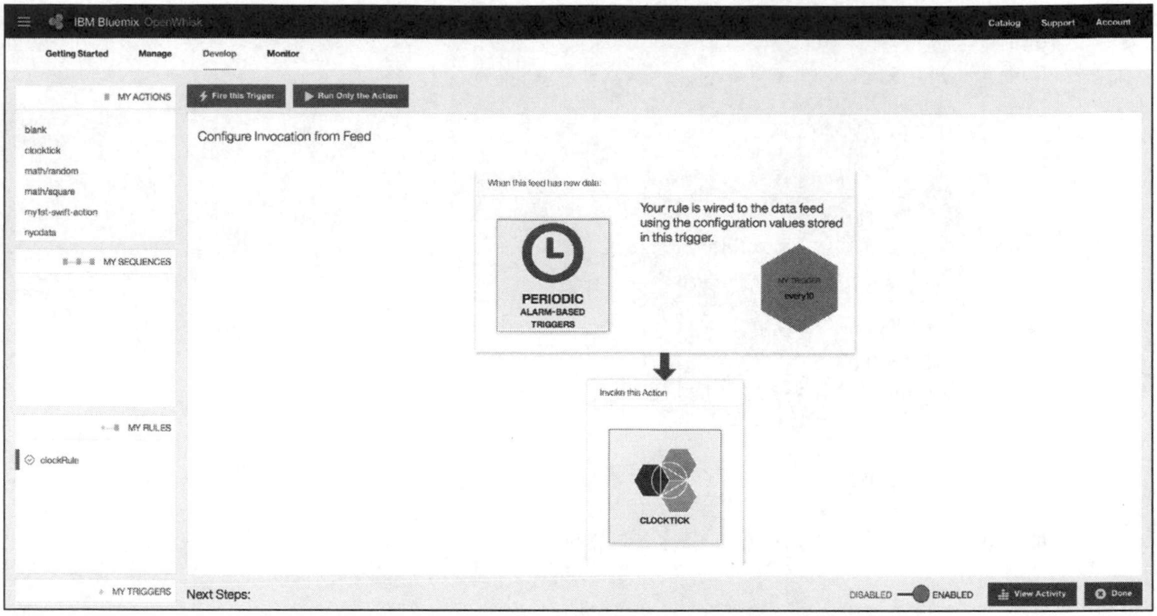

Figure 8-18: A graphical representation of the automated OpenWhisk action trigger

Figure 8-19: Monitoring your OpenWhisk activity in the Bluemix console

Figure 8-20: The expanded Activity Log view for automated OpenWhisk actions

The output produced by the clocktick action is fed into the echo action when this clockEcho sequence is invoked. Let's change the rule that you defined earlier for what happens when the every10 trigger fires. You'll change that rule to invoke the clockEcho action instead of the clocktick action. First you have to disable the existing clockRule rule so it can be modified. The wsk rule update command will fail if applied to an enabled rule.

```
$ wsk rule disable clockRule
ok: disabled rule clockRule
$
```

Next, update the rule to invoke the clockEcho action instead of the clocktick action.

```
$ wsk rule update clockRule every10 clockEcho
ok: updated rule clockRule
$
```

Now, enable the clockRule rule so that it is activated once again, linking the every10 trigger to the clockEcho action.

```
$ wsk rule enable clockRule
ok: enabled rule clockRule
$
```

You can see the new behavior by viewing the clockRule graphical representation in the OpenWhisk Develop web page, as shown in Figure 8-21.

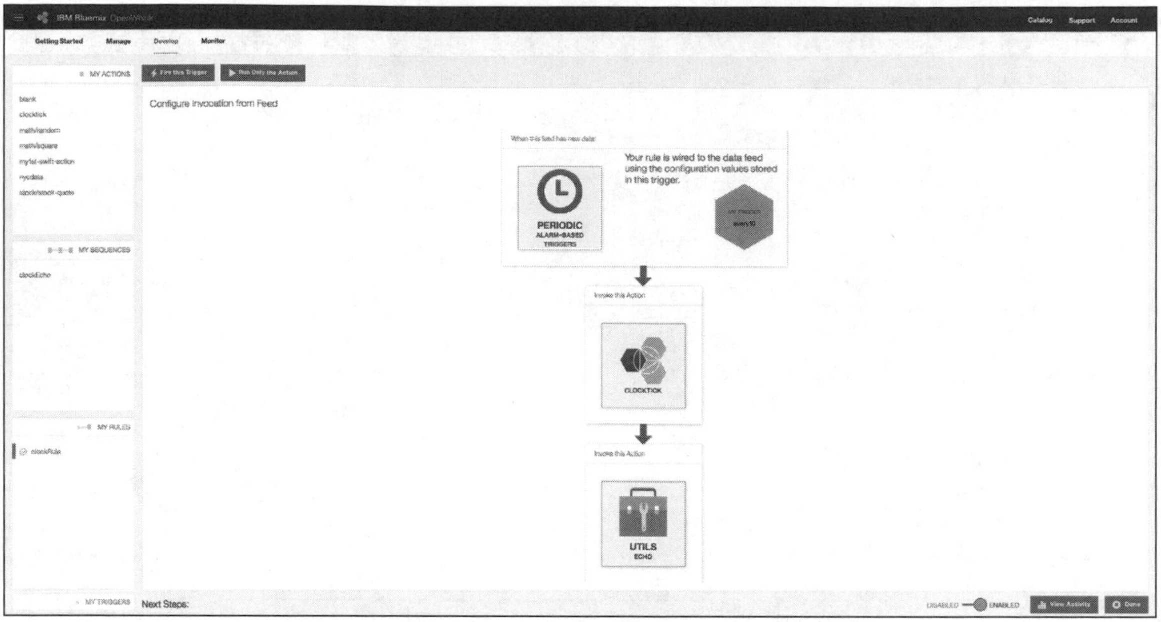

Figure 8-21: A graphical representation of the new sequence of multiple actions

Now, look at the Activity Log again, in the Monitor web page. As Figure 8-22 shows, the activity log now shows the echo action being invoked along with the `clocktick` action every 10 seconds.

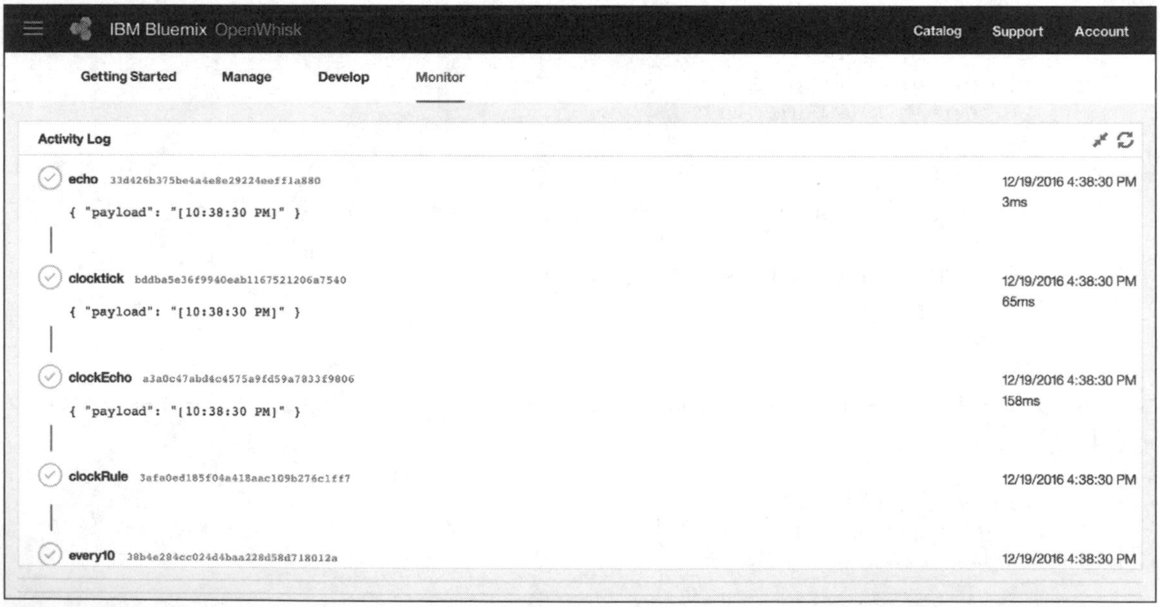

Figure 8-22: The Activity Log showing the echo action in the sequence of automated actions

Now that you've explored the basics of writing serverless OpenWhisk actions in Swift, there are dozens of examples and projects that you can examine and learn from. The Swift@IBM GitHub repository (`https://github.com/IBM-Swift`) has several valuable projects, and you'll find still other projects to study in the Awesome OpenWhisk project repository (`https://github.com/openwhisk/awesome-openwhisk`).

The examples I used in this chapter employed relatively simple Swift modules, but some of the sample projects have more extensive Swift code actions. Some developers use the Swift sandbox (see Chapter 2) to initially write and test their action code before deploying it to OpenWhisk. Remember that you can use almost any business logic written in Swift for a serverless action.

Summary

For highly scalable and economic cloud-native applications, an event-driven, serverless microservices architecture is often an excellent choice. The OpenWhisk service that is part of the IBM Bluemix cloud platform offers an open-serverless environment with many advantages, including first-class support for the Swift language. You can write your serverless actions in Swift and deploy them without having to deal with infrastructure setup and maintenance. It's easy to link your Swift actions with dozens of other pre-built serverless actions from other services in the Bluemix platform. And the applications that you build with Swift serverless actions will scale automatically, as the volume of users increases.

You can develop Swift serverless action code using the Bluemix OpenWhisk web development pages, or you can simply write the Swift action code using your favorite code editor. There is even an open source project to develop the tooling necessary for using Xcode to write and deploy your Swift actions directly to OpenWhisk. This alternative is especially appealing because your serverless Swift actions may actually originate from Swift code written for a mobile app or other client-side code in Xcode.

As OpenWhisk, and serverless computing in general, matures and gains greater support, the ability to assemble fast and inexpensive innovative solutions from multiple microservices will expand and offer great choices for developers. Your imagination is rapidly becoming your only limitation!

CHAPTER 9

Over the Horizon:
Where Do We Go from Here?

Even though this book was written just two years after the initial release of Swift, this language has made very rapid progress in that short time. It has established a firm beachhead as a client-side language for the Apple ecosystem, and it has contributed to improved quality of developer's code as well as faster development cycles. Swift has gone from a proprietary language to a fully transparent open source project with a very large and active community supporting its evolution. The 3.0 release of Swift also delivered an initial level of support for the language to be used for server-side (and cloud) software. So now the question is, where do we go from here?

In this chapter, I'll explore areas of focus for the Swift community for the next major release. I'll also peer beyond that, to examine longer-term enhancements that I know are necessary to reach the full potential of this exciting new language. As you read about these projects that will improve the story for Swift, perhaps you will be inspired to join the effort and become one of the many contributors to one (or more) of them!

Bringing Swift to the Server

A crucial value proposition for Swift is the concept of fluid migration of Swift code across the client-server (or client-cloud) network divide. There have already been projects where developers with iOS Swift experience have been able to quickly apply their front-end Swift knowledge and skill to back-end Swift server development. Knowing the language and its patterns enabled these mobile front-end developers to write Swift code for some back-end services from scratch very quickly and with a minimal additional learning curve.

While there is plenty of value in an environment where familiarity with the language syntax and development tools can bridge the client-server chasm, this is not the same thing as true code portability between front end and back end. One of the goals for Swift is code consistency between client and server. You do not want a fractured development experience based on where the code is running. Instead, one of the guiding principles for Swift is to be able to *migrate* code from client to server (and back).

The advantage of reaching this kind of client-server code portability is that application projects will no longer be dependent on different teams to build back-end and front-end software. There can be just one full stack development team, with each team member capable of writing code that is deployed to any tier—and that may, in fact, be moved from one application layer to another over the course of project development. Any developer should be able to move their code back and forth between client and server very easily. Ultimately, this will produce faster development and delivery of the overall application.

For Swift to achieve this lofty goal, the surrounding frameworks and ecosystem of tools must be enhanced so that the semantics of the language are preserved between client and server, not just the syntax. Pursuing support for this kind of capability was one of the motivations for forming the Swift.org Server API workgroup.

The need for enhancements also goes beyond common syntax and semantics. As was mentioned in earlier chapters, Swift.org releases include support for Swift language compilers, debuggers, and libraries on Linux. However, to make full use of Swift in the cloud, several additional projects are needed, and it is urgent that rapid progress be made on them.

You can see some of these projects at the Swift@IBM Git repository (`https://github.com/ IBM-Swift`). This site contains a variety of projects, including many types of helpful example applications, as well as development resources and tools for Swift. The repository also contains some important Swift server projects.

IBM Cloud Tools for Swift

Of special importance in the effort to better enable skilled Swift mobile programmers to migrate their Swift code from the client environment to the cloud (server) environment, is the IBM Cloud Tools (ICT) for Swift project (`http://cloudtools.bluemix.net/`). These software tools help developers to create projects to organize and link their client-side and server-side code as part of a single development view. You can monitor the status of your client and cloud code from a single dashboard.

Mobile app developers using Swift will have extensive familiarity with the Apple Xcode Integrated Developer Environment (IDE). In order to assist these developers with the creation of cloud-hosted Swift code, ICT for Swift complements a developer's familiar Xcode environment and therefore helps improve programmer productivity. For projects deployed to the IBM Bluemix cloud platform, the tool assists developers with the following:

- Code generation and provisioning to pre-tested Kitura runtimes, running either on your local developer workstation or in the cloud
- Unified management of cloud service credentials
- Centralized control and monitoring of assets deployed on the cloud
- Local notifications of remote actions
- Quick access to logs from the server in real time

At the time of this writing, ICT for Swift is available as a beta release tool.

ICT for Swift is packaged as a native macOS application that you download from the ICT web page, as shown in Figure 9-1. You need to be using the 8.2 or later release of Xcode if you plan to locally compile and run Swift 3.0 code. Once you've downloaded and installed ICT, you can run the application on your macOS workstation, alongside Xcode, and start using it, as shown in Figure 9-2.

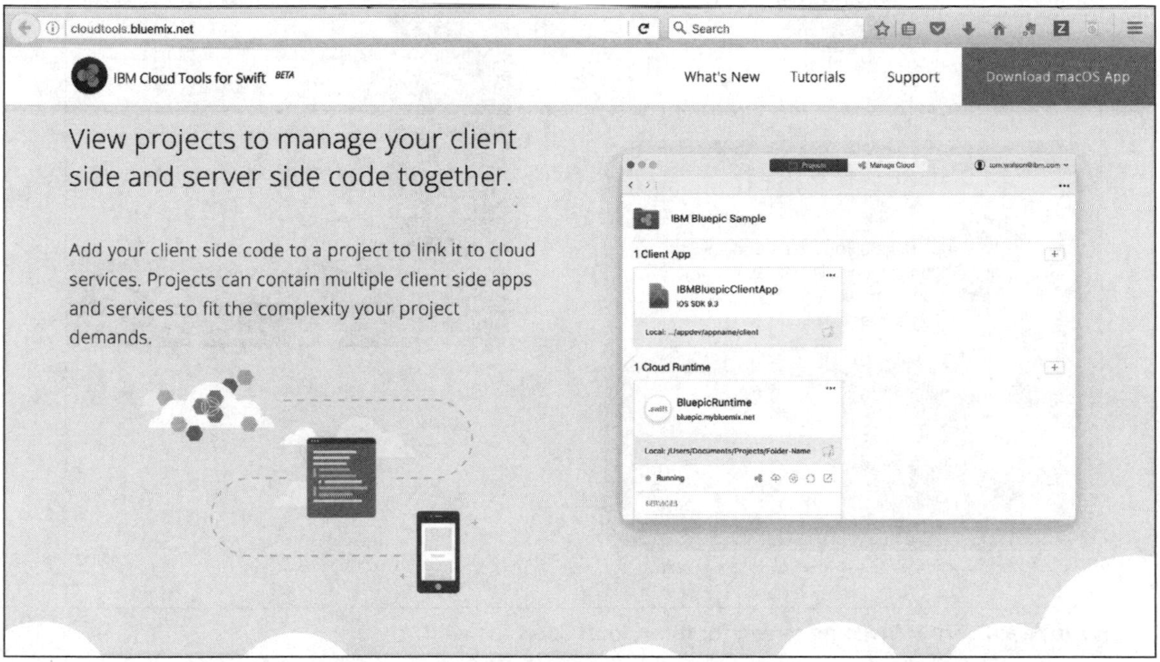

Figure 9-1: The IBM Cloud Tools for Swift web page

You can sign in to the IBM Bluemix cloud platform environment (or create a new Bluemix account) directly from the ICT main application screen. Signing in to Bluemix allows you to interact with the server side of your application directly from the ICT dashboard on your macOS workstation. You can also deploy the Swift cloud services code for your application into Bluemix from the ICT dashboard. From the ICT dashboard, you can change the Bluemix organization and space with which you are interacting. This allows you to switch between different projects that are deployed into different organizations or spaces within an organization, as shown in Figure 9-3.

When you create a project in ICT, you are creating it for both client and server Swift code. You begin the process of creating a new project in ICT by clicking the plus sign (+) in the upper right of the dashboard and then selecting from a set of pre-defined projects or choosing to create a new custom project. Figure 9-4 shows the creation of a project in the early beta release; the tool may look different by the time you use it. In particular, there are plans to organize the ICT projects based on distinct categories, and the list of starter applications is changing, evolving, and growing. In fact, it is possible for a third party to submit their own app to be featured in the list, so the selection of potential projects upon which to base your new one is likely to be quite large.

Figure 9-2: The Welcome screen for IBM Cloud Tools for Swift

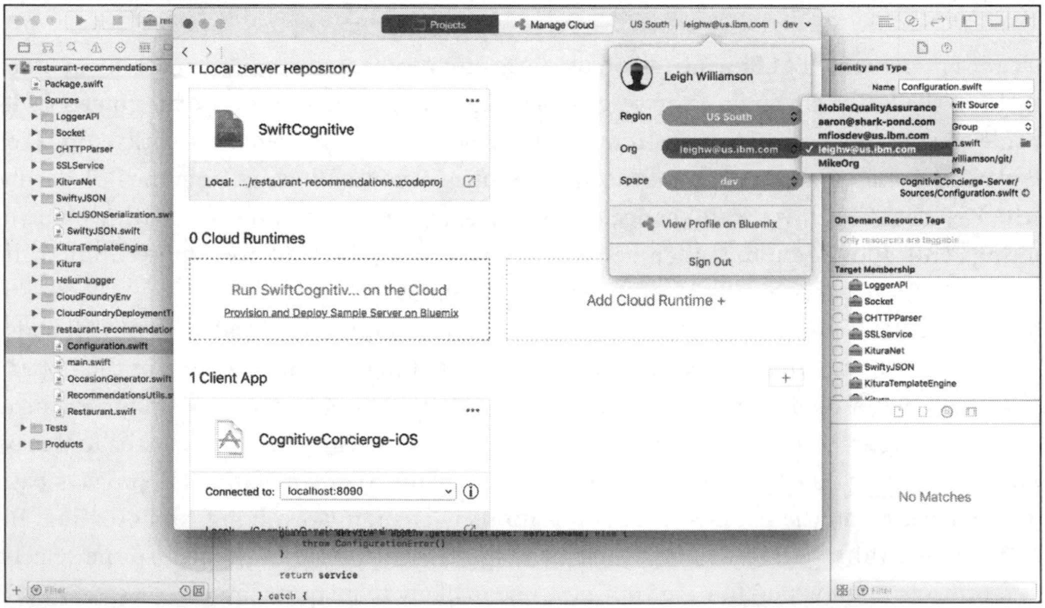

Figure 9-3: Switching between different IBM Bluemix organizations in ICT

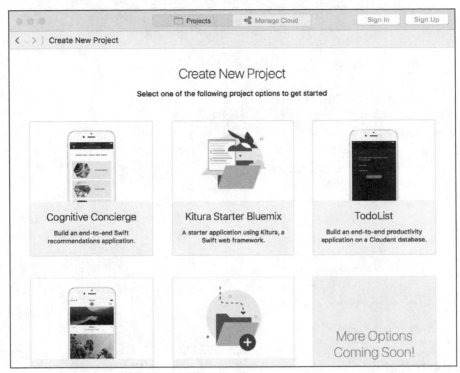

Figure 9-4: Selecting a new project in IBM Cloud Tools

The ICT project view shows you both client and server runtimes for the application, and also the source code repository for the project (see Figure 9-5). From this project view, you can open the source code in the Xcode IDE and also deploy the server code into the IBM Bluemix Cloud.

When you execute a cloud deployment from ICT into the Bluemix cloud platform, you can monitor the cloud deployment logs in ICT on your macOS development workstation, as shown in Figure 9-6. Once the deployment of the server-side Swift code to the cloud environment is complete, you can continue to view and control the cloud code from the ICT dashboard, as shown in Figure 9-7. After deployment, it is often useful to keep the log window of ICT open so that you can continuously monitor the activity of your Swift cloud service "live" while interacting with it via the Swift client application on your workstation.

Once you have set up and deployed the ICT for Swift project, you can make code changes in Xcode for either the mobile client app or the cloud services used by that app, and run both the mobile app and its associated server right on the same macOS workstation (see Figure 9-8).

At IBM, our initial target persona for ICT was iOS developers looking to move some of their Swift code to a server in the cloud. These users are experts with the Xcode IDE, so that has been the initial focus for feature development in ICT. In future versions of ICT, the command line interface (CLI) will be a much more foundational piece of the tool architecture, where the graphical user interface will be a nice veneer over the underlying installed and available CLI. In the beta version at the time of this writing, ICT interacts with the cloud without any separate command line program, but this will evolve and change with subsequent releases.

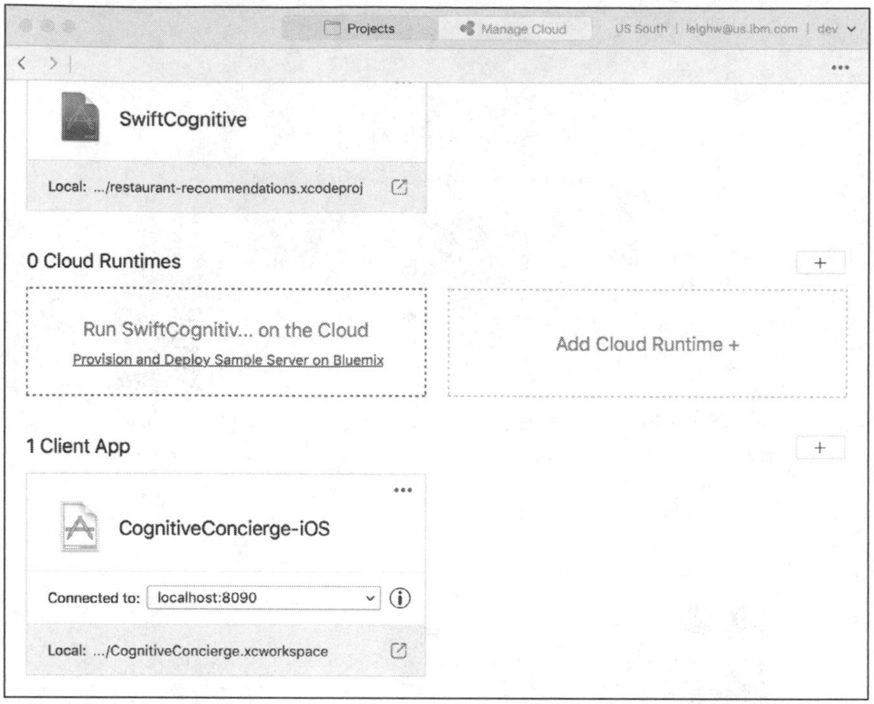

Figure 9-5: ICT view of a project—both client and server components

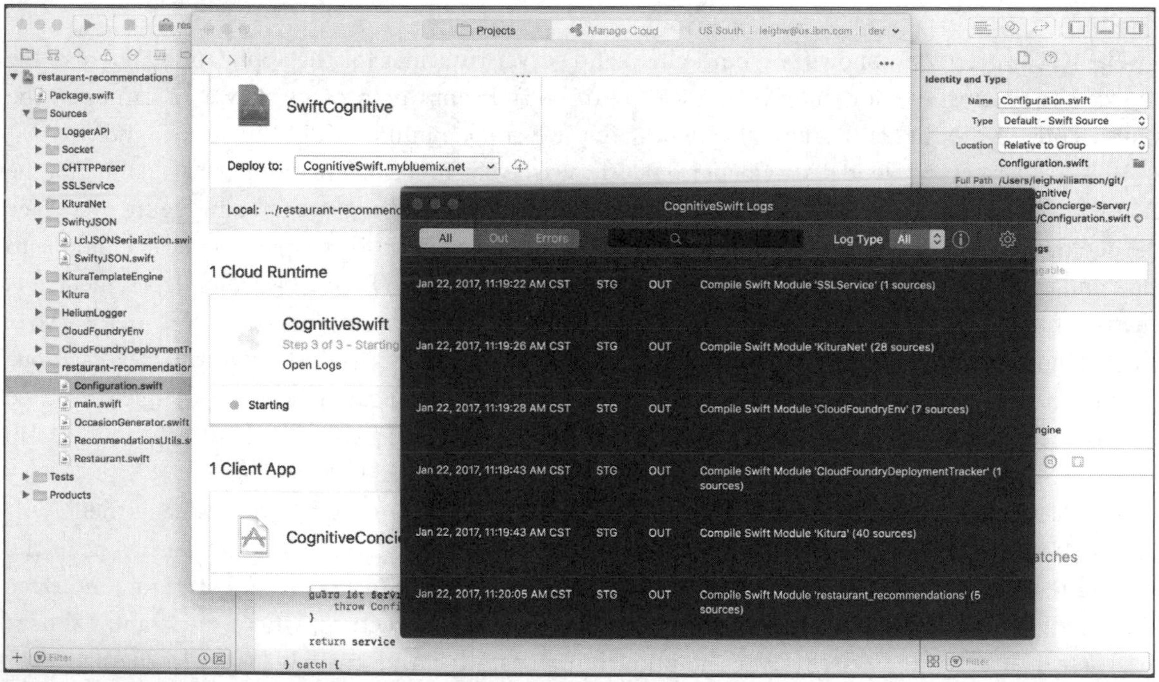

Figure 9-6: Viewing the status of cloud deployment from ICT

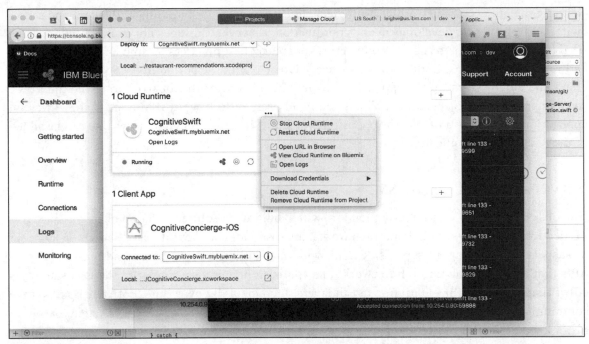

Figure 9-7: Monitoring the Swift cloud application from ICT

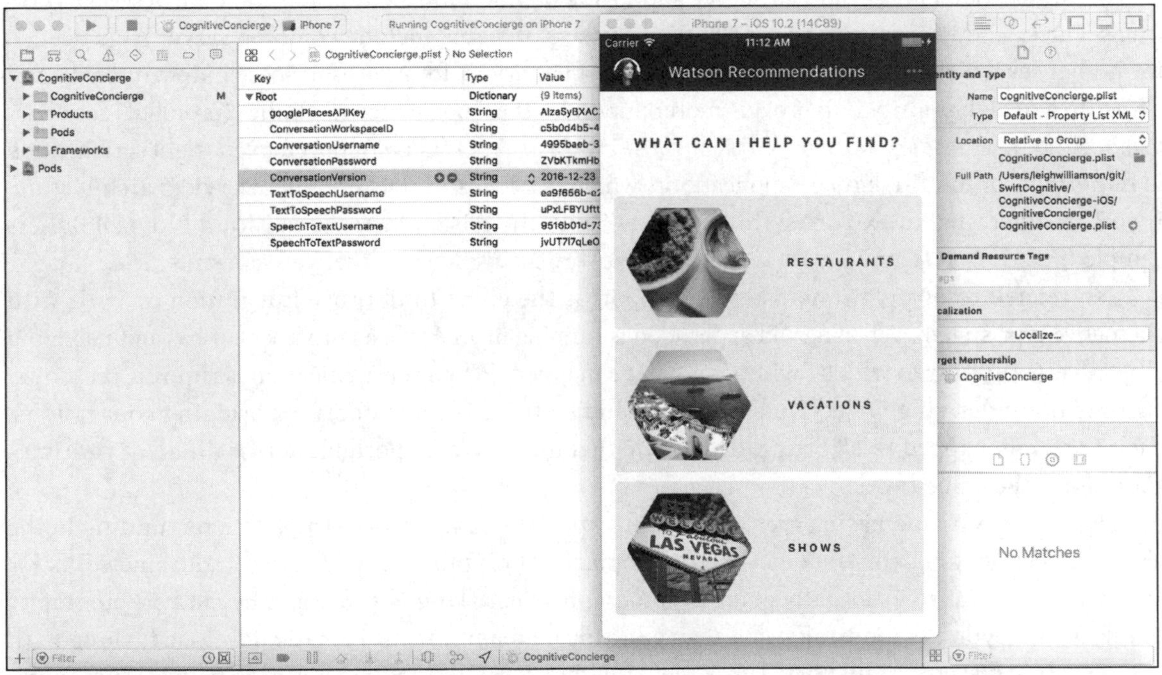

Figure 9-8: Running both parts of an application—mobile app and cloud services

Using the projects framework, ICT provides a great structure for bundling both client and server Swift code together for development and coordination. However, this does not explicitly address the need for good design patterns and architecture that reflect best practices for implementation of such end-to-end applications. Good patterns are needed to help with the portability of Swift code between client and cloud "sides" of the application. By making it easy for third parties to create their own starter application projects and publish them to all users of ICT, we at IBM hope that Swift cloud application developers will take the opportunity to build example design patterns that can be added to the ICT featured applications list.

Server-Side Frameworks

One of several critical areas of evolution for Swift is building a solid foundation of server-side APIs needed for the next wave of cloud frameworks, microservices, and Swift-based server packages. A key aspect of enhancing the server-side frameworks is to untangle dependencies, adding the missing APIs that are not in the initial framework. The approach here is very similar to the Java standards effort that produced JEE—building out in layers, incrementally over time. Both the open source community and IBM understand what it takes to get to the next wave of the ecosystem, based on history, working with customers, partners, and industry on the future of cloud development. There is broad support for further standardization of server-side Swift development via Swift.org and the Server APIs Project of Swift.org.

The initial focus for enhanced server support is on common server-side APIs for base networking, security and encryption, and HTTP/WebSockets. Benefits include common server APIs needed for higher-level web frameworks, REST API implementations for microservices, and Swift packages.

An area of high priority is to provide more support for the Google Protocol Buffer (protobuf) serialization technology (`https://github.com/apple/swift-protobuf`). This support for very tight serialization is important for multi-language applications, which is a focus of polyglot microservices architecture. If you are interested in exploring this aspect of Swift, there is an instructive Kitura Protocol Buffers sample (`https://github.com/IBM-Swift/Kitura-Protobuf-Sample`) that you can study.

Also related to polyglot microservice support is the effort to improve integration of Swift with the native type system. When a Swift application is running in an Apple environment, it has an underlying Objective-C runtime to which Swift types can be mapped. When the application is running on Linux, there is no underlying Objective-C runtime, and so there is no support for bridging conversions, such as string mapped to NSString. Swift code that intends to be portable across different runtimes should use the value types.

With security an increasing area of concern, especially for enterprise applications running in the cloud, investment is being made in the development of cryptography libraries and frameworks for Swift. The intent is to eventually make cryptography a core language feature. Beyond cryptography libraries and cypher support, keychain and certificate management is being developed, along with SSL/TLS-based secure transport. These security libraries will integrate with the networking frameworks to provide secure communication.

Across the full range of Swift frameworks, an effort is being made to improve the underlying implementations—both client and server. For instance, with more and more frameworks being crammed into iOS client code and bloating the client footprint, IBM is studying how to break out some of that code from the client and easily move it to the cloud. This should result in a lot less code on the client side, a lot less memory required in the client, lower latency, and generally better performance of the client implementation.

There is ongoing work to produce common low-level basic networking APIs, with a solid, portable HTTP and HTTP/2 layer for Swift. Also underway is development activity for datagram (User Datagram Protocol, or UDP) support, perhaps leveraging the BlueSocket project (`https://github.com/IBM-Swift/BlueSocket`). IPv4 and IPv6 support and domain name resolution are part of this effort, and these communication connections will support both synchronous and non-blocking interaction. Another area of enhancement related to communication is improved support for JSON marshalling and unmarshalling.

As that work is progressing, there is a parallel effort to rebase Kitura on top of standard APIs, especially for network functions. The goal for Kitura is to be a solid web framework for production scenarios, something that enterprises can run their business on. Much development and testing remains to be done in order to reach this goal.

Kitura isn't the only web server framework for Swift; another popular web framework is Vapor (`https://github.com/vapor/vapor`). This Swift web framework is very simple to start using, is nicely integrated with Xcode, and takes care of a lot of common concerns for developing web applications (such as object relational mapping and data model protocols). It can be deployed on a variety of cloud platforms including Heroku, Amazon Web Services, and Bluemix. So, regardless of the high-level Swift web framework you use, the intent of the work of the Swift.org Server APIs Project is to provide a common, underpinning set of libraries for server functions that is supported on all environments where Swift runs.

Server-side or cloud service code typically includes interaction with data residing in one or more data stores or databases. At the time of this writing, a multitude of Swift libraries and frameworks are devoted to supporting various data stores. A brief look at the Awesome Swift list (`https://github.com/delba/awesome-swift/blob/master/README.md`) shows the variety of Swift implementations supporting SQL relational stores, noSQL databases, CoreData, and Key-Value data stores. One of the goals for Swift.org is to develop some standards for data store interaction so that, similar to Java language standards, a fundamental common interface for data persistence becomes available. This will take considerable time, given the huge number of data stores that Swift will need to support.

Fundamental to all of these projects, considerable work is ongoing for the core Foundation framework, so that common code can be reused between client and server environments. This work is crucial to make porting Swift source code from client to server easier and more automatic. The same classes and behavior must be counted on wherever you choose to run the code.

While the list of new and improved server frameworks for Swift is large and will take several releases to address, you can expect to see initial support for many of these features in the version 4 time frame.

Concurrency

Concurrency is a critical aspect of server-side programming. Without good concurrency support, a server application or cloud service cannot scale or handle multiple users and threads of execution.

Today Swift concurrency is handled outside of the core language via libdispatch (Grand Central Dispatch). This implementation of concurrency support does not employ an explicit threading model, but instead relies on Apple operating system APIs for scheduling tasks in queues and synchronizing operations across common resources. Initial porting of Grand Central Dispatch to Linux leveraged some native libraries that made it quick to map the common concurrency APIs to operating system–specific functions.

In the future, we at IBM will explore how we can work with the community to directly integrate concurrency into the language. This brings in other topics, including memory management and Automatic Reference Counting (ARC). From a server code perspective, it is crucial to continue to improve high-throughput Swift concurrency and optimize its performance. Specific areas of focus for concurrency improvements include enabling thread-specific storage to optimize dispatch operations and investigating the resource management and scheduling logic decisions made when executing server workloads.

First-Class Support for Microservices

Presently, there is a prevailing view that microservices architecture is the future of cloud software development. The Swift community continues to press to deliver first-class support for modern microservices development (polyglot microservices and serverless).

Cloud development is increasingly following the microservices architecture approach, and asynchronous interaction between microservices is crucial for scaling and performance. In order to enable Swift-implemented asynchronous microservices, one of the next important frameworks needed is support for WebSockets communication (less chatty communication). This need aligns with the planned common network frameworks and also with the focus on improved concurrency in Swift.

Many initial projects implementing a microservices architecture have employed Kitura as the framework for their microservices. This is effective, but additional work is needed for better runtime metrics. Depending on where you deploy your microservice, Auto-Scaling may be available and is crucial to successfully running a microservices solution. At IBM, we are working on more advanced tooling for development and deployment of microservices, including the ability to generate some of the code.

An alternative approach for implementing microservices is to leverage serverless environments, as discussed in Chapter 8. The current status of serverless support for Swift is promising, but it is still expected to require significant further development before providing impressive microservices programming model support. A key aspect of successful microservices implementation is good isolation between the microservices and graceful failure when one microservice experiences problems. Along those lines, IBM is developing integrated frameworks that support patterns such as the Circuit Breaker pattern, which avoids catastrophic cascading failures of chained microservices.

IBM would like to add support to the Swift Package Manager for languages other than Swift. This includes support for mixing and matching Swift with other languages. Specifically, we are most interested in support for C-based languages, because the existing ecosystem of Swift code is heavily reliant on C-based code—up to and including Objective-C runtime support in Swift itself on Apple platforms. However, the ability for Swift to be combined with Node.js JavaScript logic and traditional Java server code will be vital for broader microservices implementation.

Improved Package Support

It is also critical that Swift should have a vibrant package ecosystem that delivers a large variety of features and functions in an easy-to-consume package format. Existing Swift package management has delivered the first wave of support for this ecosystem in the Package Catalog, but a centralized Package Index is a crucial next feature that will allow enhancements to this area of the ecosystem.

A central Swift Package Index will support impact analysis between dependent packages originating from different unrelated sources. A central Package Index can also act as a naming authority, designating certain packages with canonical names. A centralized index service would have the responsibility to ensure the integrity of packages that it distributes, the security of identities related to the packages, and the availability of supporting resources, as well as the ability to revoke fraudulent or malicious packages.

As Swift package management (SPM) matures, it is important to consider the security conventions for how consumers and producers of packages can safely publish and share or consume the packages. Among other features motivated by this need, is the concept of a mechanism to sign and verify packages. Prior to downloading a package, the SPM could use such a mechanism to verify that the package had not been tampered with since it was published, and warn the user if it is an unsecure package. An even more sophisticated concept is to add a "chain of custody" or chain-of-trust mechanism to the package management system.

Because the Swift Package Manager is a tool that supports development, another area of focus for its evolution is improved integration and support for other tools in the Swift development ecosystem. Adding a test harness to the Swift package system will encourage the best practice for package developers to include tests with the package code, and a means for automatically executing those tests against the packages when they are updated or when they are added to another project as a dependency. Exploration is ongoing for explicitly supporting XCTest, from the Swift Core Libraries, as the native testing library for the package testing mechanism.

Along with automated testing for the Swift packages, a mature package management system should include automated generation of documentation for every package. A key to effective usage of the packages is clear and understandable documentation, and establishing a standard markup and mechanism for Swift packages will go a long way toward increased ease of use for developers.

Support for other version control systems besides Git, for other build systems, and for other programming languages is all on the table for Swift package management enhancements. A proposal for better cross-platform (multiple operating system) package support and for the notion of package "flavors" (essentially different package build configurations) will help to make progress toward the goals of making portability of Swift packages easier and of expanding the range of Swift, both on the client side and for multiple cloud platforms.

You can read more about a Package Index for Swift, and follow the Swift.org plans for improved package management, by visiting the Swift Package Manager Community Proposal website (`https://github.com/apple/swift-package-manager/blob/master/Documentation/PackageManagerCommunityProposal.md`). This website provides both an excellent background and the philosophy behind Swift Package Manager (SPM). After the section on SPM philosophy, there is a long list of potential future features.

Making It Easier to Learn and Share

Key to the success of Swift, whether targeting client or cloud environments, is that it be increasingly easy to learn and share Swift code. As described in Chapter 2, the Swift Sandbox really helps to accelerate learning Swift programming by enabling rapid experimentation with the language and immediate feedback of the execution results. But imagine how effective a communication and code sharing mechanism it would be if you could send "live" Swift code snippets to someone or even post a chunk of Swift code into `stackoverflow.com` in order to seek help with a coding problem.

Although it has long been helpful to send the text for various programming languages back and forth, in order to exchange information with a common understanding of the code, what I am describing now is a step beyond simply the programming language text. Soon you will be able to add the IBM Swift Sandbox as an embedded component to any web page. As illustrated in Figure 9-9, this upcoming ability to provide running (or failing) live example code to another person will dramatically increase the productivity of Swift developers. The possibilities for exploiting this capability are limitless and mind-boggling!

In addition to new approaches for learning and sharing Swift code, the flagship Xcode IDE is being enhanced to provide better support for cloud services (server) development. Expect to see integrated tools in the Developer Tools list that support cloud service simulation, testing, and other coding tasks similar to the existing integrated developer tools for client platforms.

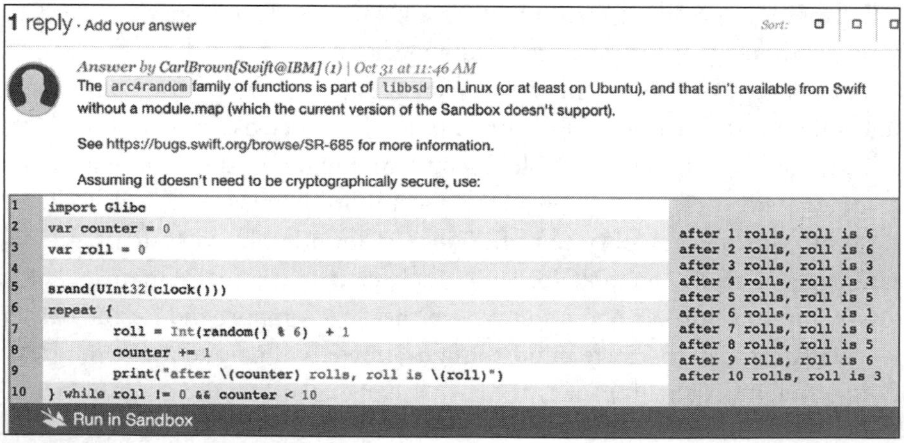

Figure 9-9: Embedding live Swift code into a web page

Expanding the Range of Swift

Another goal of the Swift community is to expand the range of Swift development across the spectrum of front-end and back-end deployment targets from the Internet of Things (IoT), through the cloud, and even including mainframe environments. An effort is also focused on expanding the range of supported client-side platforms, with the obvious targets for client platform support including the Android ecosystem and Microsoft Windows clients.

Swift Support for Linux

In the context of the Swift language, when we speak of "server-side" code, generally we are referring to Linux systems. I've heard more than one server code developer talk about Linux environments as "where we live," and this is one of the reasons why the Swift.org open source effort is so crucial. The relationship and dependency between the Swift open source project and the Linux open source project is natural and intuitive. Therefore, support for Swift on Linux is an obvious top priority.

Some of the current areas of community emphasis center on making it even easier to develop Swift on Linux with enhanced desktop tools, including expanded support for desktop testing and debugging.

Developers using Swift to create mobile app software are very familiar with the iOS Simulator tool that is integrated with the Apple Xcode IDE. This simulated mobile device environment allows developers to run and test their Swift iOS mobile app code on their macOS developer workstations without needing a real mobile device on which to run the code. It is a great convenience and saves a lot of time to be able to execute the build-deploy-test cycle for the mobile code all on the developer's computer, and in a matter of minutes. For mobile-targeted Swift code, the iOS Simulator is an essential tool.

Work is now underway to create a different kind of simulator tool, one that mimics the Linux cloud back-end environment but runs on the developer's local workstation. You can leverage Docker containers to run a Linux "Cloud Simulator" tool on macOS—integrated with Xcode like the iOS Simulator—to test and debug Swift server-side code running in this Cloud Simulator. An additional benefit of this Linux Cloud Simulator is that both sides of the client-server application can be debugged on the same computer. A programmer can step through Swift code instructions one at a time as the logic bounces back and forth between the application client environment and server environment.

Work is also underway to support use of ICT for Swift on Linux development workstations. With the increased support for command line interaction with ICT, the goal is to broaden the range of full stack Swift developers whose chosen development environments include Linux.

The Internet of Swift Things

While one side effect of open sourcing the Swift language has been an intense focus on scaling it up on the server, in the cloud and even on "big iron" systems (see the next section), another path that developers have taken the language on is to scale it down by creating Swift packages for the ARM architecture systems. This means that Swift can now be compiled to execute on systems such as Raspberry Pi, BeagleBone, and others.

However, in order to make the language truly effective for the ARM-based Internet-of-Things (IoT) world, more work will be needed. Library implementations for using the Raspberry Pi peripherals are needed, for the GPIO (general purpose input/output) pins, I2C, SPI (Serial Peripheral Interface), and serial port communication. A lot of device-specific I/O frameworks will be released over the next few years.

The notion of implementing Internet-of-Things solutions using Swift goes all the way back to the origin of the language. Apple offers a range of smart devices such as Apple Watch and Apple TV, and quickly brought out Swift support for its HomeKit smart home solution framework. So, regardless of the ecosystem of devices that your IoT solution employs, Swift can be your programming language of choice.

An advantage that Swift brings to the table, as an IoT programming language, is that it can be used end-to-end to implement the system. You can use the same encryption libraries in the smart devices on the edge of your system as are used by the cloud services that collect the data produced by the devices.

Big Iron Swift

IBM mainframe computers, or z Systems, have been serving mission-critical business applications and data for decades. With its ultra-high scalability and security, significant performance enhancements over each generation of System z processors, and continual commitment to open source, mobility, agility, and efficiency, this is an ideal platform for enterprise transactions, systems of record, and application workload for a hybrid cloud.

High availability, resiliency, and hardware cryptography support have been the strength of IBM z Systems through software and hardware co-design. Z Systems deliver standard features such as large pages, hardware transactional memory, and hardware runtime instrumentation, allowing further optimized usage of the underlying hardware infrastructure. Runtime instrumentation is enabled automatically, and transactional memory can be exploited by middleware and applications. Additional accelerators for compression (zEDC), memory access (Flash Express), cryptography (Crypto Express), and IP communication over RoCE (Remote Direct Memory Access over a Converged Ethernet) have all made z Systems the most reliable, efficient, powerful, and trusted workhorses in existence today.

Linux on z Systems also provides the flexibility and benefits of running Linux, with the advantages of fault-tolerant mainframe hardware. Linux has been the world's fastest-growing server operating system for several years. IBM has officially supported Linux on z Systems since 2000. Red Hat and SuSE ship enterprise Linux distributions for z Systems, and the Debian and Fedora distributions also support the architecture.

Building on the successful experiences of thousands of customer engagements and deployments, IBM has delivered a new portfolio of systems, solutions, and services called IBM LinuxONE. IBM LinuxONE is the IBM Linux server, a responsive service delivery platform capable of provisioning new virtual Linux servers in seconds. The LinuxONE environment allows users to share and over-commit system resources to meet client expectations for unlimited access to existing and new services. LinuxONE enables enterprise-grade Linux servers that are more robust and trusted for critical workloads, and have higher performance and throughput to deliver a solution that incurs lower cost per transaction.

LinuxONE is designed to deliver 100-percent uptime, ensuring continuous operations even in the case of hardware faults. LinuxONE systems and solutions provide users with a flexible yet powerful infrastructure that helps ensure that a business receives the performance, reliability, security, and processing power it needs to address increasingly sophisticated and demanding application requirements.

In a hybrid cloud, LinuxONE typically plays a key role as the core system-of-record because it has the processing speed, scale, availability, and security to handle business-critical applications and high-value data. IBM has ported Swift to LinuxONE and contributed code back to the community. Why? Because running Swift on LinuxONE delivers a consistent end-to-end experience for application development while opening new paradigms and programming models for applications that span hybrid clouds.

With the z/OS proven transaction processing capabilities, such as Customer Information Control System (CICS) and Information Management System (IMS), proximity to and re-use of enterprise data such as DB2 on z/OS can help you preserve your investments in COBOL and PL/I by continuing to extend your old applications with Swift code.

Typically, you have different developers working on user-facing client applications, on premise services, and on public cloud services, as they are most likely using different languages. By bringing Swift to the cloud and the LinuxONE platform, the end-to-end application development is significantly simplified because Swift developers can write applications across the entire hybrid cloud, from the smart phone, to the cloud, to the LinuxONE back-end system. This streamlines the development process by allowing the same developers to write the full end-to-end solution.

Figure 9-10 shows the Swift framework on LinuxONE and z Systems, where Swift can be integrated naturally with core back-end systems such as CICS, IMS, and DB2 for z/OS, as well as programs written in COBOL, PL/I, and C++. Swift programs on LinuxONE can interact with these back-end systems through the REST protocol via IBM z/OS Connect Enterprise Edition, or the z/OS Connect feature in the WebSphere application Liberty profile.

In the near future, look for z/OS support for CICS packages for Swift, as well as additional Swift packages that integrate the language more deeply with the System z environment. To explore Swift on z further, check out the following blog, Try Swift on z/OS: `https://developer.ibm.com/swift/2016/12/05/try-swift-on-zos/`.

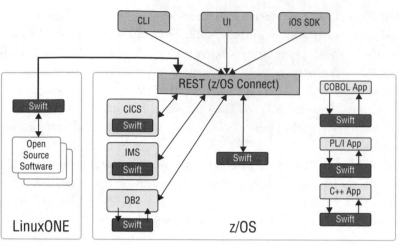

Figure 9-10: Architecture for Swift on System z

Swift DevOps

When it comes to enterprise production deployment of any software, the level of DevOps support is key to broad adoption of the language and frameworks. Improvements in DevOps capabilities are needed for simplifying Swift cloud development that spans multiple deployment models (virtual machines, containers, Cloud Foundry runtimes, and serverless microservices). No matter which model of cloud deployment you choose for your project, the software processing pipeline for your Swift code should be as configurable as possible, with all workflows easily automated.

The Swift cloud deployment story needs attention, with the goal being to "get it running and keep it running." Improvement in failure-handling design is very important for server stacks. One key aspect of improved DevOps for Swift is advanced server-side monitoring and metrics services, including metrics for HTTP traffic, databases, CPU, memory, and the general operating environment. You will be able to embed this monitoring in your own Swift code and frameworks, creating a capability similar to Instruments for Swift.

At IBM, we are currently working to ensure that capabilities that developers have come to expect when using runtimes like Node.js, Java, or Liberty in the cloud are also available for Swift in the cloud. Such capabilities will significantly improve the readiness of the Swift language for the enterprise.

In a future version of the IBM buildpack for Swift, developers will be able to remotely debug (using LLDB) their Swift applications running as Cloud Foundry apps on Bluemix. They will also have the capability to copy any core dump files generated in the Cloud Foundry container to their development system, even if the Swift application crashes. The buildpack will be responsible for compiling the Swift application using the debug configuration, for starting the LLDB-server, and for starting a proxy agent to ensure the Cloud Foundry container is not destroyed if the Swift application crashes.

Having implementations of design patterns in the Swift language that are commonly used in enterprise solutions should empower developers so they can deliver more resilient applications for their customers. Our team is currently working on a new Swift package that implements the Circuit Breaker and Bulkhead design patterns. Using this package, developers will be able to protect critical functions, avoid making calls to components that are currently unavailable, and also limit the number of concurrent invocations for a given component.

We are also updating several of our cloud services for a better integration with Kitura-based applications. For instance, an updated Bluemix Availability Monitoring dashboard will include a dashboard for visualizing the CPU, memory, and HTTP response, as well as HTTP throughput metrics for Kitura-based apps. Also, a new version of the Auto-Scaling service on Bluemix will allow developers to write rules for automatically scaling (up and down) their Kitura-based apps. These rules will be definable on memory utilization, CPU usage, and HTTP utilization metrics.

We plan to add the ibmcom/swift-ubuntu image to the official Bluemix public registry, thus making this image even easier to access for Bluemix users. We also plan to create an additional new image that only contains those libraries required for running Swift applications. This implies that this second image will not contain SPM, or Clang, or any of the build tools, which should make the image smaller and faster to upload to Bluemix.

Summary

As the improvements described earlier in this chapter are delivered, IBM will be looking into the future to build an even bigger ecosystem with more mature components. The enthusiasm and contributions from the Swift open technology community have produced really impressive and rapid growth in Swift-based code assets and frameworks. There is every indication that this momentum will carry forward for many years to come.

Given the initial focus of Swift on client platforms such as iOS, watchOS, and tvOS, the existing default developer journey for Swift has been as follows: Start applying your client-side programming skills using Swift, and eventually move into back-end cloud services development while still leveraging the same programming language. But with all of the progress that has been achieved with cloud services, and with all of the server-side enhancements on the way, it will soon be reasonable to expect that a developer might start with back-end development using Swift and then leverage their Swift expertise to move to the front end of the application—the client.

The Swift@IBM team is looking forward to that day, and we are working every day to improve the cloud development capabilities of Swift. If you can define the history of information technology in terms of generations of IT that build and improve upon the previous ones, then right now is very much the "Swift and Cloud Generation"!

Index

Index